THE
HARLEM
RIOT OF
1943

THE HARLEM RIOT OF 1943

by Dominic J. Capeci, Jr.

TEMPLE UNIVERSITY PRESS PHILADELPHIA

Temple University Press, Philadelphia, 19122
© 1977 by Temple University. All rights reserved
Published 1977
Printed in the United States of America
International Standard Book Number: 0-87722-094-8
Library of Congress Catalog Number: 77-70328

Per i miei genitori
Mary Rita Cashin Capeci
e
Dominic Joseph Capeci, Sr.

Contents

Acknowledgments

Throughout my research and writing, I have benefited from the assistance of others. I am deeply indebted to Professor Van L. Perkins of the University of California, Riverside, who guided this study through its first stages and provided important suggestions for its revision. At a crucial point in preparing the manuscript for publication, the encouragement and judgment of Professor Gerald D. Nash of the University of New Mexico were invaluable. Reorganizing and revising the manuscript would have been impossible without the advice, assistance, and friendship of Professors Frederick J. Blue and James P. Ronda of Youngstown State University and Professor James N. Giglio of Southwest Missouri State University. Professor Donald D. Landon of Southwest Missouri State University offered valuable suggestions for Chapters 7 and 10. My efforts have been constantly encouraged by Professor Agnes M. Smith of Youngstown State University and Professor Robert B. Flanders of Southwest Missouri State University.

The University of California, Riverside, provided an Intercampus Opportunity Grant for the summer of 1967 and a University Fellowship for 1967–1968, which greatly facilitated my research. I owe special thanks to William B. Liebmann of the Herbert H. Lehman Collection and to

Maria Grab and Idilio Gracia Peña of the Municipal Archives and Records Center of New York City. I also received much-appreciated help from the staffs of the Columbia Oral History Collection, the Library of Congress, the National Archives, the Franklin Delano Roosevelt Library, the Southern Collection at the University of North Carolina Library, and the Schomburg Collection of Negro Literature and History. Charles Poletti and Roy Wilkins took time from their busy schedules to give interviews. The members of the History Department of Southwest Missouri State University generously reduced my teaching load during the spring semester of 1974 so that I could make necessary revisions. The Research Committee of Southwest Missouri State University provided financial assistance for typing the final draft. Betty Hindman typed the manuscript, while Georgia Brunner handled my correspondence. As usual I am most thankful to Norma Donoghue and our sons, Dominic Edward and James Joseph, who reminded me that their humanity was as important as that about which I was writing.

Introduction

The summer of 1943 found racial tension brewing in numerous cities throughout the United States. As Malcolm X commented about the atmosphere in Harlem, "One could almost smell trouble ready to break out."[1] When it did on August 1, Harlem joined other communities—including Mobile, Los Angeles, and Detroit—that fell prey to a race riot. In twelve hours, six persons died, several hundred were injured, and approximately two million dollars' worth of property was damaged. Though less numerous and, with the exception of Detroit's, less serious than the riots of World War I, racial violence during World War II reflected the continuation of deep-seated antagonisms.[2] In fact, certain developments after World War I served to augment and confuse tensions between the races. Increasingly, many black Americans experienced paradoxical feelings of hope for future equality and despair over existing injustice.

During the Great Depression, black people everywhere—but particularly in urban centers like New York City—suffered more heavily under the strain of economic crisis than did white citizens. Yet the Great Depression also promoted hope for progress. The need for greater solidarity within AfroAmerican communities nurtured race consciousness, mass action, and positive outlets for frustration.

Economic boycotts, for example, were organized against businesses that refused to hire black personnel.[3] Relief programs enacted after 1933 indicated concern on the part of some white officials for the plight of black citizens. On the national level, President Franklin D. Roosevelt included black Americans in his New Deal programs, albeit paternalistically and indirectly, and in New York, Governor Herbert H. Lehman and Mayor Fiorello H. La Guardia went even further in committing state and municipal governments to the economic and civil rights of black residents.

World War II heightened these tensions and expectations. Despite the emerging national property, blacks continued to suffer economic depression because of the curtailment of relief programs and the discrimination practiced in the booming war industries. Insult was added when whites indicated that blacks were neither wanted nor needed in the armed services. Nevertheless, civil rights protest and, more significantly, manpower needs eventually drew blacks into unprecedented economic and military positions. Better treatment in the postwar period seemed certain.

In 1943, these feelings of hope and despair collided. Despite the gains, blacks were despondent. Their morale was dampened by the slow pace of integration, by the hypocrisy of fighting abroad for something they did not have at home, and by the degrading treatment they received in industrial and military centers. As a result, riots ignited in several cities. In late June the worst of these disorders occurred in Detroit, perhaps the nation's most important war-industry center. The Harlem riot took place six weeks later.

This study of the Harlem riot is intended to provide an understanding of race relations between the periods of depression and war. Although it emphasizes conditions and attitudes in New York City from 1933 to 1943, drawing when possible from views of black residents, this work is not of Harlem from the inside looking out. Rather, it focuses on the relation between black citizens and white society—particularly public officials—during a war that stressed democratic and egalitarian aims. Such an approach helps to explain the simultaneously positive and negative impact of World War II on AfroAmericans and race relations, while indicating why progress continued to be limited.

Much of this impact is embodied in the personalities and actions of Adam Clayton Powell, Jr., and Fiorello H. La Guardia. As an indigenous leader with deep roots in black Harlem's historical, political, and religious heritage, Powell provides a mirror of the frustrations and expectations held by many blacks. Although he represents the thinking and strategy of only one of many segments of black leadership, better than anyone else he speaks for the lower class. The political ideology and style that Powell later followed as a controversial congressman developed in this period. La Guardia embodies the official government position, but not one that always represents the view of most white New Yorkers. In varying degrees, his mayoral decisions reflect the thinking of Walter White, executive director of the National Association for the Advancement of Colored People, and of other black leaders who advocated the gradualist approach to civil rights.

In addition to living conditions, leadership, and municipal policy, black attitudes were affected by circumstances outside New York City—for example, the Detroit riot of 1943. Black feelings about that upheaval, as well as the responses of La Guardia and Roosevelt to it, partly influenced the situation in Harlem. Understanding of the larger, national crisis places the Harlem riot in a sharper perspective.

THE
HARLEM
RIOT OF
1943

1
The Mayor and the Councilman

From 1933 to 1943 race relations in New York City were not ideal, but they were more harmonious than in other urban centers. This was partly due to the combined efforts of black leaders and white public officials. While national figures like President Roosevelt and Walter White of the NAACP influenced local concerns, it was those leaders most directly associated with the city who determined how the races lived together. Of these, Adam Clayton Powell, Jr., is a key to understanding the hope, the militancy, and the diverse perspectives of black New Yorkers. Mayor Fiorello H. La Guardia, who also lifted black morale and advanced civil rights, was the most important white public official. A study of Powell and La Guardia provides insights into the variants of racial attitudes that existed in New York City during the Depression and war—as significantly, it explains why each man responded as he did during the Harlem riot of 1943.

La Guardia was, in Arthur Mann's words, "a fighter against his times."[1] Personal experiences rather than careful thought account for his liberal beliefs. Born in 1882, the son of Italian-Protestant and Italian-Jewish parents, he experienced ethnic discrimination early in life. Later his father's health was destroyed by "embalmed beef" served to soldiers in the Spanish-American War, and his mother was denied a pension because the government wrongly determined that her husband's death was not the result of a service-incurred disability. Most tragic, in 1921 La Guardia's first wife and their only child died of tuberculosis. In between the tragedies, he served immigrants as a consular agent in Fiume and Budapest, and as a lawyer in New York City, where he witnessed their exploitation by officials and private citizens. Although he understood the plight of immigrants better than that of black citizens, as a congressman he opposed racial discrimination and had a sincere concern for all minorities.

In 1933, La Guardia was elected mayor of New York, ending twelve years of corrupt Tammany Hall rule. Although greatest support for his anti-machine, reformist campaign came from the middle class and wealthy, some blacks and other minorities were part of La Guardia's "crazy-quilt coalition."[2] "He found mutual interest in the problems we . . . faced," a representative of the Brotherhood of Sleeping Car Porters reminisced, " . . . becase he had always been a champion of the underdog."[3] For this reason, efforts to include black residents in all municipal plans were undertaken during La Guardia's first year and a half in office. Before March 1935, for example, the Harlem River Houses were being planned as part of the New Deal–sponsored public housing program.

La Guardia's closeness to the black community, however, really began on March 19, 1935, when a minor incident involving a young black shoplifter and a white store manager ignited a riot that swept through Harlem. Almost immediately, La Guardia appointed a biracial Mayor's Commission on Conditions in Harlem to investigate the disorder. Chaired by Charles H. Roberts, the commission divided itself into six subcommittees, each based on "a special phase of community life," conducted twenty-five hearings, and listened to the testimony of 160 witnesses. In order to gather authentic information on the socioeconomic factors that fostered riot, the commission provided Howard University sociologist E. Franklin Frazier with a staff of thirty. These efforts produced "The Negro in Harlem: A Report on Social and Economic Conditions Responsible for the Outbreak of March 19, 1935."[4]

The Mayor's Commission clearly defined the plight of black New Yorkers.[5] It concluded that the black economic position could be improved if more aggressive administration efforts were taken to prevent discrimination in municipal and related employment. In addition, the relief system should be made more equitable. To combat overcrowded, overpriced housing, it suggested that the housing code be strictly enforced and a building program planned for Harlem. Moreover, it advised that the community's substandard health, inadequate education, and high crime rate could be altered significantly if its medical, educational, and recreational facilities were made equal to those elsewhere in the city. Finally, the commission suggested that racial tension could be drastically reduced if a community committee was created to investigate complaints against the police department.

La Guardia found himself in an awkward position. Although the abject conditions of slum living were least attributable to his administration, the Mayor's Commission severely criticized some of La Guardia's appointees—particularly Police Commissioner Lewis J. Valentine and Hospital Commissioner Sigismund S. Goldwater—and some of the municipal departments. Furthermore, some of the commission's findings disregarded the basic problem of financing new and additional municipal facilities in Harlem. La Guardia opposed municipal actions by persons operating outside the realities and limitations of government. Consequently, he considered the commission's report a guide rather than a blueprint. To have accepted it verbatim would have committed him to a rigid plan for reform by which critics could measure progress. Nor could La Guardia solve the problems of Harlem by making the municipal commissioners and their departments scapegoats. They alone possessed the machinery needed to ameliorate slum conditions.

Hence La Guardia sought to unite his administration.

Each municipal department commissioner was asked to comment on the commission's report, "showing where there are misstatements of facts or where conclusions have been made on erroneous facts."[6] Valentine, Goldwater, and Edmond B. Butler, the Relief Administrator, harshly faulted the report.[7] Although they were the commissioners most criticized by the report, La Guardia neither reprimanded nor dismissed them. Nor did he authorize release of the commission's report, although portions of it had been leaked to the press.[8] The Mayor also disregarded certain recommendations, most notably the creation of a citizens' committee to investigate the police.

La Guardia, nevertheless, was sincere about improving the living conditions in Harlem. "Owing to the conflict of facts" between the Mayor's Commission and his department heads, he requested Professor Alain Locke of Howard University to evaluate the material.[9] Locke, editor of the famous *Survey Graphic* study of "the New Negro" and presently engaged by that magazine to write an article on the findings of the Mayor's Commission, was given access to all reports on the riot. Indeed, La Guardia must have been baffled by the discrepancy between these reports. The Mayor's Commission, for instance, contended that Valentine was "too busy, unsympathetic or uninterested" to cooperate with its efforts.[10] More critically, it concluded that police tactics and brutality promoted resentment among black citizens and the belief that their lives, "in the estimation of the police," were cheap.[11] Valentine countered that police courage, efficiency, and integrity had won "the confidence of the law-abiding citizens."[12] In fact, only hoodlums resented the NYPD.

Locke tended to support the Mayor's Commission. In a confidential report, he urged La Guardia to publish the commission's findings immediately, he concluded that Valentine was in serious error, and he called for immediate remedial action in certain areas of health, housing, education, recreation, and police-community relations. Abject conditions in Harlem were due to long-standing in-

consideration, "considerable civic neglect," "some discrimination," and the Depression.[13] Because the situation
was grave, he advised against department heads quibbling
over the findings of the Mayor's Commission. Indeed, that
report must become "the basis of a new civic program." In
his article, "Harlem: Dark Weather-Vane," Locke objec-
tively described the riot, summarized the commission's report, and recorded what municipal action had been taken
to meet the crisis. He emphasized that La Guardia had
inherited the conditions that sparked disorder and listed
several preriot plans that had been "seriously delayed by
lack of capital funds or federal subsidies." He refrained
from criticizing municipal commissioners or departments.
Since La Guardia was "losing no time in acting to improve
the Harlem situation," he was optimistic about Harlem's
future.[14]

La Guardia did not implement all of Locke's recommendations, but he did agree with the remarks about quibbling
and the need for constructive action. By August 1936,
when Locke's article was published, significant programs
were already in progress. Four years later, the Harlem
River Houses, the Central Harlem Center building, the
Women's Pavilion at Harlem Hospital, and two Harlem
schools were completed.[15] Also, the number of black
nurses and attendants of the Hospital Department doubled
and that of black physicians and medical board members
tripled. Moreover, they were being assigned to hospitals
whose staffs had previously been all or nearly all white.
Blacks were also receiving better employment opportunities in the civil service. Further health and educational
facilities were planned for the near future.

Perhaps most important were mayoral appointments of
blacks. Before the riot, Tax Commissioner Hubert T. Delany and a few other blacks had been held over from the
previous administration. After the disorder, however, Afro-
Americans received more serious recognition. In 1936, the
Reverend John H. Johnson was named to the Emergency
Relief Board.[16] Equally important, La Guardia appointed

Myles Paige the city's first black magistrate and Jane Bolin the first black woman judge in American history.[17] Blacks were also placed in the offices of the city marshal, corporation counselor, and district attorney. Accordingly, the *Amsterdam News'* first editorial for 1940 praised La Guardia for appointing "more Negroes to big, responsible jobs in the city government . . . than all the other mayors of the city combined."[18]

La Guardia's decision to improve the living conditions of black New Yorkers was partly political. Anticipating the riot as an issue in the 1937 mayoral campaign, he had Locke prepare material describing how far his administration had gone toward implementing the recommendations of the Mayor's Commission.[19] His confluent motives were again evident in 1941, when he appointed Samuel J. Battle parole commissioner. One columnist astutely concluded that the appointment was "good for the Mayor in an election year, good for the Negroes of New York who needed just such a hypodermic, and good for Battle because he deserved advancement."[20]

As a result, numerous white liberals and black residents sincerely respected La Guardia. In 1940, officials of the New York Public Library's Schomburg Collection and the Association for the Study of Negro Life and History honored him, along with five other whites and six blacks, for improving race relations.[21] Walter White wrote that local officials as far away as California were influenced by La Guardia's position on civil rights.[22] And nowhere was black admiration more clearly displayed than during a mayoral campaign.

On the eve of the 1941 mayoral election, La Guardia bustled into Harlem. A crowd of 20,000 black supporters jammed Colonial Park for a political rally that more closely resembled a "party among friends."[23] Against the background of music by Cab Calloway, the enthusiastic audience greeted La Guardia: "Yeah Man!" "Hi Butch!" "That's our Mayor!" These salutations were repeated by individuals in the crowd and "hundreds of persons . . .

hanging out of the windows of surrounding apartment houses." Visibly impressed, La Guardia announced what everyone knew: "My administration and myself have not treated Harlem any different than any other section of the city, but we have insisted on giving Harlem what any other section gets." As La Guardia concluded his talk, Bill Robinson arrived from Boston. "The Mayor of New York now welcomes the Mayor of Harlem," La Guardia shouted, pulling his friend and the most popular entertainer in Harlem to the microphone. Clearly the Colonial Park gathering's size, spontaneity, and warmth reflected far more than political payment for a progressive administration.

La Guardia's relationship with black society transcended political campaigns—for example, in the field of crime and delinquency. Early in 1940, he approved a Plan for Prevention of Juvenile Delinquency in the City of New York submitted by Justice Stephen S. Jackson of the Domestic Relations Court.[24] Fiscal limitations prevented the full implementation of Jackson's plan, which was designed for a section of West Harlem. La Guardia, in fact, seemed to dismiss the project until an alleged "Harlem crime wave" occurred late in the following year. Although initial statements by the Mayor and municipal officials gave credence to reports by white newspapers that crime was rampant in Harlem,[25] the administration eventually moved publicly to defend the character of black residents. Personnel and funds were now made available for Jackson's plan, though meager in relation to the problem.[26] Attempts were also undertaken to improve the socioeconomic conditions fostering criminal and delinquent behavior.[27] Again, financial limitations retarded any meaningful reconstruction.

As the war progressed and the white press periodically sensationalized a black "crime wave," La Guardia continued to support AfroAmerican society. He praised Harlem's fine families and reproved their critics.[28] His actions were motivated as much by self-interest as by personal belief. Since environment affected crime, criticism of a "crime wave" was also criticism of government services in black communities. When in 1943, for example, the Kings County Grand Jury criticized the crime and slum conditions in Bedford-Stuyvesant, La Guardia marshaled evidence to document the improvement made in that area by his administration.[29] In defending black New Yorkers, he defended his record, challenged the concept that crime and race were synonymous, and aligned himself with the black community. Such an alliance, however, could not have existed if black citizens had not already respected the Mayor.

Mayoral efforts in the field of employment also drew AfroAmerican respect. Early in 1941, La Guardia, like other officials, believed he lacked authority to compel defense industries to hire black workers and questioned the effectiveness of such authority. In response to urgings by the local Urban League, La Guardia gently inquired about discriminatory employment practices at Brewster Aeronautic, Grumman Aircraft Engineering, and Republic Aviation companies.[30] His inquiry carried no governmental force or threat of governmental force. Nonetheless, Urban Leaguer Charles Collier, Jr., was optimistic about Republic Aviation's plan to experiment with black labor and thanked the Mayor for assisting to make such a policy possible.[31]

As black demands increased, La Guardia considered compelling defense industries to employ black workers. His role in the negotiations of the March on Washington Committee (MOWC) with President Roosevelt prompted him to rethink the entire issue. Before Roosevelt yielded to A. Philip Randolph's demands for a Fair Employment Practices Committee (FEPC), La Guardia was brought into the negotiations. Aware of the Mayor's popularity among blacks and of the MOWC's New York City origins, presidential aides hoped he could avert a march on the nation's capital.[32] Following a conference with black leaders and presidential representatives on June 13, La Guardia advised the White House that nothing short of "the President's presence and direction" would prevent the march.[33] Roosevelt then agreed to confer with the MOWC on June

18. At Randolph's request, La Guardia attended the conference, where he broke the impasse by supporting Randolph's proposal that the march would be called off in exchange for a meaningful executive order.[34] Encouraged by the Mayor's mediation, Roosevelt appointed him to chair a committee to recommend a solution for racial discrimination in defense work.[35] Subsequently, the committee drafted an executive order, but before issuing it Roosevelt instructed La Guardia to make a final attempt to dissuade Randolph from marching without promise of the order. That failing, the President issued Executive Order 8802. It was based on a draft submitted by La Guardia and probably suggested by his committee.[36]

La Guardia's role in the MOWC negotiations marks his new willingness to commit government to civil rights. Executive Order 8802 reaffirmed a federal policy opposed to discrimination in the employment of workers in defense industries or government and created apparatus to enforce that policy. Randolph and White now pressured Roosevelt to appoint the Mayor FEPC chairman. "La Guardia's standing among colored people and his reputation for getting things done," White argued, "make it imperative that he be named Chairman."[37] La Guardia apparently was willing to serve, at least temporarily, but Roosevelt refused to appoint his liberal friend to the politically sensitive FEPC.[38] Instead, southerner Mark Ethridge, liberal editor of the *Courier-Journal* (Louisville, Kentucky), became the first chairman.

La Guardia quickly adopted Executive Order 8802 as New York City's official municipal policy. He thought about creating a local body to deal with discrimination in employment, but decided against it and referred complaints to Governor Herbert H. Lehman's recently established Committee on Discrimination in Employment and to the FEPC.[39] In keeping with the Mayor's personal style and politics, however, complaints relating to municipal departments or municipally funded programs were investigated by mayoral personnel.[40]

Although La Guardia came to believe that state and federal government were responsibile for preventing discrimination in public and publicly supported employment, he believed as strongly that hatred could not be removed by law. Civil rights legislation should goad individuals toward better race relations rather than reinforce antagonism: if brotherhood was not "in your heart and head," the Mayor testified before the FEPC, "all the laws" would not cure discrimination.[41] Partly because of this reasoning, La Guardia delayed enactment of Local Law No. 44 until the penalties for its violation were reduced. Introduced by Anthony J. Di Giovanna, it forbade any employer engaged in municipal or municipal-related work to refuse employment of or to discharge "any person on account of . . . race, color or creed."[42] La Guardia would see that all laws were "obeyed and enforced," but education, not coercion, was the way to rid society of prejudice.[43]

La Guardia doubted that government possessed the authority to compel private employers who were not receiving government contracts or funds to hire minorities. Here, he relied on moral suasion and personal influence. He asked Daniel Higgins of Eggers and Higgins, Architects, for example, about possible employment for a black man who came "highly recommended by Marian Anderson."[44] But as the war progressed, La Guardia sought to impose some mayoral jurisdiction. Since private employment agencies played an important role in the hiring practices of private enterprise and since they were licensed by municipal authorities, he acted to prevent their running discriminatory employment ads that did not disclose the employer's name. For over a year, La Guardia and License Commissioner Paul Moss attempted first to persuade, then to order, private agencies either to refrain from placing such advertisements (which were sometimes derogatory) or to publicize their clientele.[45] The logic, of course, was to expose those discriminating and, in the process, press them to change their policy. Eventually, in May 1942, the City Council enacted Local Law No. 11, which required the agencies to record discriminatory placement orders, to open their records to the license commissioner, and to identify the clients of such advertisements.[46]

Civil rights legislation aside, World War II provided La Guardia with a democratic atmosphere and positions of influence more conducive to aiding black New Yorkers. As Civilian Defense Director and chairman of the Joint Permanent Defense Board, he placed black volunteers in air raid service, which was previously closed to them, and secured the war materials that were necessary to keep operating a plant that employed over four hundred black workers.[47] Nevertheless, New York City's marginal position in the war economy and the scarcity of finances and materials limited his efforts to improve socioeconomic conditions throughout the metropolitan area.

Handcuffed during the war, La Guardia began laying plans for the coming peace. He instructed the City Planning Commission, for example, to prepare a postwar program that would include the completion of housing projects suspended because of war exigencies.[48] Sensitive to the needs of black residents, he later urged Governor Thomas E. Dewey to press the state legislature for housing appropriations that would permit the city to purchase land and draw plans for four state projects, two of which—the Abraham Lincoln and the James Weldon Johnson houses—were to be built in Harlem.[49]

Yet in his zeal to expand New York City's living facilities, La Guardia committed one of the gravest errors of his career. On the eve of the riot-torn summer of 1943 and after several years of effort, he contracted the Metropolitan Life Insurance Company to construct Stuyvesant Town.[50] Parks Commissioner Robert Moses was most responsible for this quasi-public housing project in lower east Manhattan. The Metropolitan's traditional discriminatory employment practices and a public statement by its chairman, Frederick H. Ecker, led many to believe that black applicants would be excluded from the project. It is doubtful that La Guardia knew very much about the contract's specifics until critics brought them to public attention; yet he was the mayor and, in the final analysis, responsible for the contract.[51] Concerned about the housing problem and looking to the future, he supported Moses' position that it was more important to commit private enterprise to public housing than to jeopardize that effort by insisting on non-discriminatory tenant selection. He hoped eventual litigation would ensure against discriminatory practices. Indeed, in 1940 he unified the subway system and in 1942 he signed Local Law No. 11, both on the assumption that judicial review would substantiate his controversial actions.[52] His critics, however, feared Stuyvesant Town would set a precedent for discriminatory tenant selection in future quasi-public projects. La Guardia's progressivism and the war's democratic purpose made the issue that much more appalling to them.

Despite public criticism and opposition from councilmen Adam Clayton Powell, Jr., and Stanley M. Isaacs, the contract was promulgated.[53] In time, the City Council acted upon a bill originated by Powell and Isaacs, which forbade discriminatory tenant selection in all future public and quasi-public projects. In time, too, La Guardia committed the Metropolitan Life to build a project in Harlem, but the litigation he assumed would integrate Stuyvesant Town ensured its segregation into the 1950s. Stuyvesant Town marked the beginning of a farsighted concept that committed private enterprise to public housing. Perhaps the price was higher than La Guardia had anticipated, for clearly he compromised his beliefs in racial justice. "Can it be, Mr. Mayor," asked an incredulous housewife, "that you, of all people, are . . . approving discrimination?"[54] At the same time, Stuyvesant Town reflected the impact of the war on democratic-minded residents of both races who opposed the contract. It promoted unprecedented legislation in the field of quasi-public housing, which further committed government to defending civil rights.

Despite La Guardia's generally solid civil rights record, the Stuyvesant Town incident reveals that the Mayor's understanding of the struggle for equality had limits. La Guardia lumped all discrimination, hate, and prejudice together without perceiving the uniqueness of racism or comprehending fully what it meant for black society. Discrimination, he wrote in 1941, "does not always lie in any one locality . . . or against any one group."[55] He believed that time and education would accomplish the assimilation of all racial and ethnic groups into American society. Whites must acknowledge the constitutional rights of blacks, who, in turn, must "meet competition."[56] Ideally, everyone should practice and teach good will. It was also necessary for "members of . . . minority groups to deport themselves in such a manner that there will be no basis for criticism."[57] Education programs would publicize the contributions of minority groups and "the good, human qualities of individuals as individuals."

Assimilation could be advanced, he believed, if he himself set the example and if "the different minority groups" took advantage of available opportunities. He would get "fed up with the talk about the problems of Harlem" and praise "the fine families in this section of the City."[58] By appointing talented black citizens to important posts, he was providing an opportunity for them to display "good, human qualities." Serving on a committee to honor James Weldon Johnson or to assist the Colored Locomotive Firemen, he was ever-present.[59] In sorrow, he attended the funerals of a black patrolman and of Fred R. Moore, publisher of the *Age;* in bliss, he entertained the Walter Whites or married the Hubert T. Delanys.[60] Nor did it matter whether La Guardia attended the funeral of patrolman John Hall out of sympathy or expedience. What counted was his obvious desire to honor a martyred black policeman—who was accidentally slain by fellow officers—just as he would a white policeman.

La Guardia also relied on black leaders for their judgment on racial matters. He called on Lester B. Granger of the National Urban League and on A. Philip Randolph of the Brotherhood of Sleeping Car Porters, among others, for advice. Often he relied on persons associated with the administration, perhaps Battle, Delany, or Paige.[61] Regularly, he turned to his intimate friend Walter White. No other public figure of his stature made more of an effort to consult black leadership or learn the problems confronting black residents.

La Guardia consulted only traditional black leadership, however, and only on issues involving race relations. His caution, often a refusal to consult with more aggressive leadership, isolated and alienated him from important segments of the black community. He dealt with black leaders who, like himself, believed that overly aggressive tactics were harmful to the racial struggle. Well-intended, La Guardia's reliance on the advice of black leaders solely for race-related areas defined black input in a limited, even segregated, way.

Perhaps the war, more than anything, affected mayoral activities in all areas. La Guardia wanted desperately to participate more directly in the war. He expressed interest in cabinet, ambassadorial, and administrative posts, especially to direct Italy's reconstruction. Unwilling to deprive New York City of La Guardia's services and leary of his maverick disposition, Roosevelt appointed him to part-time positions as chairman of the American section of the Joint Permanent Defense Board and, then, as Civilian Defense Director.[62] The early part of each week he spent in Washington on civilian defense duties; then he returned to govern New York City. Newbold Morris, the City Council president, recalled that defense obligations kept La Guardia "away a great deal and I assumed the administration responsibilities."[63] A four-day work week as mayor, plus the pressures of additional federal positions, compounded the difficulty of each task and exhausted La Guardia. From the outset, his final term was hampered by part-time leadership.

The war's priority also affected La Guardia's view of civil rights. He made sincere efforts to impose the "Double V" standard: Victory at Home, Victory Abroad. But if the choice was between the war effort and civil rights, La Guardia consistently sided with the former. In early 1943, he lent the United States Navy facilities at Hunter College for the purpose of training United States Navy and Coast Guard Women's Reserves, both of which excluded blacks. Unlike other white liberals, however, La Guardia did not desert blacks completely, or even frequently.

La Guardia's administrative style and personality also restricted his approach to civil rights. Although he consulted black advisers regularly, his desire to govern completely sometimes resulted in costly errors. Apparently, no one conferred with black leaders about Stuyvesant Town. Then, too, La Guardia opposed nonofficial persons or organizations conducting official business. Hence he permitted commissioners to investigate charges of discrimination in their own departments, a policy containing obvious shortcomings. If La Guardia had been less trusting of his own administration, he could have been more effective in combating institutional racism.

Incapable of handling criticism, La Guardia gave no quarter to those he considered adversaries. In race relations, he feared that self-serving demagogues would retard progress. "There are those," he wrote, probably with Powell in mind, "who try to use this issue to manufacture a problem so as to give themselves a cause, an interest and perhaps even a livelihood."[64] He also jousted constantly with journalists, whom he accused of slanting the news.[65] This attitude, of course, prevented him from appreciating or utilizing the constructive ideas and abilities of his critics. Pride and achievement deluded La Guardia into believing that progess was greater than it sometimes was.

Yet La Guardia contributed to the quest for equality. Even though his emphasis on gradualism reflected the period in which he lived, his struggle for racial justice reflected the morality he believed in, and it was in advance of the times. Complex and capable, La Guardia was at once an administrator, a politician, and a progressive; he advocated civil rights on many levels and for many reasons. Most black people saw in him more friend than politician. On the eve of riot in 1943, they would have agreed with Samuel J. Battle that "La Guardia . . . is the greatest mayor New York City ever had."[66]

Somewhat similar to La Guardia in personality and temperament, the handsome and charismatic Adam Clayton Powell, Jr., was the darling of most black New Yorkers.[67] Thirty-two years old in 1940, he was everything but an average black man. His AfroAmerican and Cherokee ancestry reflected the slavery experience of some of his ancestors, but in appearance he revealed the English and German side of his genealogy: light-skinned, hazel-eyed, aquiline-nosed, and brown-haired, he could have passed for white. Sheltered and spoiled as a youth, Powell had witnessed the deprivation, despair, and permanency of ghetto life, but never experienced it personally. He received an exceptional education, earning a Bachelor of Arts at Colgate University in 1930 and a Master of Arts in Religious Education at Columbia University a year later. Between these academic pursuits, he traveled in North Africa, Asia Minor, and Europe.

As a boy, Powell was conscious of his light complexion.[68] While at Colgate, he passed for white until his father came to lecture on race relations. Powell must have thought deeply about the destructive ramifications of passing for white, for later he wrote that "the attitude that fostered it represented the most ruthless form of division."[69] In fact, he considered the black-mulatto schism in all periods of United States history as the major impediment to the struggle for equality. Thereafter, Powell would take every opportunity to assure black people of his allegiance. "One of the things that gives me strength," Powell admitted in later life, "is that people say, 'Here's a guy who could live white, be white; but he isn't—he's part of our community.' "[70]

Powell was most influenced by his father and the church. Adam Clayton Powell, Sr., was responsible for building the Abyssinian Baptist Church into the largest black Protestant

congregation in the United States. In 1937, Powell fulfilled his father's wishes by succeeding him as pastor. He also inherited the elder Powell's political ability and his concept of the church as "a mighty weapon" for achieving social justice.[71]

Claiming a membership of thousands, the Abyssinian Baptist Church served as Powell's power base.[72] Early in the Depression he directed the Abyssinian relief program, which fed, clothed, and sheltered thousands of Harlemites. He also became involved in protest at this time, successfully leading a delegation before the New York City Board of Estimate to oppose the banning of five doctors from Harlem Hospital. Powell considered the experience "heady wine for a youngster of twenty-two" and, for the first time, realized the potential of mass action.[73] In 1936, he joined other black leaders to form the National Negro Congress for the purpose of stimulating political and economic action. Two years later, the Reverend William Lloyd Imes, A. Philip Randolph, and Powell organized the Greater New York Coordinating Committee Employment for blacks. As director, Powell employ boycott and picketing tactics, gaining jobs for black and popularity for himself. Using identical technique 1941, he led the Harlem Bus Strike Committee to an precedented employment agreement with the private companies and the Transportation Workers Union. Ac ing to Powell's estimates, which are greatly exagge four years of picketing brought "ten thousand jobs "ten million dollars" to Harlem.

Powell worked to become a grassroots leader. Wl tional figures were required to move about and wo influential members of both races, Powell concent Harlem and direct, personal contact with its r Magnetic and militant, his eloquence and achie captured the feelings of many blacks, who easily with him. His personality and style set him others, like Reverend Imes, who were also leaders and pastors of large Harlem congregati

Powell was more aggressive, ambitious, and politically sagacious than other local leaders. In 1941, he successfully ran for City Council. Under the existing proportional representation system, it was especially difficult for an Afro-American to be elected. Every voter in each borough chose from all the council candidates regardless of their districts, and only six candidates (in Manhattan) would be elected by a complicated process of elimination; a large majority of black votes and a significant number of white votes were necessary for victory. Entering the race without official party backing, Powell engineered an impressive victory. First he convinced rival black candidates Channing Tobias, the Republican, and Max Yergan, the American Laborite, to withdraw in favor of his candidacy. As his popularity increased, major black and white leaders and organizations, including La Guardia, the GOP, and American Labor Party, endorsed him.

Powell took advantage of the collapse of machine politics that had begun with La Guardia's 1933 victory over Tammany Hall. As reform brought an end to black politicians serving uptown white bosses, a more wide-open multiparty process emerged.[75] Powell provided the leadership, and the Abyssianian Baptist Church furnished the infrastructure of human and financial resources necessary for political success at a time when blacks were denied access to party mechanisms and when those very mechanisms were collapsing.[76] Early in the campaign, Powell transformed the Greater New York Coordinating Committee into The People's Committee, which supervised 1,800 campaign workers and eight offices.[77] Its aim was to make Harlem "Powell Conscious" by stressing his record, particularly in attaining employment for black workers. His endorsements, popularity, record, and publicity kept Herman C. Stoute, the black Democratic candidate, from seriously cutting into the black voting bloc. Powell was easily elected the first black councilman as blacks and liberal whites gave him the third largest number of votes among Manhattan's candidates.[78]

Powell wore no specific party label. He "always liked the guy who was nationally a Democrat, locally a Republican, theoretically a Socialist, but practically a Communist."[79] Accordingly, he endorsed Harold C. Burton, a Republican, and Hulan Jack, a Democrat, for Assembly, and Socialist Layle Lane and Communist Benjamin J. Davis, Jr., for Congress. Although some politics was involved, he generally supported candidates who would best serve the public interest and favored a "swing vote" strategy. "We are open to all parties," he announced prior to the New York gubernatorial election, "but we will not be dominated by any one."[80]

Party labels aside, Powell was unpredictable but not enigmatic. He believed that only an independent could be trusted by the masses to act in their interest. Like several other independents, black and white, he was influenced by the Communist Party and its Popular Front. Hence he sought to forge a biracial political coalition of the common people along popular, though non-Communist, lines. Therefore he opposed black separatism and anti-Semitism and worked "to smash Hitlerism, both domestic and foreign."[81] It was not by chance that his volunteers were designated "The People's Committee," his campaign "a people's crusade," his election "a victory of the people," or, later, his newspaper, the *People's Voice*.[82] Indeed, the latter, which was begun in February 1942 and became Powell's political mouthpiece, was "open to any organization engaged in the great fight for complete emancipation of all people."[83]

In opposing separatism, Powell made it clear that he championed blackness. Whatever the issue, Powell was first committed to black people, for they comprised his immediate constituency, the nucleus of his coalition, and the source of his power. "I am not seeking a political job," he campaigned before the Colored Baptist Convention.[84] "I am fighting for a chance to give my people the best representation in the affairs of their city." Consistently, he endorsed AfroAmericans for public office and opposed a black candidate only when one competed against another.

Yet Powell sought integrated coalitions when they were possible. He opposed, for instance, Randolph's decision in 1943 to bar whites from the March on Washington movement. He emphasized, however, that "Negro mass organizations . . . should be led, directed and supported *in the main* by black people."[85] Rather than contradicting himself, Powell brought his integrationist philosophy in line with the realities of his community and the needs of his constituency. Among 200,000 black residents, integration was an ideal, not a reality.

More than any other leader, Powell related the racial struggle to the people's crusade and both of those to World War II. When war came, he emphasized the correlation of national and universal aims: America could not defeat Hitler abroad without defeating Hitlerism at home.[86] Powell contended that black citizens struggling for racial justice were creating new white citizens, who together would found—in Wendell Willkie's phrase—"One World."[87]

In part, Powell's thoughts were influenced by Communist doctrine. The Depression, the emphasis on class rather than caste, the attractiveness of an ideology preaching brotherhood and racial justice attracted Powell to Marxist-Leninist theory. As a result, he associated with Communists and the Communist Party (CPUSA) organizations. Powell stressed economics as the key to racial equality. He contended that black society needed a second emancipation, "an emancipation from the shackles of economic slavery."[88] Speaking about the war, he used jargon that may have appeared to some as Communistic: Hitler was "the product of a western culture based upon greed, dictatorship, privilege"; the war could be lost because "we haven't a strong people's base."[89]

Not a Communist, Powell was, in his own words, "a radical and a fighter."[90] Despite his presence at Communist-sponsored rallies, his endorsement of Communist office-seekers, and his support of the campaign to release CPUSA president Earl Browder from prison, Powell's primary motive for associating with Communists was to advance justice. The rallies promoted the Double V campaign, the office-seekers advocated civil rights, and Browder, like the Scottsboro Boys, was a victim of "the Un-Americans."[91] Powell accepted the Communist Party emphasis on social justice and economics, but never its Russian allegiance or revolutionary ideology. Upset by the German-Russian Non-aggression Pact of 1939, which he considered "the most classic doublecross in history," Powell contended that democracy was "the only thing left in the world for the masses to depend on."[92] His aspirations were tied to the United States, where he sought civil rights through the existing political process. Nor as an ordained minister could he have accepted the implications that Communism held for Christianity or nonviolence. Then, too, Powell had been socialized in a capitalistic, bourgeois value structure. He found in Communist thought some corollaries that paralleled his own thinking and used the Communists to advance the struggle of black people.

Powell's tactics were closely related to the Depression experience. Mass participation and grassroots organization, which reflected the Communists' as well as the Depression's influence, were the keys to his People's, Harlem Bus Strike, and Greater New York Coordinating committees. His strategy was to use the direct nonviolent "pressure of an increasing horde of people who knew they were right."[93] After election to the City Council, Powell regularly addressed or sponsored gatherings to protest injustices. In addition, he was now in a position to promote civil rights from within the government.

From the outset, Powell worked hard to build a machine that would augment the influence he initially lacked as a black independent. For mutual benefit, he and La Guardia attempted to establish a political relationship. Powell later reminded La Guardia, "You promised to look into the appointment of four or five key workers in our campaign in Harlem."[94] Shortly thereafter, Powell again requested municipal employment for some members of The People's Committee. More striking, he asked La Guardia to support his efforts to be appointed minority leader of the City Council. La Guardia disapproved of Powell's increasingly bold efforts to accumulate power. To encourage The People's Committee, the Mayor recorded, would be "to encourage a permanent headache."[95] Any advice or assistance for Harlem's population, he elaborated, "should be *through existing* or newly established City depts. and agencies." The suggestion that he assist Powell to become minority leader was "terrible and n.g."

The relationship continued into February of 1942, but shortly thereafter it collapsed. Powell's attacks on discrimination in higher education, in quasi-public housing, and in police activities directly associated the administration with racism. His involvement in the Double V campaign also seemed to threaten municipal tranquillity. Moreover, his boisterous, intimidating manner appeared to some to be self-serving demagoguery. The inevitable break between La Guardia and Powell came as a result of the councilman's first major proposal, which concerned discrimination in the faculty of city-owned colleges.

During the previous decade, only a very small number of blacks were appointed to administrative, research, or teaching positions in the city's private and public colleges. Dr. Max Yergan, director of the Council on African Affairs and president of the Communist Party–controlled National Negro Congress, was one of these. Following an investigation into subversive activities in New York City's educational system by the state legislature's Rapp-Coudert Committee in 1941, he was not reappointed instructor of Negro History at the City College of New York (CCNY).[96] College officials denied that Yergan was dropped because of his political affiliations and announced plans to replace him with a more qualified black scholar.[97] But most Afro-Americans, regardless of their politics, protested in Yergan's behalf.[98] Though Yergan was not reinstated, Powell's Greater New York Coordinating Committee for Employment commenced a drive to secure positions for black teachers in the city's colleges.

A few months later, immediately following the council elections, Powell decided to discuss the issue with the City Council. On February 3, 1942, he introduced Resolution No. 31, which called for an end to the practice of "obvious discrimination" in faculty appointments to the tax-supported municipal colleges and the adoption by the Board of Education of a policy making all such appointments "solely on the basis of merit, regardless of race, color or creed."[99] On February 13, the Committee on Rules conducted a hearing on the subject.

The presidents of the city colleges—CCNY, Hunter, Queens, and Brooklyn—and of the Board of Higher Education testified in opposition to Powell's charge, asserting that all faculty appointments were made on the basis of qualifications. On the strength of their testimony and the failure of Powell to marshal sufficient evidence, the Committee on Rules concluded that no evidence substantiated the charge of discrimination and recommended that the resolution be filed. The City Council complied by a vote of eighteen to two, Powell and Peter V. Cacchione dissenting.[100]

Soon Powell was being criticized by persons of both races. Some Council members believed he was seeking to smear the college presidents.[101] The *Age* editor, always a critic of Powell, agreed that Powell had failed to prove his charges.[102] In contrast, the *Amsterdam News* criticized him for failing in his attempt rather than for filing false charges. Discrimination in the city colleges did exist, the editor contended, "despite the fiasco the Harlem Councilman made of his unsupported charge."[103]

Clearly, Powell's debut as a councilman was unimpressive. He had made the serious charge of racial discrimination against an educational system noted for its progressivism and then had been unable to substantiate his allegation. Having failed, he played down his own inadequacies and argued that the Committee on Rules catered to the college presidents. Moreover, his premature and incompetent handling of the issue tended to weaken it, to make it seem facetious, as if racial discrimination in the city's colleges was out of the question.

In fact, racial discrimination did occur in the appointment of instructors to the municipal colleges. There was at least one documented instance of discrimination against a highly qualified, Harvard-trained black man, William H. Dean, who applied for a position in the city colleges.[104] The question was, in Dean's words, "if qualifications like mine are rejected, what chance . . . has a colored man to be appointed in the institutions of higher learning in New York City?"[105] No doubt, this example of discrimination was indicative of others. Councilman Cacchione pointedly asserted that "it matters not whether a single case of legal discrimination can be proved," for the fact remained that none of the city colleges' 2,000 permanent faculty members with the rank of professor or instructor was black.[106]

Still, Powell had a positive, though limited, effect. Within a year of his allegation, three of the four city colleges added or planned to add blacks to their faculties. However token, this was no small feat. According to most of the college presidents, the war—which was decreasing student enrollment and with it the need for additional professors—would prohibit progress in this area. It would also, the Reverend William Lloyd Imes cautioned, give some an excuse to withhold black appointments.[107]

As Powell continued to agitate for civil rights he increasingly isolated himself from La Guardia and most council members, who considered him an opportunist seeking issues and scapegoats. Some members of La Guardia's administration came to consider him a genuine threat to racial harmony. On May 17, 1942, Powell sponsored a rally at the Golden Gate Ballroom to protest the police slaying of Wallace Armstrong. "One More Negro Brutally Beaten and Killed," read an inflammatory handbill: "Shot down like a Dog by the Police."[108] Because the Armstrong affair was before a grand jury and because Powell's techniques smacked of demagoguery, the Police Commissioner advised La Guardia "that this type of rabble rousing is dangerous and might result in serious disorder."[109] In the public interest, the commissioner argued, Powell should be urged to cancel the meeting and await the grand jury's decision. On instructions from La Guardia, who was out of town, mayoral secretary, Lester B. Stone, unsuccessfully attempted to dissuade Powell from conducting the meeting.[110] Despite the administration's apprehension and police surveillance, no incidents occurred as a result of the gathering, but the La Guardia–Powell relationship was now severed permanently.[111] "The Mayor," Powell editorialized on May 23, " . . . is one of the most pathetic figures on the current American scene."[112]

La Guardia, no doubt, felt the same about Powell. "No greater mistake can be made," the Mayor wrote in an anniversary note to the *People's Voice*, "than to seek to make an issue where an issue does not exist."[113] Other white officials, and some black leaders, distrusted Powell. Councilwoman Genevieve Earle recalled that he "ran out on me" on at least one matter of council. Few members got along with Powell.[114] Besides, his charges seemed to most whites and a few blacks less important if not petty when compared to wartime problems.

In reality, Powell alerted residents of both races to the issues. He protested against racial discrimination wherever it appeared, in the city colleges, in police-community relations, and in several other areas. In every instance, there was evidence to substantiate his charges.

And though Powell's council contributions might be difficult for some people of both races to distinguish, they were well understood by most black New Yorkers. No doubt Powell exaggerated when he contended that each of his objectives "eventually came through victoriously."[115] Yet some of his efforts did result in important civil rights gains.

Powell's appeal and, in some ways, his most significant contribution was that of racial awareness. Symbolically, he promoted a day of honor for Crispus Attucks, black patriot of the American Revolution.[116] His cries of discrimination, his cool bravado, self-righteousness, and singleness of purpose defied "the Man." Others also confronted white society, but Powell did it more dramatically and publicly. He gave a sense of participation to thousands of black people by saying things they could not say without "getting into some trouble."[117] He was a surrogate who fulfilled the psychological needs of his followers. Powell's independence maximized his appeal and, according to NAACP lobbyist Clarence Mitchell, personified "the conflict between what whites think a Negro ought to act like and a Negro who intends to act as he wishes."[118] He excelled where few other blacks and certainly no white man could have.

Of course, Powell was not without faults. His intelligence and political ability were marred by arrogance and opportunism; his understanding of blackness, its meaning and struggle, were hindered by a selfish unwillingness to share leadership; his verbal harassment in public and friendly persuasion in private created mistrust among those he needed most; his sensational oratory, which enthralled most blacks, too often smacked of demagoguery; his aggressiveness, so necessary to making any meaningful racial progress, was often overplayed and on occasion irresponsible. He did not always marshal his evidence effectively, and further weakened his charges by his arrogant, ballyhoo tactics. Powell concentrated on getting the administration to enforce laws and improve living conditions for blacks. Hence he adopted issues as they arose, haranguing about one until another emerged, but he rarely followed one through.

Although an independent, Powell was hampered more by his personality, political style, and congressional ambitions. In trying to prove his independence to the people, he spoke "fearlessly on any subject" and focused "attention on wrongs that would have to be righted."[119] His rhetoric served a useful purpose, but it de-emphasized the cooperation needed to right such wrongs. His congressional ambitions, too, made him seek the limelight. As a congressman, in fact, Powell contended that the "primary and overriding responsibility of each Member of the House . . . is to get reelected."[120] It was easier to speak out, sponsor protest rallies, write sardonic columns, and challenge municipal officials than to work behind the scenes for a local ordinance.

To a significant degree, Powell's evaluation of earlier black leaders is a key to his own concepts and actions. Booker T. Washington was "subsidized" and "acceptable" to whites, while W. E. B. DuBois had failed to utilize the church or reach the masses.[121] In contrast, Marcus Garvey was "one of the greatest mass leaders of all times." From him, Powell came to understand the masses, the divisiveness of the black-mulatto schism, the dangers of black separatism but the need for awareness. Just as Garvey stirred imaginations, excited hearts, and promoted solidarity, so would Powell. Opposed to separatism, however, Powell would use Garvey's methods to achieve DuBois' aim of being "integrated into every part of American life."[121]

Powell, then, was in somewhat of a dilemma. His political style was molded by his interpretation of black citizens' needs, depending in large part on appeals to the principle of racial justice and on the presence of an "enemy."[122] Both the difficulty of compromising sacrosanct principles publicly and Powell's stridency left him with little political room in which to maneuver. If Powell had been more sensitive to leaders and officials, he might have accomplished more. That, however, would have depended as much on them. In refusing to admit flaws in an administration that he rightly considered one of the best in municipal history, La Guardia probably appeared paternalistic to Powell. As mayor of all New Yorkers, La Guardia did not share Powell's singlemindedness. Since mayoral success necessitated compromise and the delivery of tangible benefits, Powell's rhetoric sounded hollow to the Mayor. Police surveillance of the councilman and La Guardia's support of Stuyvesant Town must have reinforced Powell's worst assumptions. In the City Council, only Cacchione and Isaacs consistently supported Powell. Nor is there evidence to indicate that Powell would have received more support if he had adopted a more traditional style. Some council members may have used his personality to rationalize their positions when in fact they really opposed his concern for racial justice.

Their differences aside, Powell and La Guardia epitomized what most black New Yorkers felt a black leader and a white public official should be. Both were political mavericks who stressed independence, sought coalitions, and challenged machines. Powell, like the black community, was on the outside looking in; La Guardia represented the power structure. Together, their efforts and concern for social justice dampened the emergence of the deep-seated racial tensions that were blatant in other cities. Yet the hope generated by Powell and La Guardia was offset by the wretched living conditions and institutionalized racism that confronted black residents daily. First Depression, then war created circumstances that accentuated this hope and despair.

2

Ghetto Life during the Depression

Most of La Guardia's and Powell's black constituency were part of a relatively recent mass migration. Since 1890, economic insecurity and racial discrimination had prompted black people to migrate from the rural south to the urban north. During and after World War I, they crossed the Mason-Dixon line in increasing numbers. From the beginning, New York City was a prime target for this in-migration and by 1930 housed the nation's largest black community. That year, author James Weldon Johnson viewed Harlem as "a large-scale laboratory experiment in the race problem."[1] Blacks still had "very far yet to go and . . . very many things to gain," but because citizenship rights were guaranteed and protected "the Negro . . . ought to be able to work through discriminations and disadvantages."

New York's liberal tradition buoyed the hopes of black people everywhere. Indeed, the state's civil rights legislation was the most advanced in the nation. As early as 1909, racial discrimination was forbidden in jury service, law practice, public school admissions, and some areas of public accommodation. Civil rights were extended to various fields of public employment, work relief, and public works projects during the Great Depression. By 1937, the legislature had created the Temporary Commission on the Condition of the Urban Colored Population. A year later, a constitutional provision forbade the denial of equal protection of state laws to any person "because of race, color, creed or religion."[2]

To black migrants of the Depression and war decades, New York City was the promised land. Between 1930 and 1940, more than 145,000 black migrants entered New York alone.[3] By the decade's end, almost 7.5 million persons resided in the city, of whom 458,000, or 6 percent, were AfroAmerican.[4] Since New York City contained 90 percent of the state's black population, it provided the laboratory for race relations of which Johnson spoke.[5]

Blacks were segregated and unevenly distributed throughout New York City's five boroughs: 107,000 blacks lived in Brooklyn, while another 52,000 blacks resided in the Bronx, Queens, and Richmond.[6] But Harlem was, in the words of author Claude McKay, "the Negro capital of the world."[7] Covering 397 city blocks of northern Manhattan, it extended south to north between 110th and 155th streets, east to west between Third and Amsterdam avenues. Italian and Spanish families also lived there, but over 80 percent of its inhabitants were black and, in Central Harlem alone, accounted for 63 percent of the borough's entire black population.[8]

Increased migration caused blacks to extend Harlem's boundaries, north beyond 155th Street, south below 110th Street, and west across Amsterdam Avenue. It also compelled them to move to the other boroughs. Brooklyn's Bedford-Stuyvesant and Brownsville sections became predominantly black, while similar neighborhoods emerged in sections of Queens.[9] With the onset of war, the Bronx became the new residential target and by 1945 part of it had become a sizeable black community.

This influx of southern blacks intensified the "colored problem" in northern cities. As the migrants became aware of their numbers and the modes of redress available in northern society, they organized and made their presence felt, if not respected, by white men. Blacks soon realized that the promised land was a slum and that a sharp distinction existed between civil rights legislation and abject living conditions.

Despite attempts by President Franklin D. Roosevelt, Governor Herbert H. Lehman, and Mayor La Guardia to ameliorate the effects of the Depression with public assistance programs, blacks found the long delay in their inclusion in these recovery efforts intolerable. On March 19, 1935, riot swept through Harlem. The outburst, a subcommittee of the New York County Lawyers' Association charged, "surprised no one who has been in touch with the condition under which we have permitted our Negro citizens to live."[10] Eventually the report of the Mayor's Commission on Conditions in Harlem revealed the deepseated racism that permeated every aspect of society and had nurtured the frustration which exploded into riot.

On June 3, 1937, more than two years after the disturbance occurred, the state legislature created the Temporary Commission on the Condition of the Urban Colored Population. Despite the state commission's claim that "three years of concern on the part of State officials and members of the Legislature" was the reason for its creation, the commission was established in response to the Harlem riot.[11] In 1934, at the time state officials and legislators were said to be concerned for blacks, Governor Lehman contended that the state should not conduct an investigation of "only one racial group of the many that make up our general population."[12] Doubtless a few officials and legislators were sincerely interested in the plight of black residents; Lehman, for instance, perhaps New York's most liberal governor, was closely associated with Walter White of the NAACP and was himself a long-time member of that organization. Nevertheless, few officials fully comprehended the needs of black residents. Until Harlem's disorder they were unwilling to extend to AfroAmericans treatment that would appear to many voters as preferential.

Formulated along the lines of La Guardia's commission, the state commission was chaired by Assemblyman Harold

P. Herman and assisted by Lester B. Granger, ranking official of the National Urban League. By extending its investigation beyond Harlem and New York City, the state commission supplemented the findings of the Mayor's Commission and showed that similar conditions prevailed throughout the state. Bolstered by independent studies, the reports
and hearings of the commissions described the slum conditions that blacks in the state had been experiencing during
the previous decade, even in the previous century.[13]

Racial discrimination has always clearly been the key to
ghetto living, or more accurately the "vicious cycle."[14]
Then as now it consigns many lower-class AfroAmericans to
the most menial, lowest paying, and least secure occupations. Economic deprivation and residential segregation, in
turn, force them into dilapidated tenements. High rent and
increased population also prompt them to take in lodgers,
some of whom are irresponsible or worse. Since rent con-
sumes much of their already scant income, little remains for
food and clothing. Because they are undernourished and
ill-clad, living in congested and unsanitary quarters, their
health suffers. Racial prejudice, meanwhile, reduces the
quality and quantity of available medical facilities. For
some blacks, home life becomes matrifocal. The un- or un-
deremployed men, further humiliated by their wives' employment, find raising a family frustrating. Broken homes,
illegitimate children, and mental depression can result.
Children grow up without supervised recreation. Vocational training rather than liberal arts prepares them for
menial employment. Together, these factors promote juvenile delinquency, later adult crime. In turn, the insensitiv-
ity of police to black people increases their resentment toward white society. The cycle is complete.

Economic factors bear heavily on the cycle. Most of "the
problems confronting the colored population," asserted
the state commission, "arise primarily out of inadequate
incomes."[15] Discriminatory hiring practices deprived Afro-
Americans of adequate employment and, accordingly, of
nourishing foods, decent lodging, necessary medical care,

and a healthy family relationship. Hence many became wards of the state, depending on others, often the discriminators, for charitable assistance.

Relief and employment statistics for the Depression revealed the low economic status of black people. During the first week of September 1935, 43 percent of Harlem's black families were on relief.[16] Throughout the state that year, two-and-a-half times as many blacks as whites were on relief because of unemployment.[17] In the next two years, the city's black residents continued to be displaced from employment faster than whites, but were re-employed in positions supplied by the Emergency Relief Bureau's employment service at only half the rate. "Negroes," a high-ranking bureau official commented, "have one-half a bad chance."[18]

Verifying relief statistics, the New York State Employment Service (NYSES) recorded that blacks registering as unemployed in 1937 constituted 40 percent of all gainful AfroAmerican workers, while the corresponding percentage for all other groups was 15.[19] Since fewer blacks registered, their unemployment was even greater than the NYSES indicated. Moreover, blacks who did find work engaged in domestic and unskilled jobs. The unemployment problem was augmented by discrimination in fields which AfroAmericans had been readily accepted before the Depression forced whites into "nigger" work. Private employers discriminated openly. A representative of the Hotel and Restaurant Employees International told the state commission that many of New York City's larger hotels, such as the Astor, employed blacks only during times of labor difficulties, while major restaurants, like Childs, refused to hire blacks at all.[20] Discrimination was also reported in other menial positions, particularly among elevator operators and counter clerks.

In quasi-public businesses and public utilities the situation was worse. Fiduciaries were among the most obvious discriminators. In 1935, for example, the Metropolitan Life Insurance Company, with over 100,000 black policyholders in Harlem alone, still refused to employ black men in or out of that community.[21] The very size of utilities and their association with the public made them important employers. In New York City, utility employees comprised nearly 5 percent of all gainfully employed residents. Of approximately 135,000 utility workers in the metropolitan area, however, slightly over 1 percent were black, and most of them held janitorial positions.[22] The Mayor's Commission considered this pattern "a caste system."[23]

Nor were public employment services free of discrimination. The New York State Employment Service, largest single agency in the state, placed a significant percentage of black registrants, but almost all in "traditional jobs." A spokesman admitted that racial identification was required on applications and that only menial jobs were listed in the Harlem offices.[24] Vocational schools further relegated black workers to specific occupations by refusing to train them in fields reserved for whites. AfroAmericans, the state commission declared, "cannot find jobs without training and they are refused training because they might not be able to find jobs."[25]

The only hope appeared to be the city and state civil service systems, of which the former was commended by the state commission for its overall fairness.[26] Nevertheless, some irregularities were present at both levels.[27] In most cases, these resulted from civil service employees imposing their prejudices on the system's nondiscriminatory code.

Labor unions discriminated, too. A. Philip Randolph, founder and president of the Brotherhood of Sleeping Car Porters, estimated that the constitutions of twenty unions contained race clauses.[28] Others discriminated in more subtle ways. Some unions, he noted, refused to issue cards until blacks had jobs, knowing they could not get work without the cards. In spite of nondiscriminatory resolutions by the state leaders of large unions, the autonomy granted each local permitted its members to decide the issue for themselves. Those unions that did not discriminate were few and uninfluential.[29]

AfroAmerican business opportunities were limited even more than those of labor. In Harlem, where one would expect to find the most and the largest black enterprises, blacks ran less than 19 percent of the 10,300 businesses, all of them in fields requiring little capital.[30] Enterprises dealing with food and other necessities were owned by whites. Noting the black-owned personal services in Harlem, author Carl Offord remarked that "the only businesses which are still left to the Negro are those of pruning himself and burying himself—businesses which continue to be his only by virtue of race prejudice."[31] And since these fields required few employees, black businessmen could not assist their brethren in a meaningful economic way.

In most cases, racial prejudice was the reason for excluding blacks from certain types of employment, unions, and business. The Mayor's Commission attributed the employment problem to attitudes that restricted black people to positions symbolic of their inferior status, that judged them less efficient than whites, and that assumed the races were incapable of working together.[32] Most employers, the state commission concurred, were "fearful of injuring their business prospects by running counter to what they presumed to be a public prejudice."[33] Blacks were not employed as telephone operators, admitted Walter Williams, the New York Telephone Company's traffic manager, because they were incompetent. "Business judgment over a number of years" provided the reason why none of Manhattan's 4,500 operators were black![34] Williams denied that New York Telephone was breaking the law. He sympathized with the justice of hiring blacks, but concluded that the world was unjust and that business was a difficult and serious enterprise.

As a result, black employment opportunities were grim. Equally disturbing, both races had come to accept it. Many blacks failed to apply for positions because past experience and present discrimination convinced them that filing applications was useless. Consequently, as the Bureau of Labor remarked about New York City in 1937,

"The poorer half of the colored population must live on an income which is only 46 percent of that achieved by the poorer half of the white population."[35]

Housing, the second most important problem confronting black society, was directly affected by inadequate income and racial discrimination. Residential segregation forced blacks of every economic class to live in specified neighborhoods. Indeed, both violent and subtle measures were used to keep them there. The process was so effective that the state commission could find no section in New York State where residential segregation was not practiced.[36]

As expected, the segregated communities were the most run-down. Late in the 1930s, for instance, 30 percent of Harlem's dwellings were without bathing facilities.[37] Deterioration was accelerated by faulty maintenance, violation of municipal codes and laws, overcrowding, and, in some cases, by ignorant tenants.[38] In addition, residential segregation forced blacks to pay exorbitant rents. Most blacks were paying higher rents than whites for similar accommodations elsewhere in Manhattan.[39] Inadequate incomes increased the hardship of paying unreasonable rents, particularly for AfroAmerican relief recipients, whose housing allowances fell considerably below the rent demanded by landlords.[40]

Segregation, poverty, and high rents, in turn, fostered overcrowding. Between 1910 and 1935, black Harlem's population increased 600 percent while its boundaries expanded only twenty blocks north and south, three blocks east and west. As a result, a "population equal in size to twice the entire population of the state capital" was confined in an area of 262 blocks.[41] Langdon Post of the Tenement House Department noted that legislation forbidding overcrowding "can not possibly be enforced."[42]

Landlords renting to AfroAmericans did so on the profitable basis of supply and demand. This forced poverty-stricken tenants to engage in unlawful and unhealthy activities in order to raise rent money. Blacks sold numbers, staged rent parties, engaged in prostitution and theft, often with their landlord's knowledge. "We are forced to do things of that sort," a Harlemite testified, "because we must have a place to live."[43] But the primary means of collecting rent money was to take in lodgers. In one block of seventy-five Harlem families, boarders constituted 38 percent of the occupants and contributed almost 35 percent of the total family incomes.[44] These money-making methods, coupled with the congestion, created significant problems in other areas. Illness and death, especially that caused by contagious diseases, was disproportionately greater among blacks than whites. Comprising less than 7 percent of the total population in 1940, for example, blacks accounted for 27 percent of the city's 3,600 tubercular deaths.[45] Equally significant, improvement in the health of black people was not keeping pace with that of whites.

Low incomes, high rents, overpriced and inferior groceries compelled blacks to live on meager budgets and subjected them to malnutrition.[46] Inferior and discriminatory health facilities contributed to the problem. Private and public agencies assigned to the Central Harlem Health Center dealt inadequately with the problems of that community. Tuberculosis and veneral disease were not being treated in proportion to their importance. Harlem Hospital, the community's basic health facility, was overcrowded, unsanitary, and, at times, poorly supervised. Black physicians and nurses were denied policy-making positions and segregated in city hospitals that served black patients. Jim Crow policies also limited the training and experience they received. Black doctors and interns refused admittance to hospital staffs were—in a Harlem physician's opinion—denied the experience necessary "to keep abreast of the progress in medical science."[47] The same was true of the nursing profession.

Health, in turn, influenced education. Undernourished, hungry children no doubt slept more than they studied in the classroom. Nor were black students motivated by the fact that education would not improve their socioeconomic status. Despite the city's progressive educational system, which the Mayor's Commission commended as "the one institution in which democratic principles . . . tended to break down racial . . . differences," significant discrimination was prevalent.[48] Dilapidated and aged school buildings, inadequate teaching materials and overcrowded classrooms, unsympathetic white teachers, reflected real limits of progress.

More obvious forms of racial discrimination were practiced in the zoning of school districts, the curriculum offered AfroAmerican students, and the images they received of black and white societies. The Reverend John W. Robinson, chairman of the Permanent Committee for Better Schools in Harlem, asserted that the line of public school zoning was gerrymandered to assure segregation.[49] Most Harlem students attended Wadleigh, Textile, Haaren, and De Witt Clinton high schools, where the curriculum relegated them to a marginal economic status in society. Blacks, moreover, were ignored and degraded in academic studies. Robinson's committee found that almost four hundred books used in the city's schools depicted blacks as slaves, "lazy, shiftless."[50] Elsewhere in the state these practices were present on a lesser scale, doubtless because black populations were smaller.

Inferior and discriminatory education, combined with inadequate employment, indecent housing, poor health, and the lack of discipline that resulted from exposure to these factors, produced high rates of crime and delinquency. One contemporary though exaggerated description of Harlem focused almost exclusively on lawlessness in the tough sections. "Beale Street" (133rd Street between Fifth and Seventh avenues) was considered the worst area, "where a knife blade is the quick arbiter of all quarrels, where prostitutes take anything they can get."[51] Other black neighborhoods in Manhattan, as well as white ones experiencing similar socioeconomic and environmental conditions, encountered like problems.[52]

The high number of black delinquents was partly due to

aggressive police activity in ghetto areas and partly to definitions of "delinquent" and "neglected" children, particularly in New York City, where more facilities were available for the former.[53] Neglected and homeless children reflected the inability of some families to cope with the socioeconomic pressures. Insufficient play areas also promoted delinquency. Crime among black adults, particularly women, was also widespread.[54] Broken homes and inadequate incomes were clearly associated with crime rates. In Harlem, the Mayor's Commission noted that most offenses were in areas of economic profit, especially the numbers racket and prostitution.[55]

Despite the high rates of delinquency and crime, most blacks viewed policemen as the boldest examples of northern racism. At a public hearing conducted by the Mayor's Commission, the police were constantly booed and jeered by the black audience. The commission itself reported that police incompetence and brutality helped to ignite and spread the Harlem riot.[56] Critics of the police compared large concentrations of patrolmen in black ghettos to "an army of occupation" and complained of constant brutality.[57] The New York Police Department (NYPD) was also accused of not protecting blacks from criminals, of being "on the take," and of ignoring crimes involving only blacks.[58] Illegal police searches and other abuses of civil liberties produced further complaints.

The despair and frustration of these conditions notwithstanding, some New York blacks were hopeful during the Depression. Several times since 1890, various observers had recorded the presence of a "New Negro." In comparison with the behavior of blacks in earlier periods the "new" individual appeared racially aware and politically mature, sometimes even revolutionary. In the 1920s, this newness was seen in Marcus Garvey's Universal Negro Improvement Association.

The depression accelerated the New Negro movement. Black leaders, already aware of blacks' marginal economic position, used the crisis to promote solidarity and awareness. In particular, the clergy stressed self-help and unity. "We must spend our money among our own people," the Reverend John H. Johnson of St. Martin's Episcopal Church instructed his Harlem congregation.[59] And with the "Don't Buy Where You Can't Work" strategy of 1934, he began a successful drive to force Blumstein's Department Store to employ black sales personnel. The rival Abyssinian Baptist Church sponsored similar employment drives and quartered a Works Progress Administration for Women. "Most of them," the Reverend Adam Clayton Powell, Jr., said in reference to his parishioners, "would be as much at home on a picket line as they are in church."[60]

The New Deal, in turn, generated hope. For the first time since Lincoln, a president appeared genuinely concerned for black Americans. Whatever Roosevelt's motives, which ranged from paternalistic humanitarianism to political expediency, blacks were included in New Deal programs. Robert C. Weaver and other presidential advisers became known as "the Black Cabinet," while agencies such as the National Youth Administration employed blacks in administrative and supervisory capacities. Even in the segregated Civilian Conservation Corps, FDR gave the impression that AfroAmerican participation was not to fall below 10 percent.[61] A few New Dealers, notably Secretary of the Interior Harold Ickes, who guaranteed equitable employment of blacks in the construction of public housing, anticipated the government's future role in civil rights.[62]

The New Deal's impact on black life was significant, though not as immediately or materially beneficial as it was to whites. Roosevelt bolstered the identity of blacks as Americans and their hope for future progress. "Jesus leads me and Roosevelt feeds me," ran the lyrics of a popular Harlem song, "and I will follow 'cause ah must be fed."[63] Accordingly, black voters in New York City and elsewhere voted overwhelmingly for Roosevelt's third term, for a continued New Deal.[64] "The Negro," a commentator summarized, "has been quickening his pace ever since 1932, urged on first by the punch of depression, then by the push of government aid and social experiment."[65]

The pace of blacks in New York City was further influenced by the Harlem riot of 1935, which fostered unity. The Reverend John W. Robinson's Permanent Committee for Better Schools in Harlem was created as a direct response to the disorder. So was the economically oriented Greater New York Coordinating Committee for Employment organized by Randolph and the Reverends Imes and Powell. Symbolically founded on Lincoln's birthday, 1938, the committee was allegedly composed of more than two hundred organizations that represented 15,000 persons and epitomized black unity.[66]

The riot also brought to the surface aggressive, resentful feelings. Unlike earlier disorders in which whites attacked blacks, Harlem's was a hostile outburst "against racial discrimination and poverty in the midst of plenty."[67] The public hearings of the Mayor's Commission and, later, the state commission offered black society for the first time a captive white audience, a sense of unity, and a hope that something positive was to be done. The riot also informed whites that the "colored problem" was no longer sectional or regional. In fact, the New Negro was more of an urban than a rural product.

The New Negro, of course, did not symbolize the entire population of Harlem. At one hearing of the Mayor's Commission, for example, which ghetto residents called "the People's Court," an older witness was reluctant to speak about police brutality. Fearing reprisal from the NYPD, he testified in a low, muffled voice. "Aw man, talk up," the audience goaded, "you ain't down south!" The young man who followed him, on the other hand, exemplified the New Negro.[68] Asked if he had seen anyone throw milk bottles at the police, he gamely retorted: "Who the hell is gonna throw . . . bottles at a cop who's got a forty-four staring him in the face?" Then, turning to the audience, he quipped: "Am I talking loud enough?" The attitudes of most blacks were somewhere between the reticent elder and the intrepid youth. As late as 1942, the Office of Facts and Figures reported that a survey of more than one thousand blacks in New York City showed that the respondents more often replied "I don't know" to white questioners than black ones, a hesitance not characteristic of the New Negro.[69] Some blacks could have been demonstrating contempt by not speaking to whites. Nevertheless, a government official interpreted it as a reluctance to speak positively to whites.

Nor were most of those who resembled the New Negro chauvinistic or separatist. Letters by Walter White and A. Philip Randolph, among others, to La Guardia and Lehman emphasized biracial methods for achieving civil rights. Powell, among the most militant of leaders, declared, "let's stop trucking nationalistically and start streamlining inter-racially for our only salvation is in world brotherhood."[70] Most black leaders doubtlessly agreed with the contention that racial unity was necessary for progress, but cautioned that too much solidarity would be counterproductive.[71]

New York City's black and, especially, white leadership, moreover, was atypical in its concern for the welfare of black citizens and its receptiveness to national organizations. The Brotherhood of Sleeping Car Porters, the National Negro Congress, the National Urban League, and the National Association for the Advancement of Colored People maintained headquarters in the city and were active in local affairs. A few leaders, like Walter White, occasionally influenced the civil rights decisions of La Guardia and Lehman. Furthermore, prominent citizens and officials were associated with the national organizations and, thereby, influenced by them in their daily work. Of the forty-five members of the NAACP's Board of Directors in 1940, for instance, almost half were New York residents, including Governor Lehman, Lieutenant Governor Charles Poletti, City Tax Commissioner Hubert T. Delany, and the Reverend John H. Johnson.[72]

Local religious and secular leaders, and their organiza-

tions, were also active. Unlike many black clerics elsewhere, the ministers of New York City, as exemplified by
Powell in Harlem and the Reverend Thomas Harten in
Bedford-Stuyvesant, played significant roles in the struggle for racial equality. Similarly, the black press—*Age,
Amsterdam News,* and, later, *People's Voice*—espoused
the cause. At times, religious and secular leaders closed
ranks, as in the Greater New York Coordinating Committee for Employment.

During the Depression, tactics were as diverse as
leadership. Meetings, labor parades, soap-box oratory, and
boycotts were in wide use. Emphasis was clearly on mass
participation, on providing the average black citizen with
a sense of pride and unity. By 1940, the middle-class–
oriented NAACP even adopted some mass tactics. "Did
you hold a mass meeting during . . . October?" queried
the *Youth Bulletin* in reference to protest against the segregated armed forces.[73] Shortly before Pearl Harbor, civil
disobedience became the logical outgrowth of previous
tactics, and was manifested in A. Philip Randolph's plans
to march on Washington.

As the depression decade came to a close, civil rights
advocates were aware of the hope and despair that sur-
rounded the position of black New Yorkers. Certainly the
abject conditions and widespread discrimination un-
covered by the mayoral and state commissions were de-
spairing; but the very creation of those bodies was hopeful.
No doubt, disappointment occurred when only two of the
state commission's fourteen bills were enacted by the legislature, but La Guardia's continued action fostered expectations.[74] Also the state commission's reports and proposals,
according to Lester B. Granger, "shaped the way for later
consideration of legislative action which was more successful."[75] Altruism, necessity, and particularly the emergence
of a more aggressive black leadership spurred some white
leaders to press for the welfare of black residents. On the
eve of World War II many anticipated further improvement
in race relations.

3

Black Response to World War II

World War II, like the Depression and New Deal, served as a catalyst to accelerate the struggle for racial justice. Both the rhetoric and circumstance of war offered black Americans unprecedented opportunities for protest. Responding to the crisis as blacks and as Americans, their attitudes and actions were far more complex than those of whites. Moreover, their energies were divided between the struggle abroad and the one at home. Only belatedly included in the war economy, blacks found their patriotism related to—and often in conflict with—the fight for equality.

Like other citizens, AfroAmericans foresaw United States involvement in World War II and reacted similarly. In 1940 and early 1941, most black leaders advocated armed neutrality and aid to England, but opposed America's direct intervention. Columnist Alfred A. Duckett wrote, "I would like to see the folks in this house stay home, lock the windows, tighten the shutters, man the doors and look so tough that no one will come around our way."[1] Although some blacks opposed any government role in the war, black leaders sought full participation in the nation's defense. On June 5, 1940, a spokesman for the Greater New York Coordinating Committee for Employment requested AfroAmerican representation on Sidney Hillman's Advisory Commission to the Council for National Defense.[2] By late 1941, the Republican *Age* and the Democratic *Amsterdam News* called for black support if the anticipated war should occur.[3]

Four days after Japan attacked Pearl Harbor on December 7, 1941, the United States was officially at war with all the Axis powers. "Harlemites Rush to Aid Country at War," read the *Age* headlines, as scores of men volunteered for duty as air raid wardens and soldiers.[4] To Roy Wilkins of the NAACP, America was home. This did not mean that the nation was perfect, but "that for better or worse . . . no one is going to shoot at her or bomb her and get away with it if we can help it."[5] Both before and after Pearl Harbor, Afro-Americans made significant contributions to the war effort. They volunteered for war-related projects and contributed finances to relief agencies and war expenditures. "If our country suffers," explained a Harlem graduate of the Lincoln Hospital Nurses Training School, "we suffer, too."[6] Perhaps for this reason Charles Noble, black chairman of the Harlem Riverside Defense Council, raised $70,000 during the Third War Bond Drive.[7] Even before passage of the Burke-Wadsworth Selective Training and Service Act of September 16, 1940, blacks volunteered for armed service in record numbers.[8] Nor did their enlistments slacken after the fighting began. On Armistice Day, 1942, Harlemites honored the 25,000 members of the community who were serving in the armed services.[9] Although the local press tended to exaggerate the total number of black men in uniform, AfroAmericans served valiantly and in proportion to their population.

Blacks were among the loyalest of American citizens. Mary McLeod Bethune of the National Youth Administration declared, "We are proud of our record of loyalty and . . . recognize our responsibility and duty to share in all of the expanded activities which defense planning entails."[10] Two-and-a-half years later, in December 1942, four Harlemites associated with the Ethiopian Pacific

Movement, a pro-Japanese organization, were convicted of subversive activities. The *Amsterdam News* contended that they were the first blacks to be convicted in the 150 years since the sedition law had been enacted.[11] Black and white authorities assured the public that the incident was an exception to the unquestioned loyalty of AfroAmericans. One columnist reminded his readers of the many white villains in the nation's history and reasoned that "the existence of a Hitler" in no way lowered "the dignity and prestige of the white race."[12]

Nevertheless, AfroAmericans were dissatisfied with the war effort. Early in the preparedness program Harlem leaders contended that black support was unenthusiastic.[13] "If I was drafted," remarked one New York porter, who no doubt spoke for many, "I'd be given a menial job. . . . If I was killed it's just another 'black boy' gone to meet his maker."[14] The situation worsened during the first year of American involvement, when black citizens were asked to share in the sacrifices but not the benefits of war. Shortly after Pearl Harbor, several major black leaders met in New York City to establish a united front for the war crisis. "We believe," read a resolution submitted by William H. Hastie, civilian aide to the Secretary of War, "the colored people are not wholeheartedly and unreservedly all-out in support of the present war effort."[15] By a vote of thirty-six to five, the resolution was adopted by the National Coordinating Committee. A few blacks challenged the resolution's validity, but most leaders verified it. Certainly the morale of New York City's black population was low.

The depressed morale of AfroAmericans resulted from both traditional and war grievances. Their major complaint, however, was with the contradiction of denouncing race superiority, second-class citizenship, and authoritarian rule abroad while ignoring it at home. Given southern lynch law and northern discrimination, a black Brooklynite asked Roosevelt in 1940: "What is the Negro expected to defend?"[16] After Pearl Harbor, another New Yorker told the President that if his people were too black to go to beaches,

restaurants, and hotels with white people, then they were "too black to go to the battlefields and fight and shed [their] blood."[17] For this reason, a scattering of the city's black draftees refused induction into the armed services.[18] Others deliberately avoided the draft. Malcolm X, then Malcolm Little, donned a loud zoot suit, brushed his hair into "a reddish bush of conk," and appeared for induction.[19] After role-playing as a misfit and telling the Army psychiatrist of a desire to organize black soldiers in the south to "kill . . . crackers," he received a 4-F classification. It is not possible to ascertain how many blacks reluctantly served in the armed forces. "I'm not a spy or a saboteur," remarked a Harlem youth awaiting induction, "but I don't like goin' over there fightin' for the white man."[20] While most of New York's black population did not go to the lengths Malcolm X did, resentment was widespread.[21]

Most objectionable was discrimination in the armed forces. Every branch of the military practiced segregation and discrimination; some, like the Marine Corps, excluded blacks completely. State militias followed similar traditions. Despite the drive for recruits and the Selective Service Act's antidiscrimination clauses, AfroAmerican volunteers were turned away, draftees deferred until separate accommodations were available, and discrimination practiced by some draft board officials.[22] Moreover, discrimination in rank and treatment increased black resentment. It was typical for white physicians, instead of black doctors with reserve commissions, to be paid $15 a day to examine the men of New York's famous all-black 369th State Guard Unit.[23] More intolerable was the harassment and beatings of AfroAmerican soldiers by white police and civilians. Except for officers, commented a Harlem reporter, "I haven't found a single black soldier who is convinced that he's fighting for democracy."[24]

Discrimination in the defense industries also bred despair. In 1941, a prominent Harlemite declared that New York's black citizens were frustrated because "our sincerest and most earnest efforts to become a part of the . . .

defense program have met with evasion and even forth-right rejection."[25] Nor was he exaggerating the frustration, which several residents expressed to La Guardia. As late as 1942, Olzaria Blackburn informed the Mayor that she had been filling out applications for defense work for three months without results. How could she be a true American "if I can't even get a defense job or a job to buy bonds to help win the war?"[26] Was she to think that "Democracy" was like an overcoat, either worn or discarded as it suited white men?

Next to discrimination in the arsenals of democracy, morale was most affected by the treatment black people received in the south. Every AfroAmerican was aware of southern exploitation and violence. With good reason, black expatriates who witnessed Nazi-occupied Germany compared it with life in the south, and black editors con-stantly compared southern leadership and justice to Hitler and Nazism. Blacks were especially distressed by the re-ports of vigilante law. In 1941 and 1942, lynchings were reported in Florida, Texas, Missouri, Arizona, and Missis-sippi.[27] Black New Yorkers protested the well-publicized lynchings.[28] A depressing cartoon in the *Amsterdam News* perhaps represented the sentiment of all blacks: Hitler, reading about the lynching and murder of blacks in the south, exclaims, "And they've got the nerve to tell me how to run my business!"[29]

A few blacks, probably remembering their own experi-ences as newcomers, were disturbed by the treatment of southern migrants.[30] Foreign refugees were well-received in New York City, but black migrants, whose flight from the South was analogous to that of the European Jews, were not similarly welcomed. "Do you suppose," Roy Wilkins asked in reference to a fund-raising campaign for refugee young-sters, "that you or I . . . could get the schools of the United States to set aside any period in which we might collect money for the aid of Negro children?"[31] Others contended that refugees were pushing black residents out of employ-ment, that the city would be unable to absorb AfroAmerican migrants.[32] Many blacks, including Wilkins, nonetheless believed in and contributed to the relief of refugees. It was when black migrants were not treated the same as white refugees that blacks were indignant.[33]

Morale was also dampened by other reminders to Afro-Americans of their "place." The American Red Cross refused to accept plasma from blacks, and even after protest changed this policy, the donations were separated according to race.[34] These policies were especially insulting because the plasma discoveries of a black physician, Charles R. Drew, had made the blood bank concept possible. Nor did the racial slurs of Allied propaganda reduce resentment. "All these radio announcers talking about yellow this, yellow that," complained a Harlemite shortly after Pearl Harbor.[35] Did the broadcasters think the Chinese, Filipinos, and other Allies were "all blondes." In New York City, blacks experienced humiliation daily. "The Birth of a Nation," perhaps the most racist motion picture, was scheduled to be shown as a means of raising money for Britain![36] Most degrading, however, was the discrimination that some AfroAmericans incurred when they sought to participate in the war effort. Three Brooklyn women, who volunteered for emergency first aid training, were informed by a WPA instructor that they would treat only black patients.[37]

Many blacks remembered that during World War I they had shelved racial grievances and, in W. E. B. DuBois' words, "closed ranks" behind the war effort only to be abused and insulted during the conflict and the reactionary postwar period. For this reason Malcolm S. MacLean, president of Hampton Institute, informed Roosevelt during the presidential campaign of 1941 that "the majority of Negro opinion about defense is colored by their bitter experiences of the last war."[38] Indeed, black leaders pressed for civil rights throughout World War II. "Once burnt, twice careful," summarized a Harlem columnist.[39]

Disillusioned blacks were patriotic, but they also found ironic satisfaction in certain aspects of the war. By challenging European colonial powers, and later America, the Axis exposed the flaws in democracy. In mid-1940, military necessity forced England to abolish discrimination in her armed services. *Crisis,* the NAACP's official publication, judged it ironic that "Hitler, the bitterest enemy of the democracies, is forcing a democracy to be democratic."[40] Perhaps more important was the shattering effect that Japanese victories had on the myth of white supremacy. "One thing you've got to give those Japs," declared an admiring black cab driver in New York City, "they showed the white man that a brown hand could handle a plane and a machine gun too."[41] World War II provided black, brown, and yellow people with the military experience that bolstered their confidence and their demands for a share of the peacetime benefits. Walter White contended that it would be "exceedingly dangerous" for white men to assume that the postwar world would be determined and directed exclusively by themselves.[42] The seeds for America's black revolution and for African and Asian nationalism and independence were permanently sown.

AfroAmericans, nonetheless, had little use for the Axis powers. During the Battle for Britain, an editorial in A. Philip Randolph's *Black Worker* warned that if Nazism won, "a new slavery and barbarism, terrorism and darkness will triumph."[43] Most blacks probably had heard or read of Hitler's refusal to honor Olympian Jesse Owens, his alleged order to sterilize 15,000 blacks, his reference to black people as half apes, and his treatment of black prisoners. Certainly such information was available in articles by G. G. M. James and Hans Habe, and brought to the attention of Harlemites by the local press.[44] Firsthand reports by AfroAmericans who experienced Nazi rule were also publicized periodically. "I'd rather be lynched any day," declared musician Johnny Russell, "than go through with what Jews are faced with in Europe."[45] After American entry into the war, this view was held by most blacks, who considered Hitler just "another poor cracker who got into power."[46] In 1942, a cross-section of New York City's black population was asked by government interviewers if they would be "treated better under German Rule?" Only 1 percent of the respondents answered "yes."[47]

In contrast, blacks viewed Japan with considerably less anxiety and some admiration. Certainly the efficiency of Japanese propaganda does not account completely for the affinity that some blacks felt for Japan. Since the black press warned of Japan's evil intentions as it did of Germany's,[48] racial sympathies probably account for the difference. As self-declared champion of all peoples of color, Japan played the major role in destroying the myth of white supremacy. In New York City, better-educated blacks were offered scholarships in Japan, while average residents were attracted to street-corner rallies conducted by pro-Japanese organizations.[49] In response to black questioners from the Office of Facts and Figures, 18 percent of New York City blacks questioned stated they would be treated better under Japanese rule, 31 percent declared treatment would be the same, 28 percent said it would be worse, and 23 percent did not know.[50] "The Japanese are colored," remarked many respondents, "and would not discriminate against dark people." Indeed, white New Yorkers who were interviewed believed blacks would fare better under the Japanese than under the Germans.

But most blacks did not want to live under any Axis power or, for that matter, under any Allied power other than the United States. Totalitarianism was not an alternative. "The very fact that I, a Negro in America, can fight against the evils in America is worth fighting for," summarized author J. Saunders Redding.[51] In New York City, local leader Frank Crosswaith referred to the "growth of democracy," columnist Layle Lane to complete equality with "no ifs, ands, buts, or whens," and sponsors of the Eastern Seaboard Conference to "freedom from oppression."[52] Regardless of the phraseology, blacks sought first-class citizenship.

Black society now fought, simultaneously, for a democratic victory at home and abroad.[53] This Double V campaign took advantage of the crisis to play up the discrepancy between Allied war aims and practices. "If we don't fight for our rights . . . while the government needs us," reasoned one black New Yorker, "it will be too late after the war."[54] The Double V campaign also permitted black leaders to channel the frustration of their followers into positive outlets that linked patriotism and protest. The point was not how black men were "doing according to Hitler's standards," but according to American standards.[55] Immediately following Pearl Harbor, Walter White declared support for the war but contended that the treatment of black people must continue as "the acid test of democracy in the United States."[56] Succinctly, Powell reasoned, "You can't whip Hitler abroad without whipping Hitlerism at home"; poet Langston Hughes wrote:

> Freedom's not just
> To be won Over there
> It means Freedom at home, too—
> Now—right here![57]

Almost unanimously, black leaders endorsed the Double V campaign, refusing to declare a moratorium on the struggle for racial equality.

National and local gatherings were held before and during the war. Essentially they sought the full participation of blacks in defense industries and the armed forces, the extension of civil rights legislation, and the establishment of price and rent controls. The aim was to increase the government's role in the struggle for civil rights. A feeling of unity among black people emerged. The fight to end racial injustice and violence in the south was waged by northern as well as southern blacks: in New York City, the Eastern Seaboard Conference proposed legislation against lynching and against poll taxes; Powell sought the City Council's support for such laws; editors condemned southern lawlessness; and, most important, numerous black residents protested the beating of tenor Roland Hayes in Georgia and other incidents of southern violence.[58]

Black Americans also empathized with the peoples of color of other countries. Beginning in the 1930s and increasingly throughout the war, New York blacks read about African history, especially Ethiopia's, and heard pleas for international racial solidarity.[59] To peoples of color everywhere, freedom and a universal sociopolitical change seemed to be in the offing. In New York City, black editors and columnists considered the war "a world revolution."[60] Some black residents associated their freedom with that of colonial peoples and advocated the end of imperialism as a war aim consistent with the Atlantic Charter and Four Freedoms. The Allies could best counter Japan's racial propaganda, contended the *Age* editor, "by granting the peoples of India the full benefits of democracy, by changing their policy towards the natives of Africa and . . . by tearing down the bars of discrimination which . . . restrict Negro Americans."[61]

In order to retain advances made during the war and to press for future gains, AfroAmericans were concerned with the role they would play in the peace conferences. This concern was expressed relatively early in the war and increased after Pearl Harbor. Hence in early 1942, a black asked:

> When this war is over
> Where will the Negro be?
> Basking in the clover,
> Or down beneath the sea?[62]

A year later, Walter White reflected a similar concern by requesting that Roosevelt give careful consideration to black representation on the American peace delegation.[63]

Before the postwar world was considered, however, the war experience accelerated black protest. The inconsistencies between Allied rhetoric and practices promoted, in the words of the National Urban League's general secretary, a "righteous indignation" and an "impressive militancy" among black people.[64] These inconsistencies provided organizations for racial advancement with mass followings.[65] Blacks, declared Walter White, knew that "if the concept of the Negro as a second-class citizen is to be changed, the major part of the work . . . must be done by the Negro himself."[66] No doubt the desertion of civil rights by numerous white liberals, who associated the Double V campaign with internal strife, reinforced White's contention.[67]

An impressive example of militant black protest occurred in New York City. In 1941, a coalition of organizations formed the Harlem Bus Strike Committee.[68] Using boycott and picketing tactics, strikers refused to ride the privately owned bus lines until the Fifth Avenue Coach Company, the New York Omnibus Corporation, and the Transportation Workers Union (TWU) agreed to employ blacks as drivers and mechanics. Adverse publicity, loss of revenue, Powell's leadership, and TWU cooperation resulted in an unprecedented victory: nearly two hundred blacks were to be hired as jobs became available.

After Pearl Harbor, however, the frustration and militancy was increasingly channeled into rhetoric. In the context of the times, blacks were militant; some, like Walter White, vowed to agitate "even if it meant prison."[69] Certainly, many whites believed blacks were more aggressive than ever before.[70] But since black leaders feared whites would consider interference with the war effort unpatriotic, they carefully avoided opening black society to the charge of treason and possible repression. Powell accurately predicted that "the hour of destiny" for black protest existed only until the United States entered the war, and then "all strikes and . . . picket lines" would be illegal.[71]

After United States entry into the war limited black protest, the media played an important role in the Double V campaign. "The Negro press," wrote a government researcher, "became more politically alert and devoted more space to the symbolic and material deprivations of the Negro in the defense industry."[72] In New York City, the *Age*, the *Amsterdam News*, and the *People's Voice* supported the campaign.[73] Radio programs were also widely used to promote black participation in the war and to educate whites on race relations. As part of the National Urban League's vocational opportunity campaign, eight programs were broadcast in New York City by prominent local residents. Justice Jane M. Bolin, for example, delivered a talk entitled "Womanpower Is Vital to Victory."[74]

Though numerous AfroAmericans participated in protest, a large majority did not. Black New Yorkers who evaded questions about the war when posed by white interviewers were tactful but not typical of the "New Negro," who Channing Tobias contended "would not lie about conditions and what is in his own heart."[75] And despite the large turnouts for mass meetings, black leaders often had to goad their followers into action. Concerned with the meager showing at an antilynching rally held on the steps of City Hall in 1942, Powell warned against apathy: "We can blow so very hot one minute and so icily cold the next."[76] Most black people, however, were neither the "New Negro" that their leaders presented them as nor the subservient "nigger" that their enemies wished they were.

War economics partly affected the numbers of blacks participating in protest. Day-to-day efforts to maintain a livelihood left little time for social action, especially before 1942. By then, blacks had become more fully integrated into the war effort and physical protest could prompt the charge of treason. No doubt some blacks, convinced that changes of substance were impossible, scorned protest as a hollow ritual. Others were probably pacified by AfroAmerican participation in war production.

Like its predecessor, World War II sparked migration from farms and towns to industrial centers of the northeast, midwest, and west. Black southerners constituted a disproportionately large number of these migrants. The National Urban League estimated that between 1940 and 1944, 750,000 AfroAmericans, comprising one-sixth of the total migratory movement, crossed state lines.[77] Blacks started their trek in mid 1942, after manpower needs and white labor shortages necessitated their employment in war industries; their migration reached its peak in early 1945, over a year after that of the total migration.[78] For all migrants the primary motive was economic, but for blacks discrimination in defense training and war employment in the south was the major influence on their proportionally higher interstate and interregional movement.

Because of its labor surplus and its lack of war contracts, New York City was not a major migratory target. Unlike several old industrial centers, it atypically registered no net in-migration for the period.[79] Early in 1941, the *Age* warned that the city would be unable to absorb southern black migrants.[80] Two years later, a Brooklyn Urban League official urged black residents to consider going elsewhere to find employment.[81] Apparently some did. Sociologist Charles S. Johnson estimated that between 1940 and 1943 the city's black population was reduced by 25,000 persons.[82]

To say that New York City's teeming black population remained about the same is not to say it remained stable. As ever, migrants constantly entered the metropolitan area. Finding employment opportunities scarce, they departed, only to be replaced by other migrants who repeated the process. Even in 1943, the significant increase in the number of black women seeking employment was attributed to "recent migrants from the South."[83] Nor did the city's population patterns change. Before World War II, Harlem was overcrowded and expansion had already begun into Manhattan's Washington Heights, Brooklyn's Bedford-Stuyvesant, and scattered areas of the Bronx. This process was accelerated during the war. As a result, interracial border conflicts continued.[84]

The Bronx, however, offered AfroAmericans a new safety-valve. Late in the 1930s, several Harlem residents began crossing the East River. Small in numbers, they experienced neither slum conditions nor residential segregation, though they tended to congregate in certain areas.

But by 1943, when their numbers reached an estimated 35,000 to 60,000, the patterns of racism and ghetto living had emerged.[85] One black, who moved to the Bronx "to escape high rents and the growing vandalism of a certain Harlem element," soon found that his "social gains" were imaginary.[86] In the wake of summer riot, he requested mayoral aid to combat "the growth of conditions comparable to . . . Harlem's" and warned of "the explosive qualities of this fast growing Negro center."

Although New York City's net in-migration was far below that of industrial war centers, the problems each faced were similar. Because the city had already made adjustments for its large, long-standing black population, interracial competition was not as acute as elsewhere. The socioeconomic problems that arose from migration, however, were comparable in kind to those in Detroit or Los Angeles. For the most part, discrimination and slum conditions continued throughout the war. Several of the city's largest cafeterias and hotels violated state law by segregating or refusing to serve blacks.[87] Social contact verging on personal intimacy was also taboo. Black drivers were quickly removed whenever white women assisted the Sanitation Department in its collection of tin cans for use in the war effort.[88] Furthermore, the vicious cycle of slum living continued almost unabated.[89]

Everyone except black people benefited from the immediate prosperity the war brought. By the end of 1940, 40 percent of New York City's black population was on relief or dependent upon federal monies for temporary jobs.[90] No wonder the New York Urban League contended that blacks were being "frozen on relief rolls." Equally significant, they were excluded from the very defense work that provided justification for reducing relief expenditures. Caught in this tightening economic position, blacks opposed reductions in relief-recovery programs.[91]

Excluded from defense employment, especially before 1942, blacks sought work in positions that whites were now leaving for the lucrative war industries. In addition to

regaining the menial and unskilled positions they held before 1929, blacks made some headway in new areas. When
New York City gained control and ownership of the rapid
transit subway system in 1940, the NAACP prompted La
Guardia to forbid discrimination in the employment of mechanics and operators—positions previously closed to
blacks.[92] The following year, the Harlem Bus Strike Committee negotiated its impressive agreement.

Progress was slower in defense work. Beginning with
the first government contracts of July 1940, the NAACP
received complaints of discrimination in employment.[93]
Soon blacks sought government action. Since their taxes
financed the defense program and since they fought and
died for democracy, they argued, they should share in its
benefits. Representative of this position, Harlem Assemblyman William T. Andrews introduced into the state assembly several bills prohibiting racial discrimination in
employment.[94]

White liberals supported the aims of black citizens. In
the United States Senate, Robert F. Wagner of New York
and others introduced Resolution 75, which called for an
investigation of black participation in "the national defense program."[95] Shortly thereafter, the Committee on
Negro Americans in Defense Industries, chaired by the
Reverend Anson Phelps Stokes and including La Guardia
and Lehman, along with sixty other prominent national
figures, supported the integration of defense employment.
"Our concern for democracy in Europe or elsewhere,"
the Committee asserted in Double V jargon, "lacks reality
and sincerity if our plans and policies disregard the rights
of minorities in our own country."[96] Aggressive blacks
and concerned whites eventually achieved some government intervention in defense employment. In New York
State, Governor Lehman acted decisively. Early in 1941,
he requested legislation to prohibit "discrimination in
employment . . . in all businesses affected with a public
interest."[97] After complaints of discriminatory hiring practices increased, he created the Governor's Committee on

Discrimination in Employment "to consider ways and means for dealing with the problem of discrimination in employment on defense contracts."[98] Biracial and chaired by State Industrial Commissioner Frieda S. Miller, the Governor's Committee was established on March 21, 1941. Most important, it was formed without fanfare or pressure,[99] and predated Roosevelt's Fair Employment Practices Committee by three months. In essence, Lehman's action culminated a civil rights drive that underlined his gubernatorial administrations and set the stage for additional progress in the postwar period.

At the national level, it was A. Philip Randolph's March on Washington Committee that pressured Roosevelt into creating a similar body. On June 25, 1941, the President issued Executive Order 8802, creating a Fair Employment Practices Committee to investigate discrimination in defense employment. Ironically, Roosevelt, who was close to Lehman and was informed of the Governor's Committee on Discrimination in Employment, did not seek his former Lieutenant Governor's advice on this matter.[100]

In spite of unprecedented committees, concerned local officials, and manpower needs, employment opportunities for black New Yorkers were limited. Unlike the expanding heavy industries in Buffalo, Detroit, or Los Angeles, which received an abundance of government orders, the small manufacturing businesses in the New York City area acquired few. In 1941, a year after preparedness had begun, Lieutenant Governor Charles Poletti urged upstate defense manufacturers to hire some of the city's 375,000 unemployed persons.[101] Six months later, La Guardia feared that the curtailment of materials for nondefense industries would further reduce employment.[102] Outside the war production zone, but not considered a distress area, New York City was in a tenuous economic position, receiving few government contracts and little federal aid. "This outlook," a Brooklyn Urban League official contended in May 1942, "presents a dark picture at best and to the Negro . . . somewhat of a total eclipse."[103]

By that time, La Guardia and Lehman had acquired presidential assistance. Early in June, Roosevelt instructed several federal officials to confer with them about "the use of plant and manpower facilities in New York City."[104] Donald Nelson, head of the War Production Board, Paul McNutt, director of the War Manpower Commission, Leon Henderson, administrator of the Office of Price Administration, and Secretary of the Treasury Henry Morgenthau, along with several others, were assigned to the conference, clearly reflecting Roosevelt's concern.

Indeed, the city's employment situation was desperate. Unemployment figures for July were 368,000, an increase of 21 percent over the previous three months and 50,000 more than the same period in 1939, a depression year.[105] "I know," Roosevelt cautioned, "that . . . the solution of this problem will not be an easy one," but he assured La Guardia that the steps being planned would "assist in alleviating this situation."[106] La Guardia attempted to hasten the employment process by proposing a plan to assist the city's numerous but limited enterprises.[107] Although his Small War Plants Corporation was not adopted, government action began to record progress. A regional WMC director estimated that 200,000 of those unemployed in July were employed by October.[108]

Roosevelt's intervention was the major reason for this success. For example, 12 percent, or nearly $832,000, of all Navy contracts distributed between July and October went to New York City firms.[109] These statistics, Undersecretary James Forrestal told La Guardia, reflected the Navy's desire "to deal positively with what we all recognize to be a serious unemployment situation in the New York City area."[110] On November 10, New York governor–elect Thomas E. Dewey appointed a committee to study the city's unemployment, but Roosevelt left no doubt about who deserved credit for the recent progress.[111] Roosevelt told David K. Niles that "Fiorello" and the federal government had reduced the unemployed from 400,000 to 280,000 and were progressing rapidly. "I think," he elaborated, well aware that Dewey could be the next Republican presidential candidate, "we can show Dewey up in this first attempt of his to make political Kudos."[112]

As 1943 began, the city's unemployment problem was far from solved, but positive steps continued. Between July 1942 and March 1943, unemployment had been halved, though New York's "vast reservoir of labor" did not "seem likely to run dry" before the year's end.[113] Black morale was bolstered by increased employment opportunities. "Baby," columnist Carl Lawrence predicted, " '43 will bring us more dough than we've ever handled before."[114] By midyear, increasing labor demands led one Brooklyn Urban League official to contend that "normal full employment in New York City should be realized before 1944."[115] Six months later, nearly full employment caused his organization to shift its emphasis from placing black workers in jobs to counseling them on how to ensure economic security in the postwar period.[116] Although the jobs and incomes of many black residents were still below standard, they were better, higher paying, and enjoyed by more people than ever before.[117]

Inroads, slower but no less encouraging, were also made in the types of employment given to blacks. In 1941, the NYSE placed numerous AfroAmericans in custodial jobs.[118] Yet only 1.3 percent of all defense production workers in the state were black, and those mostly unskilled.[119] By mid-1943, blacks were getting more jobs in fields previously closed to them, but most of these were "the white man's leavings."[120] Gradually, some advances were made, particularly by black women, in defense industries and in occupational categories.[121]

Black efforts and government intervention alone, however, could not have increased employment. Activities of private organizations such as the Urban League were important but limited, while those of the Governor's Committee and the FEPC were meaningful but retarded by their emphasis on gradualism, education, and persuasion.[122] Occasionally, private and public organizations worked together. For example, the Atlantic Basin Iron Works Company—a shipyard engaged in "essential war work" in New York City—refused to hire blacks even while asking for federal assistance in filling certain jobs.[123] Information provided by the Brooklyn Urban League and the War Manpower Commission resulted in FEPC action, causing the shipyard to hire most of those who had been denied employment earlier. It was, nonetheless, labor shortages caused by industrial and military demands rather than moral suasion that placed most blacks in "white" jobs. In early 1942, a mayoral aide hoped that as labor needs increased racial discrimination would be "broken down, never again to occur."[124] Similarly Jonathan Daniels, presidential assistant on race relations, admitted that black employment was largely "a fortuitous result of the necessity of [black] labor in wartime."[125]

Blacks also found themselves victimized by an inflationary economy. Since New York City was not considered a typical war industry center, federal price and rent controls were absent. Already paying unreasonable prices for inferior foods and inadequate housing while being the least employed, blacks suffered the most during much of the war prosperity. Throughout the war, efforts were made to bring the city under some form of government regulations. Early in 1941, La Guardia (who believed he lacked authority to enact a local measure) and the City Council supported state legislation for rent control.[126] A year later, when it appeared that such a bill would be adopted, the Office of Price Administration requested the state legislature to recall the measure.[127] Federal authorities feared the bill would impair a national policy. The legislature compiled with the OPA, but since the city was not designated a war industry district, government regulation was not forthcoming.

In price-regulating, the situation was comparable. Between 1940 and 1943, prices in the black communities were higher and increased more rapidly than elsewhere in New York City. A survey conducted by the NAACP and released in August 1942 disclosed that Harlemites paid 6 percent more for food than did residents in other sections of the city.[128] Hence Walter White requested Roosevelt to extend OPA authority to eliminate price differentials in black neighborhoods.[129] No action was taken. Nor did the situation improve in the coming year.

Other important areas were also influenced by the war. Construction of the State Housing Program's first project, the Fort Greene Houses in Brooklyn, was delayed because materials were unavailable. Materials were finally obtained on "the condition that defense workers would be considered for... these houses."[130] Still, Fort Greene Houses were not completed until 1944. Unlike that project, most slums, particularly in the Harlem area, were not located in a war production zone and, therefore, not in a position to obtain building materials even if such were available.

Despite fourteen low-rent public housing projects built for 17,000 families by the New York Housing Authority between 1935 and 1943, housing was inadequate.[131] Such was true especially in black communities, even though 15 percent of all NYCHA tenants were AfroAmerican. Some black workers benefiting from the war economy were even evicted from municipal projects for earning more than the prescribed maximum income.[132]

Black health and education continued to lag behind the overall advances of white citizens, and complaints of discrimination in Harlem Hospital recurred periodically. Advances, however, were made in certain areas. A new Outpatient Department for Harlem Hospital was dedicated in 1942, and a year later the Health Center was opened to care for the children of working mothers.[133] Private plans were also made to integrate Sydenham Hospital's patients and staffs.[134] Labor needs, meanwhile, forced an end to discrimination in the training of nurses by the Department of Hospitals.[135] The armed services' demand for physicians also accelerated the internship program at Harlem Hospital.[136]

Less was achieved in education. Community pressure compelled the city administration to construct the long-awaited annex to Harlem's West 135th Street branch of the Public Library.[137] Financial limitations and material shortages, nevertheless, forced La Guardia to reduce drastically the number of teachers and curtail school construction. Five new schools seating 9,100 students had been built in Harlem between 1938 and 1942, while another was near completion; but the construction of three others was suspended.[138] Nor would the municipal budget permit special education for children in poverty areas such as Harlem.[139] Overcrowded classrooms, segregated school districts, occupational rather than academic curriculums, unsympathetic white teachers, and textbook contents continued to be criticized, though less frequently than before the war.[140]

Interracial cooperation emerged in some quarters. The City-Wide Citizens' Committee on Harlem, which had been formed as a result of the alleged crime wave in November 1941, constantly goaded private and public action toward improving the living conditions and morale of black residents.[141] Cochaired by Algernon D. Black and the Reverend Adam Clayton Powell, Sr., the committee was comprised of three hundred prominent black and white citizens. Although major tangible gains were difficult to obtain during the war, the committee did make some inroads. Most significant was its Race Discrimination Amendment, which prohibited municipal courts and departments from assigning delinquent children to discriminatory child care institutions.

In general, blacks in New York City experienced some gains during the war, albeit slower, less dynamic, and less significant than those of white residents. The democratic spirit of the Allied cause, the ideology of Nazism, and the nation's manpower needs offered black citizens the opportunity to accentuate their grievances and participate in the war in such a way that longstanding progress might result. Partly because AfroAmericans were deserted by some white liberals, who disagreed with the Double V or were absorbed in the defense effort, and partly because Third World peoples experienced a racial awakening, black awareness reached a new dimension during the war. As a result, black Americans and war circumstances largely accounted for the progress made.

Certainly, black society suffered most from the exorbitantly high rents, unreasonable prices, and uncertain employment that resulted from New York City's peculiar economic position and the federal government's slow response to it. Black residents also had poorer education, health, housing, and recreation facilities, and although inadequate finances also curtailed the improvement of the facilities in white communities, it was in the black neighborhoods that they were needed most. In time, blacks achieved more and better jobs, and by 1943 they were more completely integrated into the nation's economy than ever before, and more hopeful of remaining there after the war. Yet the racial atmosphere was not completely harmonious.

4

New Yorkers' Response to the Detroit Riot

Without doubt, World War II had sharpened racial tension. A series of race riots swept through several of the nation's largest cities, including Mobile, Beaumont, Los Angeles, and Detroit.[1] In the rural south, black servicemen clashed with white soldiers, civilians, and local authorities; in the industrial north, midwest, and west, black and white workers competed—often violently—for jobs and living facilities. As the war progressed, the situation worsened. Nowhere was this more evident than in Detroit.

As a major industrial center, Detroit quickly became the destination of migrants searching for defense work. Between June 1940 and June 1943, more than 500,000 persons entered that city.[2] Of these, 50,000 were AfroAmericans who came during the last fifteen months of the period. Beginning in 1941, racial tensions were already mounting as black and white workers were pitted against each other in a strike at the Ford River Rouge Plant.

Early the following year, antagonisms increased over the Sojourner Truth Homes.[3] The federally built project was designed to house black workers, but in the face of protest it was rumored that the government was going to reassign the project to white workers. Counterprotest prevented a reassignment, but government ambivalence convinced angry whites that they could bar black tenants from occupying the project without interference. On February 28, whites and police officers assaulted blacks who attempted to move into the Sojourner Truth Homes. Although blacks eventually occupied the projects, the Office of Facts and Figures warned that Mayor Edward J. Jeffries was incapable of handling the situation. Unless "socially constructive steps" were taken, "the tension . . . is very likely to burst . . . into active conflict."[4] Presidential action was considered the only means to avert upheaval.

As black migration and the competition for living facilities increased, government leadership failed to emerge. The races clashed more frequently. By October of 1942, many city officials, industrialists, and black leaders considered Detroit a "keg of dynamite with a short fuse."[5] Indeed, throughout the nation racial tensions neared a critical stage. Riots began the following spring. Finally, on June 20, 1943, Detroit erupted.

On that sweltering day blacks and whites sought relief at Belle Isle.[6] Soon pent-up antagonisms spilled out onto the beach and picnic areas. By evening, rumors of a riot spread into Detroit proper. As police turned traffic away from the Isle, blacks destroyed white-owned property and assaulted whites in the ghetto. Meanwhile, white mobs attacked blacks caught outside their neighborhoods. Riot, and now looting, raged into the second day as Mayor Jeffries, Republican Governor Harry F. Kelly, and presidential officials dickered over who should take the initiative for sending federal troops to Detroit. That evening white mobs attempted to invade the ghetto area of Paradise Valley and police exchanged continuous gunfire with black snipers on the ghetto fringes. Violence increased. More than a hundred fires burned out of control as riot activity covered three-fourths of the city. Finally, federal troops entered the fray and restored order by late the following morning. In the riot's wake, thirty-four lay dead—including twenty-five blacks, most of whom were killed by policemen—more than seven hundred were injured, and more than two million dollars' worth of property was destroyed. "The long expected riot," Walter White recalled, "had come."[7]

New Yorkers of both races were alarmed by all the disorders, but particularly by that in Detroit. The size and kind of riot that occurred in the "arsenal of Democracy" demonstrated the possibility of a national race war. What happened in Detroit, Walter White wired Roosevelt, "climaxes a condition that can be checked only by your personal intervention."[8] Perhaps the Baltimore *AfroAmerican*'s New York correspondent most accurately reflected the attitude of blacks when he observed that the riots "have sapped Negro morale, changed Negro attitudes towards the war, America, and race relations."[9]

The city's black press was equally outraged. At times its indignation bordered on understandable sensationalism. "Hell Breaks Loose in Eight Cities" read the *Amsterdam News* headlines for June 26, while the front page of the *Age* featured pictures of blacks being beaten by white mobs in Detroit.[10] Editors were infuriated by the national scope of race rioting, its similarity to German anti-Semitic tactics, and the government's failure to protect AfroAmericans. "The most horrible Nazi atrocity stories," cried the usually calm *Age* editor, "are no worse than these home front outrages."[11] In the face of mob violence, the *Amsterdam News* editor urged his readers to retaliate: "It's far . . . better to die fighting as a man than to perish like a caged animal."[12] Such words were reminiscent of Claude McKay's poem "If We Must Die," written during the racially violent Red Summer of 1919: "If we must die—let it not be like hogs / . . . If we must die—oh, let us nobly die . . . fighting back!"[13]

Certainly the press adequately reflected the alarm of black residents, but one leader worried La Guardia. Immediately after news of the Detroit riot spread, Councilman Adam Clayton Powell, Jr., wired La Guardia that the tense racial situation demanded a mayoral meeting with the biracial group he represented.[14] In a form letter "My dear

Fellow Citizens," he announced the next day a Citizens Emergency Conference to discuss the crisis. "What has happened in Detroit," he asserted, "can happen in New York City."[15] Distrustful of Powell, La Guardia wanted no part in his meetings. An aide suggested that he undermine Powell's efforts by meeting with the City-Wide Citizens' Committee on Harlem instead, but this was not done.[16]

In the City Council on June 24, Powell charged that if riots occurred in New York City "the blood of innocent people . . . would rest upon the hands" of La Guardia and Police Commissioner Valentine.[17] The Detroit riot, he quoted the highly respected Walter White, was the result of a weak mayor and irresponsible police. Since La Guardia had not acknowledged his request for a biracial meeting to consider means of combating tension, he was weak. Since Valentine had ignored the acts of "unwarranted brutality" against black residents by whites, he was irresponsible. Moreover, just as Detroit's police cooperated with hoodlums and Ku Klux Klanners so did the New York police. By implication, a riot was possible in New York because officials and circumstances were similar to those in Detroit. To avert the impending crisis, Powell recommended a council discussion to establish "some type of mechanism . . . to squelch rumors" and a pledge to track down "all rumors as quickly as possible."

A mayoral informant attended the Citizens Emergency Conference that was held in Powell's office after the council adjourned. (Sometimes detectives were sent to Powell's meetings when municipal officials considered his activities threatening to public order, even though surveillance of a city councilman, however intermittent, was insulting at best and a dangerous precedent at worst. Such tactics revealed La Guardia's suspicious and self-righteous nature, and doubtless accounted in part for Powell's unrelenting criticism of the administration.) It was obvious, the partisan informant reported, that the meeting's real purpose was for Powell to show "Harlemites that he alone has their interest at heart."[18] Indeed, the majority comprised

"Adam's own people" and, as expected, he "ran the show." Except for the appointment of various committees to visit officials about a possible riot situation, no significant proposals were forthcoming. After the meeting, the informant spoke with Charles Collier of the National Urban League, Assemblyman William T. Andrews, and another black leader, all of whom agreed that "Adam called this meeting for his own purpose" and that the few responsible people who attended did so to keep tabs on him. If the meeting had been called by the City-Wide Citizens' Committee on Harlem, the informant believed it would have had "real value."

Others were also concerned about Powell's activities. One Harlemite felt that the publicity given to race riots by some preachers and politicians was "a smoke-screen . . . to incite racial disputes."[19] A more excited and biased correspondent begged La Guardia to place the churches of Powell and the Reverend Thomas Harten under surveillance. They were "agitators," wrote Monsignor John L. Bedford, a prejudiced priest, who had reason "to believe . . . that they will arouse the Negroes on Sunday, 27th June."[20] Most alarming, though least reliable, was an anonymous, confidential letter that "A Former Associate" of Powell sent to the City Council on July 3. The correspondent considered Powell "a notorious demagogue" and political opportunist, who "doesn't give a hoot in hell for colored people."[21] He contended that the *People's Voice* was "Communist-controlled" and made special note of its sensational coverage of the riots. If a disturbance occurred in the city, he predicted, Powell would be the instigator. If the City Council gave Powell "an opportunity to crucify police officials before a Council investigating committee and subject them to his abuse," racial attacks would be provoked. All these critics, including La Guardia, seemed to object more to Powell's methods than to his politics. Only the "Former Associate" condemned his leftist leanings.

Nor would Powell's critics concede that he could be constructive. On July 3, for example, Powell chided La Guardia, the "Prima Donna," for not meeting with his biracial committee.[22] "Get rid of your inferiority complex," he lectured the Mayor, "and appoint an inter-racial committee" that represents "the masses and we won't have a Detroit in New York." On July 10, he editorialized that the "greatest danger" confronting black citizens was "the temptation to resort to violence."[23] Self-defense was necessary for survival, but aggression by blacks was untenable. In a sense, Powell's criticisms of La Guardia and his admonition to Harlemites may have served to quell black fears and displace black frustration in the wake of Detroit's upheaval.

From the perspective of Powell's critics, however, the councilman was irresponsible. After being relatively silent through most of July, Powell spoke out on July 24. "Klan Threatens New York Negroes" read the sensational headline of the *People's Voice*.[24] An accompanying story exposed a letter to Powell from a Klan official, who warned: "Ugly rumors have reached us that unless colored folks stay by themselves, the Detroit affair will happen here." The letter had been delivered three weeks earlier, but Powell refrained from publishing it then for fear of inciting violence.[25] Apparently he did not consider discussing its contents with other black leaders and municipal officials or, more significantly, never publishing it! Indeed, Powell contradicted his own, earlier concern about squelching rumors.

Frank Crosswaith, formerly of the Harlem Labor Committee and presently a member of the New York Housing Authority, was deeply disturbed. "I presume," he wrote to La Guardia, "you have seen current copies of the *People's Voice* and other papers published in Harlem."[26] Several persons were "greatly concerned with the very obvious efforts of the politico-minded people behind these newspapers to stir up trouble." Crosswaith believed "there are . . . individuals and organizations who feel that only in a disturbed atmosphere can they effectively peddle their spurious wares" for the election in November. Doubtless he was referring specifically to Powell and perhaps, to a lesser degree, to the Democratic *Amsterdam News*. La Guardia was concerned about Crosswaith's letter.[27]

From Powell's perspective, it was not his actions but those of La Guardia, Valentine, and various black spokesmen that were suspect. He perceived Detroit's disorder as ominous for New Yorkers. When La Guardia did not respond to his urgent request for a meeting with his biracial citizens committee, it might have appeared to Powell that—as usual—he could not hope for mayoral cooperation. Although La Guardia was deeply concerned about the Detroit riot and engaged in extensive activity designed to prevent racial upheaval in New York City, he neither publicized it nor consulted Powell about it. By warning of racial tension and criticizing La Guardia publicly, Powell sought to goad mayoral action and promote citizen involvement, but his sense of urgency, aggressive personality, and isolation as councilman reinforced his propensity for the dramatic.

Powell's charge against the police department did prompt La Guardia to instruct Valentine and Investigation Commissioner William B. Herlands to submit reports on the matter. Valentine described the accusations as "baseless" and denied that cases of alleged brutality by whites against blacks were "white-washed."[28] In reference to Powell's allegation that a complaint he submitted to the Department of Investigation was ignored, Herlands called the charge "misleading" and "unequivocally incorrect."[29] No one, however, denied that altercations had occurred or that past police-community relations lent credence to Powell's assertions. Powell knew that the Mayor's Commission on the Harlem riot of 1935 had severely criticized Valentine and the NYPD, that police brutality cropped up periodically, and that the Detroit riot had been compounded by disgraceful police activity. Therefore, he may have overstated his charge of racial conflict; but the NYPD treated it routinely rather than urgently.

Powell was constructive in warning of racial tensions, criticizing the administration, and suggesting ways to avert disorder. It could have appeared to him that the administration was unconcerned about the fears numerous black residents felt in regard to Detroit's riot. Nevertheless, Powell was irresponsible for failing to follow up the formation of citizens' committees and, more deplorable, for publicizing the Klan letter. Both actions placed his intentions in doubt.

Powell aside, La Guardia and others were concerned about black newspapers in general. Although the critical days of June ended without incident, some tension continued into the following month. Press coverage was usually accurate, but it may have angered some readers. Because twenty-three of the twenty-five dead blacks in Detroit were slain by the police, who killed no whites, the disorder was described as a police attack on AfroAmericans.[30] Black people, Roy Wilkins summarized, were "the victims of the riot, and particularly the victims of the Detroit police."[31] Surely every Harlemite could recall an instance of police brutality and recognize the similarities of ghetto conditions everywhere. Another commentator contended that racial conflict was not new and would recur "unless the people of this country take positive steps to wipe out discrimination, segregation and jim crowism."[32]

Comparisons were also made between the United States and Nazi Germany. A front-page cartoon in the *People's Voice* illustrated a Nazi officer happily conversing with an American policeman, while in the background loomed two ravaged piles marked Poland and Detroit. The caption read: "This Must Not Happen Here!"[33] Langston Hughes was even more poignant in "Beaumont to Detroit: 1943":

> Looky here, America
> What you done done—
> Let things drift
> Until the riots come
>
> Now your policemen
> Let the mobs run free.
> I reckon you don't care
> Nothing about me.

You tell me that hitler
Is a might bad man.
I guess he took lessons
From the ku klux klan.

You tell me mussolini's
Got an evil heart
Well, it mus-a been in Beaumont
That he had his start—

Cause everything that hitler
and mussolini do
Negroes get the same
Treatment from you.

You jim crowed me
Before hitler rose to power—
And you're still jim crowing me
Right now, this very hour.

Yet you say we're fighting
For democracy.
Then why don't democracy
Include me?

I ask you this question
Cause I want to know
How long I got to fight
BOTH HITLER—AND JIM CROW.[34]

The truth of these lines, of course, was all too obvious to any black American.

Some black editors continued to advocate self-defense. According to the *Amsterdam News*, blacks were determined to fight and, if necessary, die for their rights. W. E. B. DuBois instructed his readers "to protect our victims, encourage our weak and scared."[35] The thought of violence, even as a defensive measure, no doubt concerned La Guardia and some AfroAmericans.

Powell, considered by many the major offender in sensational exploitation, which at times he was, was not, however, alone. Black newspapers sensationalized, but never to the degree practiced by the white dailies—including the respected *New York Times*—during the alleged Harlem "crime waves." Nor was the sensationalism of the black newspapers as divisive as first thought by La Guardia, Crosswaith, and others. A very small survey conducted by psychologist Kenneth B. Clark after the Harlem riot of 1943 concluded that the black press did not appear to be a significant factor "in developing . . . attitudes which would lead to the acceptance of group violence among Negroes."[36] While sensationalism from any quarter cannot be excused, that of the black press must be understood within the context of racial violence and from a black perspective; throughout the spring of 1943 and culminating in Detroit, AfroAmericans had been the victims of unwarranted and senseless white aggression. Black journalists had ample cause for their indignation and fears.

Despite the apprehension of many, a riot did not occur in the wake of the Detroit disorder or in the month of July. It was averted in part because most New Yorkers, black and white, were outraged by the events in Detroit and made sincere efforts to prevent such an occurrence in their city. Following Powell's charges in the City Council, separate resolutions were introduced to appoint a committee to investigate individuals and groups suspected of creating racial or religious antagonisms.[37] Since the council's session terminated the following day, June 25, this action was pointless.

The determination of private citizens to avert a riot was partly induced by the war experience. An AfroAmerican informed La Guardia that throughout the nation a war of "righteousness and justice" was being fought, which, she asserted, "has to be settled before you can even hope to win against your external foe."[38] She pleaded for an end to the racial injustices that marked Detroit. Emphasizing national more than racial interests, whites were also influenced by war. Typical of many, a Brooklynite believed that riots gave aid and comfort to the enemy, disrupted war production, and negated "the very principles for which so many American men and women are working, fighting and dying."[39] Religious and democratic ideals affected the thinking of others. New York ministers, priests, and, especially, rabbis—who drew analogies between Nazi anti-Semitism and white racism—called for unity.[40] Parents and teachers alike offered their assistance to La Guardia because racial conflict "threatens our aims in war, as well as our basic democratic ideals."[41]

Blacks were aware of another, more realistic reason for maintaining racial calm: they would be the inevitable losers in interracial combat. Powell, for one, was keenly aware of AfroAmerica's exclusion from the power structure. Noting the difference between violence and self-defense, he contended that violence was "an impossible position for Negroes to hold."[42]

Leaders and organizations of both races promoted racial harmony. Independently, local NAACP and Urban League officials joined quickly with interracial groups to launch "preventive action" programs in race relations.[43] On a larger scale, the Governor's Committee on Discrimination in Employment began plans for a radio program on minority groups.[44] The most comprehensive effort to avert further riots, either in New York or elsewhere, was made by a group that included Walter White and Wendell Willkie. On July 24, Willkie and famous stage, screen, and literary personalities were featured in the first of a series of national radio broadcasts to improve race relations. "An Open Letter to the American People" told of Detroit's riot, described the socioeconomic conditions of black people, and pleaded for unity.[45] The *People's Voice* accurately called the program "a milestone in the nation's broadcasting history."[46] Even at the individual level, many—like Justice Jonah J. Goldstein, who admonished July's grand juries to be "on guard" to prevent racial disorder—participated in efforts to ease tensions.[47]

Every black leader, despite the anger, sensationalism, or opportunism that Detroit provoked, sought to avoid a racial conflict. Powell cochaired an "It Must Not Happen Again" rally at the Golden Gate Ballroom. Sponsored by his People's Committee and the Negro Labor Victory Committee, the gathering was attended by 3,000 persons.[48] Also in early July, an *Amsterdam News* article recommended a biracial program to prevent riots.[49] Later that month, more than two hundred Brooklynites assembled at the Ashland Place YMCA to continue plans for the Negro Freedom Rally scheduled for early August.[50] The Reverend Thomas Harten, whom Monsignor Bedford had dubbed a rabble-rouser, conducted the meeting.

Individual residents also demonstrated concern, some silently in the conduct of their private lives, others publicly suggesting ways to promote harmony. From the Detroit riot in late June to that of Harlem in early August, La Guardia's mail reflected these activities. John O'Hara recommended the distribution of a poster depicting a black and a white family indulging in identical but separate activities. One caption read: "Mindin' My Business."[51] One correspondent advised that civic leaders of all races meet, keep a close watch on newcomers, and emphasize the detrimental effect that riots had on the war effort; another counseled La Guardia to "personally call the editors of every New York newspaper into a private conference on racial tolerance."[52] Several individuals urged him to involve civic and religious leaders as lobbyists for legislation and preachers of tolerance, while a Brooklyn housewife encouraged the use of air raid wardens to promote unity in their districts.[53] Columnist Max Lerner suggested that a biracial committee be created to promote understanding, and the Young Communist League called for an interracial conference open to all interested persons.[54]

Most impressive was black and white participation in unity gatherings similar to those held by Powell and Harten. On July 9, the United States Student Assembly sponsored a rally, "New York Youths Won't Let Detroit Happen Here," which featured Councilman Stanley Isaacs among the speakers.[55] That month, a representative of the Churches of God of Greater New York informed La Guardia of plans for its "March of Churches" on Labor Day.

Over fifty denominations and forty language groups, representing east side, west side, and Harlem churches and marching from separate directions, would converge at 110th Street and Eighth Avenue to pray for the United Nations.[56] Most successful was the July "No Detroit Here" rally at Poe Park sponsored by the Bronx Civilian Defense Volunteer Office, which drew 5,000 participants who pledged themselves to unity. "We must be," the Reverend Elder G. Hawkins asserted, "the hosts who will swear that race riots must not happen here."[57]

Though it is difficult to estimate exactly how many residents actively undertook efforts to improve racial harmony, the correspondence to La Guardia, the participation in unity rallies, and the fact that no riot occurred when it appeared most likely seems to indicate a significant number. Since the social climate of a community and its system of social control are among the key determinants of riot eruption, New York City's climate—which discouraged racial violence—and La Guardia's immediate and assertive response to the crisis were probably decisive factors in averting disorder at that particular time.[58]

5

Official Response to the Detroit Riot

Unlike the earlier riots, the carnage and destruction in Detroit was so awesome that public officials could no longer assign race relations a low priority. Interracial violence that might have been considered local, isolated conflicts in the spring, now appeared epidemic and obviously threatened domestic stability. As mayor of the nation's largest city, La Guardia acted decisively to maintain peace by assuaging the tension created by the Detroit riot. He provided creative leadership throughout the remainder of June and all of July, setting the tone for New York City's response. Roosevelt reacted more cautiously, hoping that the violence would pass with minimal impact on the war effort.

Following the outbreak in Detroit, La Guardia moved quickly to calm New Yorkers. On June 22, barely a day after the conflict began, he warned of its detrimental effect on black residents. A spokesman for the *Amsterdam News* reported "that something important may develop" in Harlem, where discussions and rumors about Detroit were widespread.[1] In response to a specific request by the Harlem newspaper, La Guardia issued a statement the same day. "We are in the midst of a most difficult and trying period," he began his attempt to offset rumors.[2] He urged residents to keep "cool" and "to have an understanding of the other fellow's problems." New Yorkers were warned about the provocation of unidentified "snakes who would like to see trouble started for any reason." By alluding to "snakes," La Guardia probably sought to curtail rumors and their transmission by associating them with sinister symbols. Mayoral reference to "snakes" eventually laid the foundation for blaming Harlem's riot on "hoodlums," which inherently denied the existence of black grievances and racial tension. By creating an enemy, La Guardia refocused attention from the real crisis of race relations to the imagined one of disunity by sabotage.

In response to the alarm created by whites attacking blacks in Detroit, La Guardia assured equal protection for all residents. "If any white man provokes or instigates assaults against a Negro group," he promised, "I will protect the Negro group and prosecute the white man."[3] The reverse would be true if blacks attacked whites. La Guardia cautioned against resorting to violence and reminded everyone of the prejudice and exploitation that existed in the city. Cooperation and understanding could cope with any situation. "I am," he appealed to the conscience of every resident, "depending on the good people of this city to keep our record clean."

Privately, La Guardia sought inside information about the Detroit riot. "If convenient," he wired Walter White, who was already in that city, "will you telephone me . . . tonight."[4] On the same day, June 22, a black member and a white member of the police department, Emanuel Kline and Edward M. Butler, were sent to Detroit as observers. During their four-day visit, they maintained close contact with Police Commissioner Valentine.[5] By the end of June, La Guardia possessed reports from White, who later provided him with a copy of "What Caused the Detroit Riots?," and Kline and Butler.[6] From these materials and with the assistance of biracial advisers, he formulated tactics that enabled him to handle the Harlem riot prudently. In fact, no sooner had White returned from Detroit when La Guardia summoned him and several others to Gracie Mansion on June 28 to hear the report of Kline and Butler and "to devise means of preventing repetition in New York City of the mistakes which had been made in Detroit."[7]

As La Guardia waited for the reports on Detroit, he took precautions to avoid incidents that could incite racial violence. City officials were alerted. Prior to Detroit's riot, a reputable resident had advised the Mayor of border clashes between blacks and whites in Brooklyn's Brownsville section.[8] "For goodness sake," La Guardia ordered Valentine on June 23, "please watch this section very carefully."[9] Some mayoral aides were so fearful of racial tension that they sanctioned discrimination rather than chance disorder. When Van M. Worth, a black journalist, complained about discrimination in a Coney Island restaurant, an aide informed Lester B. Stone, the Mayor's secretary, that Worth could bring legal action against the restaurant's proprietor for violating state law. The aide, nonetheless, opposed advising Worth to engage a lawyer. Nothing, she believed, could precipitate a riot more easily than "the Mayor's official sanction of whites and colored congregating in eating places."[10]

La Guardia also sought to involve the individual citizen in the campaign against racial turmoil. Accordingly, all members of the Civilian Defense Workers, the United States Defense Corps, and the United States Civilian Service Corps were designated "Good Will Deputies" and directed "to maintain a united home front . . . against all persons who, designedly or through hysteria, contribute to or incite disorders or violence."[11] More significantly, La Guardia endorsed the unity pledge campaigns undertaken by the liberal newspaper *PM* and by actress Jean Muir. Before June ended, he considered plans to climax Muir's campaign in a public pageant.[12]

During his weekly Sunday broadcast on June 27, in another effort to publicize the crisis and mobilize the populace, La Guardia appealed directly for tolerance and solidarity. "Let no snake agitator come here . . . seeking to start racial trouble," La Guardia began, building on his earlier theme of conspiratorial external elements.[13] As in his previous statement to the *Amsterdam News*, he contended that riot was not inevitable, that residents could control their fate, that disorder was the work of a common enemy, a "snake agitator." Law and order would be maintained: "I will not permit . . . any minor group to be abused by another group." Numerous persons, including five hundred white residents from the racially troubled Washington Heights area, registered approval of his broadcast.[14]

La Guardia also asked Walter White to contact every black leader and organization in Harlem and Brooklyn.[15] Mailed before July, White's letter admitted that AfroAmericans were "justifiably resentful" of their treatment in the armed forces and urban centers.[16] Nonetheless, he urged black leaders "to see that our people so conduct themselves during the next few critical weeks and months" that they will give "no cause for racial friction." He was particularly concerned about the younger, rowdier individuals. "If trouble comes," he reasoned, "let it be caused by our enemies." Given La Guardia's efforts, "we need have no fear that the police here will act as they did in Detroit." White followed the Mayor's lead, however, by warning that potential danger lay with those who "deliberately fomented" violence. In requesting leaders to check the community's temper, he made it absolutely clear that "there is . . . no slightest suggestion that Negroes when attacked should not defend themselves."

As the critical days of June passed, La Guardia was relieved that the city had endured the shock of the Detroit riot. "Thank God," he exclaimed to Roosevelt on June 27, " . . . I believe we have done more than any other city in the country."[17] Better than anyone else, however, the Mayor knew that long hot summer days lay ahead.

Throughout July, La Guardia continued to make the public responsible for its own behavior. The unity pledges of actress Jean Muir and *PM* were circulated everywhere. "In this hour of danger, when every great city is threatened by race riots," began the *PM* pledge, "I want to join you in doing my share to keep New York from being a house divided against itself."[18] To achieve this, every pledgee promised to guard against provocation, to denounce all divisive rumors, to resist "every attempt to set me against my fellow-New Yorker." As instructed, residents signed the pledge and forwarded it to La Guardia. A relative of Henry Ward Beecher, the abolitionist, was one of many who followed instructions. "What he fought for 80 odd years ago," William Ward Beecher informed La Guardia, "I'm fighting for today."[19] Jean Muir's pledge was similar and also endorsed by large groups of people, such as those at a "No Detroit Here" rally in Poe Park. "You will be pleased to hear," Muir advised La Guardia on July 19, "that at the present time . . . ten thousand pledges are distributed . . . and that the reaction has been so favorable . . . we are finding it necessary to expand considerably."[20]

Mayoral plans for racial harmony also included the clergy, whose assistance was requested in a letter of July 8. New York City had become famous because "we have demonstrated that people coming from every country . . . in the world . . . can live as good neighbors in peace and harmony."[21] Now, La Guardia returned to what would become a self-fulfilling prophecy: "Evil-minded people" might attempt to create friction, for selfish, "political," or even treasonous reasons. Perhaps the clergy would assist to prevent such friction with sermons on good will or unity. "Do please help," La Guardia concluded, revealing, as did his very appeal, that the matter was more than routine.

Besides attempting to mobilize public concern, La Guardia continued to have racial complaints investigated carefully and quietly. When the Bronx division of The People's Committee protested that a black youth was framed for a crime, Lester B. Stone looked into the charge. "Can you," the mayoral secretary asked James Harten, "find out quietly about the disposition of this case?"[22] Breaking standard procedure, he instructed the inquiry be made "without bothering the Police Department." Justice Isaac Siegel, who had decided the case, assured Stone that the contradictions of witnesses who testified in the youth's behalf convinced him of the teenager's guilt. It was recommended that the youth be placed on probation, assisted in finding summer work and in planning a school program "that will help him in the future."[23]

No doubt, it was remembered that the Harlem riot of 1935 had been ignited by an incident involving a black youth, a store manager, and the police. Perhaps for this reason La Guardia received regular reports from the police department of racial clashes that occurred throughout July, but which the NYPD had not yet investigated completely.[24] The Mayor, his staff, and the police tried to gather information on every incident that might cause a riot.

More lasting steps, which sought to correct long-standing AfroAmerican grievances, were also undertaken. On July 6, New York Urban League officials conferring with Valentine recommended an increase in the number of black policemen as a means of reducing tension. The Police Commissioner implied that he would appoint more black officers, speak publicly on the importance of using them in riots, and cooperate with any groups who would assist in recruiting blacks for the NYPD.[25] Before the month ended, the Urban League recruited twenty-two prospective police candidates.[26] Not all of these recruits may have been qualified, and certainly none of them were trained before August 1, but Valentine's attitude reflected mayoral concern.

In other areas, La Guardia did what little was possible. Late in June, he officially opened the Mount Morris Music School, which Justice Jackson's Bureau for the Prevention of Juvenile Delinquency had planned for some time.[27] During July, Edmond B. Butler, chairman of the New York City Housing Administration, announced that two postwar projects were scheduled for Harlem, and La Guardia requested the OPA to place the city under immediate rent control.[28] La Guardia also sought gubernatorial authorization "to freeze rents within the City."[29] Though not solely associated with the black community, La Guardia based his timely requests in part on the racial situation. Of course, he had taken similar steps before, but he went through the motions again, hoping to produce a positive psychological effect and, in some areas like rent control, to improve black living conditions immediately.

La Guardia also contemplated a biracial committee to promote better race relations. Between June 20, the date of the Detroit riot, and August 1, numerous individuals and organizations, both black and white, urged him to appoint such a committee. A local chapter of the State, County and Municipal Workers of America was typical in calling on the Mayor "to establish a committee . . . to investigate those factors tending to promote intolerance and disunity . . . and to take immediate prevention measures."[30] At least one organized postcard-writing campaign was conducted, perhaps by *PM*, to influence the creation of a mayoral committee.[31] Before July 1, however, La Guardia had already considered the action.

At the Gracie Mansion conference on June 28, the Mayor requested Walter White, the Reverend John H. Johnson, Channing Tobias, Samuel Battle, Herbert Delany, and Myles Paige "to submit four names for the committee of nine to deal with racial tensions in New York City."[32] Returning from a defense conference, which he attended for two weeks as chairman of the United States Section of the Joint Defense Board, La Guardia was informed that the names were available. On July 17, White submitted the names of Mrs. Anna Arnold Hedgeman of the Office of Civil Defense, Dr. Max Yergan, Tobias, and himself, with Powell and Naida Springer of the International Ladies Garment Workers Union as alternates. Such a committee, with La Guardia appointing the other five, white members, needed only mayoral approval to be created.

Apparently, White and the others had originally requested La Guardia to form the committee.[33] Most likely he was receptive because of the immediate shock of the enormity of Detroit's riot. In addition, the pattern of violence that had already occurred, the public reaction to

Stuyvesant Town, and the alarming reports by reputable black and white leaders that warned of high racial tensions in the city probably reinforced La Guardia's willingness to consider a committee on race relations. No doubt the experience of the Harlem riot of 1935, action being taken in the cities where riots had occurred recently, and normal reaction to a crisis situation also affected his thinking.

La Guardia, however, was never fully committed to appointing a committee on race relations. Submitting the names of prospective committee members on July 17, White admitted that "there is some uncertainty that you still want . . . names for the committee."[34] He recalled that "just as we were about to leave [Gracie Mansion on June 28], you asked us to submit the . . . names, but Reverend Johnson was of the impression that you had changed your mind."

Several factors probably affected La Guardia's decision not to appoint a committee. By the time he returned from the defense conference, New York's situation did not appear to be as critical as it had been immediately following the Detroit riot. Mayoral press statements, radio appeals, unity pledges, and letters to religious leaders had received favorable public response, while police surveillance and biracial leadership kept a lid on incendiary incidents. In Harlem, where tensions were the highest in June, the atmosphere appeared to be calm. There, the July 4th weekend was described as the gayest and the safest in years.[35] La Guardia, furthermore, believed that all executive undertakings should be coordinated through the existing governmental structure. Perhaps he recalled the problems associated with the Mayor's Commission on Conditions in Harlem. Indeed, White (probably with the Mayor's Commission also in mind) had informed him that if a biracial committee was to be effective "it be given sufficient authority to attack . . . the problems it is appointed to solve."[36] With tensions apparently reduced, there was no reason to appoint a committee that might limit mayoral authority. La Guardia, moreover, probably questioned

what a committee could accomplish that the combined efforts of the administration and AfroAmerican leaders, like
White, could not. Finally, as his defense assignment and
absence from the city implied, he was pressured by the
demands of different, though equally important positions.
Therefore, he allowed the decision to lapse, apparently
deluding himself into believing that the situation had
changed for the better.

La Guardia's program to avert riot was planned and implemented with the assistance of important people in the
field of race relations. Some, including White and Tobias,
were recommended as prospective committee members.
In fact, White was the most important black or white mayoral adviser. No sooner had he arrived in Detroit to observe the riot when La Guardia requested information
about his observations. He also participated in the Gracie
Mansion conference, prepared an appeal to black leaders
to assist in easing tensions, and worked with Jean Muir on
plans for the unity pledge campaign.

White, of course, was no ordinary adviser. On June 27,
La Guardia advised Roosevelt to see the NAACP official
"at the earliest possible moment."[37] White's advice to
Governor Harry F. Kelly, he asserted, was "the saving
point" of "the disgraceful situation" in Detroit. In any
case, La Guardia begged FDR not to withdraw federal
troops from that city: "Walter urges this very strongly."
After receiving White's report on Detroit, La Guardia
urged it be sent to the President. Roosevelt, nevertheless,
did not confer with White.[38]

A committee could have served a permanent public relations and psychological function; citizens who normally
considered themselves outside the governmental process
could have been involved in a significant community program. As a result, the committee could have become more
informed of the local situation and more active in promot-
ing racial harmony than the Mayor, who was already divid-
ing his time between two positions and several cities. Perhaps a committee could have better understood Powell's

urgency and made use of his leadership. Of most importance, an institutionalized vehicle would have been created to carry mayoral concerns beyond the crisis period and into the summer, perhaps throughout the war's duration.

There is no guarantee that a committee on race relations could have prevented the Harlem riot of 1943. Much would have depended on its composition, the seriousness of its members toward their task, and the extent of its authority. Perhaps such a committee could not have reduced tensions enough between its inception and the disorder—a two- or three-week period at most—to have averted riot. Yet it might have improved the situation. For that reason alone, La Guardia's failure to heed the advice of his black counselors to form a committee is unfortunate.

As August 1 drew near, although local officials were doing everything possible to prevent a riot in the city, the President was not. The many racial disorders within a relatively short time led concerned citizens to look to Roosevelt for the leadership he had provided in so many previous crises. Even La Guardia considered it a period of national crisis. "It is not over," he warned FDR in late June.[39] "The situation is still tense." It was most important "to avoid a recurrence, or the spirit becoming contagious and going to other cities."

Following Detroit's upheaval, New Yorkers joined citizens everywhere in beseeching the President to act. The situation, a Brooklyn resident urged, required presidential action, perhaps a radio address discussing "proposed remedial measures."[40] On July 3, the *Amsterdam News* asked: "Why don't you do and say something . . . before it is too late?"[41] Two weeks later, the editor criticized "FDR: The Sphinx," for failing to "give heart to America's . . . colored citizens" and promote national unity.[42] As late as July 28, Milton Bass implored the federal administration to investigate the Detroit disorders, which caused more "direct damage to our war effort than we would have suffered if a fleet of one thousand . . . German . . . planes bombed" that city.[43] Why should blacks and whites "combat fascism on foreign soil, when . . . at home . . . we have seen overt demonstrations of fascism?" Publicly, Roosevelt remained silent.

The President, of course, was well aware of the critical situation. Indeed, he had personally issued orders for the use of federal troops to quell the Detroit upheaval. Shortly thereafter, Mrs. Roosevelt passed on a message from Monroe Sweetland of the CIO War Relief Committee, declaring that nothing short of a presidential statement "would have any effect on the situation."[44] On the same day, June 22, FDR received an analysis of the crisis from aide Jonathan Daniels. "The race riots in Detroit," wrote the recently appointed presidential adviser on racial matters, "must be recognized . . . as a climax in what almost amounts to an epidemic of racial tensions in the United States."[45] Action was necessary to prevent disturbances in other areas. Nothing, he advised, "could be more effective" than a presidential statement. The war effort was being seriously disrupted, almost as if attacked by the enemy; the situation did not require a grandiose "statement of idealism" for perfect race relations, but rather a realistic appraisal of the situation and its effect on the war. "So far," Daniels reiterated the need for action, " . . . there are no signs that this ugly situation will wear itself out." Mary McLeod Bethune came to the same conclusions independently.[46] Together, they influenced Roosevelt enough for him to ask Stephen T. Early: "Don't you think it is about time for me to issue a statement about racial riots?"[47] Apparently the press secretary disagreed, for no presidential message was forthcoming.

From late June to late July, Roosevelt outwardly evaded the entire issue. On June 24, Daniels assured Lester B. Granger of the National Urban League that "throughout the government in Washington there is the gravest concern about this whole matter."[48] In reply to urgent letters from eminent citizens, such as Anson Phelps Stokes, Philip Murray, and Vito Marcantonio, Roosevelt agreed that "the recent outbreaks of violence" endangered "our national unity and comfort our enemies."[49] He, therefore, had asked the attorney general and heads of several government agencies "to give special attention to the problem." But no mention was made of concrete public action.

Behind the scenes, Roosevelt was attempting to cope with the crisis. According to Vice President Wallace, Afro-Americans were awaiting presidential action by "their friend."[50] White liberals, he reported on July 7, suggested a fireside chat, a congressional investigation, or an inquiry by eminent individuals. None of these recommendations, however, suited the President. Instead, rumors spread that he planned to curtail black migration to northern war centers and to create a special board to handle all racial problems. Black leaders responded immediately. Granger charged that restriction on a citizen's freedom to migrate was unconstitutional.[51] Walter White disapproved of a special board, believing it would shift responsibility from the President and the departmental heads to a single committee of questionable influence. In addition, the plan seemed to have been devised by inexperienced minor officials, "without consultation with responsible Negro leadership and apparently without intention that Negroes be members of the board."[52] The following day, July 22, White forwarded Daniels a copy of the views he had expressed to Roosevelt.[53] About the same time, Attorney General Francis Biddle publicly evaded the issue of black migration and denied plans to create a "super board" on racial problems.[54]

In a confidential letter to Roosevelt on July 15, Biddle had contended that the Detroit riot was "typical of what may occur in other cities throughout the country."[55] In order to prevent the overcrowded living conditions from causing upheaval in other municipalities, he had suggested restricting black migration and creating an interdepartmental committee on racial problems. He had, however, never recommended a "super board" as White envisioned it. Biddle had also advised Roosevelt to provide impetus privately for the formation of a national nongovernmental committee to promote racial unity "chiefly in the local communities." To deal with the problem of understaffed and inadequate police forces, he had urged that policemen be deferred from selective service and that a manual explaining the procedure for requesting federal troops be prepared for local officials. Finally, he had cautioned against a presidential radio address.

Biddle had originally recommended that Monsignor Francis J. Haas head the interdepartmental committee, but changed his mind because such might put "too much pressure" on the recently appointed FEPC chairman.[56] Subsequently, he suggested that Daniels chair the committee that would exchange information between departments and formulate recommendations "with regard to present race and group tensions."[57] Although Daniels agreed with the basic suggestion, he urged—obviously as a result of White's arguments—that each agency retain "full responsibility in its own field." His job would be to correlate the relevant information of each agency, review it, and provide Roosevelt with an updated report whenever requested. "A formally announced and appointed committee could not . . . do more" and would become "a pressure point for the numerous agitators in this field." Three days later, he notified White that no decision had been reached on the subject of a super board, but "it is receiving a great deal of attention."[58] Meanwhile, the *Amsterdam News* reported that Roosevelt was contemplating a committee composed of representatives from nine federal agencies to direct government policy on race relations.[59] Black leaders feared that the members would be white and inexperienced.

As July waned, the President acted on the recommendations regarding an interdepartmental committee, and in typical Rooseveltian style accepted the basic points of both Biddle and Daniels. The attorney general forwarded Daniels a suggested list of members for the interdepartmental committee, which included six AfroAmericans.[60] On July 29, Daniels informed all department heads that as a result of the recent race conflicts "the President has di-

rected me to correlate all available governmental information as to these tensions and difficulties involving minority
groups in all parts of the country and to keep myself informed as to what is being done about them by responsible officials."[61] Hence he requested the full-time assistance of a member of each department. In time, departmental heads began to comply with the request. As Harlem was about to explode, Roosevelt had finally responded
to the crisis.

But the President's action was late and meager and
failed completely to provide the leadership that most black
and some white citizens of the nation sought and needed
so desperately. The very secrecy of Daniels' committee,
which may have prevented a confrontation with militants,
did nothing to relieve the fear of blacks and white liberals.
The limits of its authority and function indicate that Roosevelt considered it little more than a means to parry pressure from those within the administration who urged some
kind of action. What the situation needed most was the
President's eloquence and activity; what it received was
his silence and vacillation.

The reasons for Roosevelt's failure to meet the crisis
head-on are not clear, though several factors help explain
his behavior.[62] One commentator attributed the President's inaction to misinformation provided by southerners.
There was some truth to this charge.[63] It was Virginia-born
Stephen T. Early whom Roosevelt asked if it was time for
him to issue a statement on the riots, and, since a public
announcement was never issued, certainly the press secretary must be considered influential in opposing such an
address. Other southerners, such as Howard Odum of the
University of North Carolina, also opposed a fireside
chat.[64] Jonathan Daniels, a southerner, however, urged
Roosevelt to make a public address, while Biddle, a north-
erner, opposed it. Roosevelt based his decision on the advice of his closest advisers, particularly on Early's, but it
was his own decision and one made with full knowledge
that opposing counsel existed.

In part, both Roosevelt and his closest advisers were influenced by politics and priorities. During the Depression, he evaded the issue of an antilynch law for fear of alienating southern Democrats, whose votes were vital to the passage of New Deal legislation.[65] In the early war years, he considered southern opposition before reluctantly issuing Executive Order 8802, and, then, his approach to the Fair Employment Practices Committee was dominated by a concern for southern reaction.[66] Immediately following the Detroit riot, Eleanor Roosevelt informed a close friend that the President "feels he must not irritate the southern leaders as he needs their votes for essential war bills." The nation, she admitted, was "sadly in need of leadership in . . . race relations."[67]

Roosevelt believed that it was better to ride out the unfortunate racial disorders than to intervene and possibly aggravate the situation. Presidential intervention might have antagonized the south and southern white migrants in the northern war centers, where further disorders would have compounded the situation. Indeed, a spokesman for the War Production Board estimated that the two days of rioting in Detroit caused absences from work totaling more than one million man-hours, a worse setback in the production of ordnance materials than that caused by all the labor disputes in the entire nation in January and February of that year.[68] The war effort was Roosevelt's paramount concern, and if less disruption would result from his silence, then so be it.

Even more tragic than Roosevelt's failure to respond to the Detroit riot was his failure to respond to the racial crisis before it erupted. Following the riot at the Sojourner Truth project, a team of investigators from the Office of Facts and Figures (OFF) was sent to Detroit. They reported that "unless strong and quick intervention by some high official, preferably the President, is taken at once, hell is going to be let loose in every Northern city where large numbers of immigrants and Negroes are in competition."[69] During the fifteen months that elapsed between the report's date and the Detroit riot, no attempt was made by the administration to improve race relations. Instead of confronting the inevitable, the administration ignored the crisis until the violence came and then chose to ride it out.

Roosevelt ignored the crisis for several reasons. Like La Guardia, he was fully conscious of the gains black people had made under his administrations. Roosevelt believed that black leaders were pressing too hard for goals that were out of reach politically and that threatened unity in wartime. As early as June 1941, when A. Philip Randolph sought an executive order, Roosevelt believed that his administration was accomplishing "an enormous amount" for black citizens in the Army and "a little" in the defense industries, that "we expect to accomplish more and on the whole progress has been relatively rapid."[70] Therefore he instructed an aide to inform Dr. F. O. Williston, "a prominent" black leader, that "the President is much upset" to hear of the proposed march on Washington and "can imagine nothing that will stir up race hatred and slow up progress more." For the same reason, he probably agreed with the comment of presidential assistant Marvin H. McIntyre on Walter White's concern over the transfer of the FEPC to the War Manpower Commission in December 1942: "I think . . . White has very little to complain about in view of the very considerable activity by the Committee."[71] In short, progress was being made in spite of black American impatience.

More important, the problems confronting AfroAmericans were not considered priority. When Edwin R. Embree, president of the Julius Rosenwald Fund, suggested that a presidential commission be appointed to lift black morale and plan for postwar civil rights, Roosevelt was unreceptive. Long-range planning, the President wrote on March 16, 1942, was important and should consider "the race problem."[72] But he feared that such planning might become a means of escape from war's realities. "I am not convinced," Roosevelt concluded his disapproval of Embree's suggestion, "that we can be realists about war and planners for the future at the same time." Two weeks after the Sojourner Truth riot, he did not appear deeply concerned about racial tensions.

Furthermore, Roosevelt's poor health, the pressures of war, and the administration's setup probably resulted in his not being fully informed about lower priorities. By 1943, he was seriously ill and incapable of dealing with all the domestic and diplomatic exigencies of the war.[73] Apparently he was not informed of Randolph's plan to march on Washington until June 6, 1941. At the conference with the MOWC, Walter White was "surprised" to learn that he had not heard of Senate Resolution 75, which had been introduced several months earlier and which provided for a committee to investigate discrimination in the National Defense Program.[74] Malcolm S. MacLean, the second FEPC chairman, believed that one of his committee's jobs was "to keep the heat off the 'Boss.' "[75] There is, however, evidence that Roosevelt was sent information about all matters long before he admitted to their existence.[76] Certainly, he may have been more coy than truthful about Senate Resolution 75. In some cases such information was screened by his aides until it became important enough to draw him away from high priority war problems. The President, for example, was alerted to the MOWC after subordinates failed to placate Randolph. Although one may assume that the OFF report on the Sojourner Truth riot was significant enough to warrant presidential attention, there is a possibility that he (and maybe even the White House staff) did not see it until after the riots had begun the following year.

None of this excuses Roosevelt. Eleanor Roosevelt as well as numerous letters and reports informed him of the depressed morale of black Americans and the increasing tensions, though not necessarily in the urgent terms of the OFF report.[77] How many of these Roosevelt read is problematic. He could have provided those cities essential to the war program with more materials and monies for the construction of badly needed living facilities. Although resources were scarce, surely areas like Detroit, which produced 35 percent of the nation's entire ordnance material in June 1943, should have been high on any priority list.[78] A series of fireside chats by Roosevelt, or presidential instructions for departments and agencies to set the example in race relations, might have established a pattern for the nation to follow. Instead, the administration's ambivalence, as in the case of Sojourner Truth, offered no direction for municipal and state governments.

Roosevelt, of course, cannot be held solely responsible. The crisis was, as Interior Secretary Harold L. Ickes noted, a national one demanding presidential leadership,[79] yet public officials of Beaumont, Chester, Detroit, and Los Angeles were equally accountable, if not more so, for failing to cope with the volatile situation. The President could not be expected to administer over every racially troubled community. Local and state officials were responsible for their communities and possessed powers, knowledge of provincial problems, and administrative experience with which to deal with such problems. Furthermore, their constituencies were easier to please than the national one that Roosevelt confronted. Incompetence, prejudice, political aspirations, and the unprecedented war situation all contributed to the behavior of local officials. In Detroit, for example, Mayor Jeffries appointed an interracial committee to investigate the 1941 riot at Northwestern High School but then ignored its report.[80] He did have the courage to protest against the administration's decision to reassign the Sojourner Truth Homes to whites, but failed to do anything to improve racial harmony in his city. Nor was there an attempt to use the police department as a force to discourage racial violence; rather it assisted whites in the Sojourner Truth riot. Ambitious for the governorship, Jeffries provided no leadership as the racial clashes became more frequent.

Whoever was at fault, and certainly thousands of citizens were as responsible as their leaders, the riots came. Unfortunately, Detroit's was not the last one. Suddenly, as if for no reason, Harlem exploded.

6

Harlem Boils Over

In the early evening of Sunday, August 1, 1943, Evelyn Seely walked through Harlem. To the white *PM* reporter, it appeared to be the end of a typical summer's day. Everyone seemed to be outdoors, trying to escape the day's heat. The atmosphere was filled with music, laughter, and "intense life." People gathered on sidewalks and stoops, went in and out of apartments, or sat on window sills. Soldiers strolled with their dates, mothers wheeled their baby carriages, and children played in the street. A small boy entertained one gathering with his guitar; a young girl urged another audience to repent. Girls in gaudy prints and bright colors appeared to be "passing exotic bouquets," and a zoot-suited youth "looked uncomfortably warm in his finery." This picture justified Seely's belief that in New York City life was a little better for black people. At 8:00 P.M. "it was a reassuring picture."[1]

Within a few hours, however, Walter White was awakened by NAACP staff member Lucille Brown, asking if he knew "there is a riot . . . in Harlem."[2] Minutes later, La Guardia requested his friend's presence at the West 123rd Street police station. Harlem, in White's words, had boiled over.

While Evelyn Seely and thousands of Harlemites were enjoying the end of a long hot weekend, an incident at the Hotel Braddock had exploded into riot. At 7:00 P.M. Marjorie Polite registered at the West 126th Street hotel, which for some time had been under police surveillance as a "raided premise."[3] She had not entered with a male companion and, in fact, may not have been a prostitute despite the Braddock's reputation. After complaining of unsatisfactory accommodations, she was moved to another room. Since the shower-bath facilities she wanted were unavailable, she demanded a refund and checked out, but before leaving sought the return of a dollar tip she had allegedly given the elevator operator. When the employee denied receiving the dollar, she became "very boisterous, disorderly and profane."

Patrolman James Collins, assigned to Raided Premises Duty inside the hotel, asked Miss Polite to leave.[4] When she refused and verbally abused the officer, he arrested her for disorderly conduct. Witnessing the altercation, Mrs. Florine Roberts, a domestic from Middletown, Connecticut, demanded Miss Polite's release. Mrs. Roberts had been staying at the Braddock while she visited her son, Robert Bandy, who was on leave from the Army's 703rd Military Police Battalion in Jersey City. Bandy remonstrated with Collins. The official police report contends that Bandy threatened Collins, who for no apparent reason was then attacked by Mrs. Roberts and her son. In the scuffle, the soldier hit Collins and ran. When he refused to halt, the patrolman drew and fired his revolver, wounding Bandy. Bandy contended, however, that he protested when Collins pushed Miss Polite, and the police officer reacted by throwing his night stick, which Bandy caught; when the soldier hesitated to return the weapon, Collins shot him.[5] Police reinforcements were notified of the incident and shortly thereafter both men were admitted to Sydenham Hospital.

Against the background of recent riots in other cities, reporters were relieved to learn that Bandy's wound was superficial.[6] Unfortunately, their relief was premature. Within minutes of the shooting, rumors swept Harlem that a white policeman had killed a black soldier, who, some said, had been protecting his mother.[7]

In response to these rumors, which created "unreasoning fury" among Harlemites, large crowds began to assemble at the headquarters of the 28th police precinct, at the Braddock Hotel, and at Sydenham Hospital.[8] Police units were quickly assigned to disperse the gatherings and dispel the false rumors, but as one crowd scattered, another formed elsewhere. At one point 3,000 persons congregated outside the 28th precinct headquarters, threatening the officer responsible for Bandy's alleged death.[9] For the next two hours, the crowd and tension increased. "The groups . . . were growing larger and merging," observed a white reporter who walked along 125th Street. Most everyone "believed that the cop had killed Bandy."[10]

Around 10:30 P.M. riot occurred, as first individuals and then groups began breaking windows. Author Claude Brown, then six years old, was awakened by loud noises that he thought were made by German or Japanese bombs. Screams and the "crashing sound of falling plate-glass windows" kept him awake for hours.[11] The chain reaction spread quickly. Centering on 125th Street, the disorder encompassed the area from 110th to 145th streets on Eighth Avenue, from 110th to 140th streets on Seventh Avenue and north as far as 136th Street on Lenox Avenue.[12]

Looting soon accompanied vandalism, though some observers believed it occurred as "an afterthought."[13] Between late evening and early morning, residents of all ages moved in and out of numerous stores "like ants around spilled sugar."[14] William Pickens observed them carting "stuff off in bundles and baskets and parcels" and taxis.[15] Protective iron gates were ripped from their hinges as looters indiscriminately stole everything available, destroying what they were unable to carry. Fires were ignited; one group set six fires in six minutes as it moved along Eighth Avenue.[16] The air was filled with screams and laughter, sounds of people running, and, as novelist Ralph Ellison remembered it, "distant fire trucks, shooting, and in the quiet intervals the steady filtering of shattered glass."[17]

Vandalism and theft continued throughout the early morning hours. At 3:00 A.M. several false fire alarms increased the chaos.[18] As dawn approached, a semblance of order began to return, and by 9:00 A.M. Harlem was relatively quiet. On Monday, crowds continued to roam the streets and sporadic looting occurred. Despite tension, the riot was over. Harlem's main thoroughfares, especially West 125th Street and parts of Seventh and Eighth avenues, "looked as if they had been swept by a hurricane or an invading army."[19] The scene was one of smashed windows, wrecked stores, and cluttered sidewalks, with broken glass, foodstuffs, clothing, and assorted debris everywhere.

The upheaval was costly. Official NYPD figures recorded six persons killed, all black, and 185 persons, mostly AfroAmerican, injured.[20] Journalistic sources placed the death toll as low as five and as high as twenty-six, while estimating the number of injured people from four hundred to one thousand.[21] Although police statistics are generally the most accurate, they probably underestimated the injured because not everyone who needed medical attention reported it. More than 550 blacks were arrested, generally for burglary or for receiving stolen goods. Estimates of damages and losses in more than 1,450 stores ranged from $225,000 to $5,000,000.[22] La Guardia's and the police department's immediate, restrained response minimized the loss of human life, prevented the riot from going out of control, and, in the long run, reduced the amount of property damage.

It was probably a little after 9:00 P.M. on August 1 when La Guardia was advised of the disturbance in Harlem. By that time crowds had already begun to form and twenty patrolmen of the 28th precinct had been assigned to the Braddock.[23] Within the hour the 32nd precinct was instructed to dispatch men to the hotel to assist the 28th precinct officers, indicating that the Bandy-Collins incident was no longer considered routine.[24] Upon arriving at the 28th precinct headquarters, La Guardia conferred with

Police Commissioner Valentine and Fire Commissioner Patrick Walsh. Accompanied by black leaders Ferdinand Smith of the National Maritime Union, Dr. Max Yergan of the National Negro Congress, and attorney Hope Stevens, he toured the riot district.[25]

Meanwhile, La Guardia ordered the Braddock closed at 11:00 P.M.[26] When shifts changed at midnight, all patrolmen were held on duty, providing a reserve of one-third of the police force.[27] Security police were also alerted, assigned to each car of the Independent Subway serving Harlem, and military policemen cleared the area of servicemen. Firemen, too, were held on duty. Shortly after 1:00 A.M., the adjoining 23rd and 25th police precincts were instructed to compile "a separate log" of all occurrences within their boundaries that were associated with the Harlem disorder and, if necessary, to supply the more critical areas with reserves.[28] In half an hour, 5,000 police were in the zone of disorder.[29]

Just after 2:00 A.M., La Guardia ordered the closing of all Harlem taverns, which forced "revellers into the streets" and, according to the *Amsterdam News,* increased the rioting, "by leaps and bounds."[30] Perhaps this order did augment the number of rioters, though probably not significantly. People not already participating in the riot were unlikely to begin that late. Nor is it probable that La Guardia's instruction decreased the number of rioters, but once the disorder subsided it helped keep a lid on the community. As far north as 170th Street, the order was issued to close all places where intoxicants were sold.[31] In time the riot zone was sealed off. Traffic was diverted around the entire area of West Harlem, from 110th to 155th streets between Fifth and Eighth avenues.

Besides saturating the district with police and isolating it from other communities, La Guardia moved to dispel the rumor that had ignited the upheaval. Returning from the tour with Smith, Yergan, and Stevens, and following their suggestion, he made the first of five radio broadcasts to New York City residents. Accordingly, at 1:05 A.M., he corrected the story of Bandy's death, asked rioters to go home, and promised to protect the lives and property "of the people of this city and that means in every section of the city."[32] Walter White soon arrived at the 28th precinct, by now firmly established as mayoral headquarters, and recommended that municipal soundtrucks carry black leaders through the community to appeal for order and to disclose Bandy's condition. Cab Calloway, Duke Ellington, Joe Louis, and Powell were out of town, but the Reverend Johnson, Battle, Smith, and Yergan responded immediately.[33]

As rioters burned themselves out on the morning of August 2, the Mayor moved to prevent a recurrence. At 9:50 A.M., he delivered his third broadcast over eight major stations. "Shame has come to our city and sorrow to the large number of our fellow citizens . . . who live in Harlem," he began.[34] Carefully avoiding any condemnation of the ghetto's citizenry as a whole, he described the riot and the measures taken to restore full order. Traffic would be limited and nonresidents denied entrance to Harlem. Liquor stores would be closed indefinitely and pedestrians would not be permitted to assemble on sidewalks or street corners. Looters, of course, would be arrested and law-abiding citizens protected. Moreover, emergency food supplies, "particularly milk for the children," would be provided immediately. "Law and order," La Guardia concluded, "must and will be maintained in this city."

La Guardia took added precautions. Later in the day he conferred with justices Bolin and Watson, Battle, police inspector Lewis Costuma, and military officials.[35] That evening, 1,500 volunteers, most of whom were black, along with 6,000 city and military police, air raid wardens, and City Patrol units secured the riot area, while 8,000 New York state guardsmen, including a black regiment, were on "stand-by" in several metropolitan armories. "All over the district policemen were stationed on street corners, in hallways, on rooftops and in automobiles parked in the streets." At 10:30 P.M. a partial curfew was imposed from Fifth to St. Nicholas avenues between 110th and 155th streets, and the wartime "dimout" was lifted so the district could be brightly illuminated. Black leaders again toured the community, urging fellow residents to maintain order. The situation "at this moment," La Guardia declared in his fourth broadcast at 9:55 A.M., "is definitely under control." Thirty minutes later, he was back on the air to plead for cooperation. Then he charged off to make another tour of Harlem.

In fact, the riot was over. That evening some Harlemites were on the streets while others peered out of their tenements. At 11:00 P.M., the district was quiet, its streets nearly deserted except for Red Cross representatives serving crullers and lemonade to the civilian and police patrols. Satisfied with the situation, La Guardia headed for home at 1:00 A.M., exhausted from a sleepless vigil.[36] As the week progressed, the curfew was pushed back an hour to 11:30 P.M., the traffic ban eased, the stores reopened, and the liquor ban lifted. The police force, too, was first reduced and finally, on August 14, returned to normal size.[37]

Reconstruction had been directed by La Guardia almost as soon as the disturbance occurred. Medical facilities and food supplies were crucial. At midnight on August 1, the Emergency Medical Service was alerted, and immediately a check was made of all hospitals in the area to determine the number of available admissions and to consider plans to coordinate facilities and manpower. After visiting Harlem Hospital, Hospital Commissioner Edward M. Bernecker expressed confidence that "the medical situation was being handled satisfactorily."[38] All interns and student nurses were on emergency duty, while visiting surgeons maintained two operating rooms throughout the early morning. Reserve surgical teams were on stand-by at Bellevue, Lincoln, and Morrisania hospitals. Additional supplies—blood, dressings, suture material, and sulfa drugs—were also available at those hospitals. Extra police were assigned to ambulances, a fleet of which was held in reserve, and volunteers of the United States Army Ambulance Corps helped register patients at Harlem Hospital. Besides that hospital, which received the most admissions, Sydenham, Knickerbocker, and Joint Disease hospitals treated individuals for lacerations, cuts from flying glass, a few bullet and stab wounds, and severe contusions. Between late August 1 and early August 3, these hospitals treated 672 patients, admitted 56, and received three Dead on Arrival. Instant first aid—for example, the presence of a surgeon at the 28th precinct—was eventually available at the riot scene.[39] By any measure, these medical operations were commendable.

Medical authorities, no doubt at mayoral instructions, were tactful as well as competent. In order to prepare Harlem Hospital's surgical wards for possible emergency use during the evening of August 3, patients were evacuated to Bellevue. The evacuation was undertaken in a manner "to avoid exciting . . . rumors" that might trigger another outburst.[40] Eight four-stretcher ambulances from six hospitals participated in a shuttle service, in which no more than two vehicles were loaded at a time. The ambulances were routed "through quiet areas," traversing only "a very small section of the area in which the disturbance was taking place."

Providing the riot area with food was another serious problem. Most of Harlem's food stores closed because their stocks were depleted by looters or because their owners feared further violence. Dealers whose drivers had been attacked also suspended operations temporarily. Early on August 2, La Guardia conferred with Markets Commissioner Daniel P. Woolley and outlined plans for the immediate replenishment of Harlem's food supply. He assured a radio audience that "we will get food up there . . . [but] it will take several days to obtain . . . the normal flow of supplies to the retail stores."[41]

Woolley set to work at once. Of approximately five hundred food stores in the area, 150 had been damaged and closed.[42] Fifty of those were damaged so badly that their reopening was questionable, while the others were operating "apparently on a normal basis." By August 3, basic foods were being delivered, though many of the sales were being transacted from trucks at regular retail prices. Fair distribution of the food was assisted by the opening of Weisbacher Grocery Store, the limited operation of two A & P's, and pushcart operators. "I don't think there is any need for real worry about food supplied in this section," the Markets Commissioner assured La Guardia a day after the riot. Indeed, milk deliveries were about 90 percent of the normal quota and meat supplies were 100 percent above normal.[43] Moreover, food salesmen were now being permitted to enter the area and take orders for future deliveries. By August 6, there was "no shortage."[44]

Action taken in the 28th precinct was representative of the administration's efforts to clean up and secure the riot area.[45] Between 4:00 A.M. and 4:00 P.M. on August 2, firemen fought eleven fires, guarded fireboxes and stores, and stood on emergency reserve. Beginning at 7:00 A.M., personnel from the Departments of Housing and Buildings boarded windows, a task ultimately requiring the assistance of 185 employees from the Department of Public Works. Also beginning early Monday morning and continuing for three days, the Sanitation Department dispatched men and equipment to clean the area. On August 2 alone, more than 1,200 men and 250 trucks worked eight hours. That day, the Department of Water, Sewage, Gas and Electricity assigned 25 employees and ten trucks to change 1,200 streetlamp bulbs, which increased illumination more than 200 percent in preparation for Harlem's curfew. Every work unit was protected by a police escort.

In addition, civic organizations assisted the NYPD to secure the 28th precinct and to hasten reconstruction. More than 530 air raid wardens, 165 members of the New York Urban League's Harlem Citizen Volunteers, and 20 members of the City Patrol Corps patrolled the heart of the riot district—Seventh and Eighth avenues and 125th Street—during the evening of August 2 and morning of

August 3.[46] Meanwhile, the American Women's Voluntary Services and the American Red Cross fed personnel on duty. Almost all 1,500 volunteers were Harlemites, which indicates the significant role blacks played in restoring order.[47] Similar civic assistance occurred in the 32nd precinct, which shared the brunt of riot.[48]

By Wednesday, August 4, La Guardia's tactics appeared to have succeeded. Detectives continued to search for stolen goods and the Court of Special Sessions prepared to judge assault cases, but the police force was reduced and the curfew pushed back.[49] With order restored, everyone now searched for the conditions that ignited twelve hours of upheaval.

Mayor La Guardia conferring with Major General Thomas Terry of the Eastern Defense Command and Captain Walter Harding of the New York Police Department after the outbreak of the riot. (Courtesy of United Press International.)

Police leading a looting suspect out of a shattered store window. (Courtesy of United Press International.)

Police with suspected rioters in custody. (Courtesy of United Press International.)

Auxiliary police receiving batons and helmets. (Courtesy of *The New York Times*.)

Tuxedo-clad youngsters being brought into the 28th precinct station house. (Courtesy of United Press International.)

Street cleaners sweeping up broken glass and debris left from the riot at Lenox Avenue and 125th Street. (Courtesy of United Press International.)

7

Police, Hoodlums, Race, and Riot

Sincere efforts by private citizens and the city government to avert riot and the conviction that ghetto conditions and racial tensions were less inflammatory in New York than in most war production centers perhaps made the general response of New Yorkers to Harlem's upheaval one of understanding. In some ways, they were too understanding: by ignoring its racial nature and by blaming it on hoodlums, blacks and whites eased their consciences and temporarily re-established harmony. This determined attitude disregarded reasons for ghetto resentment and the need for measures to improve the living conditions of black residents.

Representative of public reaction to the riot was the sentimental report in *PM* that throughout the evening of August 1 "two little boys," one black, the other white, "slept peacefully side by side" in the 28th police precinct headquarters.[1] Like the two youngsters, members of both races were tolerant of each other in their evaluation of the disorder.

Praise for La Guardia, which sometimes verged on eulogy, was especially high among blacks. The words of Thomas B. Dyett, the State Commissioner of Correction, were typical: "Mr. Mayor [you] have kept the faith."[2] Even Adam Clayton Powell, Jr., described La Guardia's action as "wise and effective."[3] Less notable citizens agreed. The spokesman of a black American Legion post, for example, considered La Guardia "a man of vision, integrity and character."[4]

Such praise was associated with La Guardia's protection of black people and containment of the riot. "We can safely say," Max Yergan spoke for many, "that the Police Department, under instructions from you, prevented another Detroit from occurring in our own city."[5] In Detroit, the riot raged for more than thirty hours; thirty-four deaths and seven hundred injuries were recorded. Of these, twenty-five corpses were black, as were three-fourths of the injured. But in New York, the twelve-hour disorder was contained in Harlem, which was a major reason why large-scale interracial fighting did not occur and why the six dead and almost all the 185 injured were Afro-American. Most of the dead in both riots were black men slain by policemen. In Detroit, however, indiscriminate brutality prevailed, while in New York looters drew gunfire only for threatening officers with bodily harm or for resisting arrest. Of the six deaths reported in Harlem, four were caused by white policemen, and one each by a black member of the City Patrol Corps and a black bartender.[6] Two of the deaths caused by policemen were clearly cases of self-defense; the other two, in which the same patrolman shot looters fleeing from a grocery store, were questionable. In general, however, the Harlem riot was contained more quickly than the Detroit riot precisely because of level-headed police action.

The police department's efficiency and restraint were due to La Guardia's early preparations, which were based on the advice of black leaders and police officials who had observed the Detroit riot. In addition, Valentine's implementation of the plans was commendable. Equally significant, policemen carried out their orders with dispassionate precision. In the process, patrolmen forced their critics to reconsider the traditional charge of police brutality, at least as it pertained to the NYPD as a unit. Police handling of the riot partly reflected the hope for better relations that some New Yorkers had previously demonstrated in their efforts to prevent disorder.

Long before the Harlem riot, La Guardia was conscious of the important role of the police in escalating or quelling a racial disturbance. On June 23, Roy Wilkins had notified him that newspaper stories about the NYPD being alerted for possible disorders alarmed black people, for in Detroit the police "murdered Negroes ... in cold blood." Black New Yorkers wanted assurances that their "police ... [would] protect all citizens regardless of race or color."[7] Condemnation of the Detroit police was most cogent in Walter White's report on "What Caused the Detroit Race Riots?" which La Guardia received in mid-July.[8] White considered the brutality and "willful inefficiency" of the Detroit police "one of the most disgraceful episodes in American history."[9] Not only had most of the twenty-five AfroAmerican dead been "shot by the police and a number of them in the back," but for years the police had permitted racists "to operate without check or hindrance." White, therefore, recommended federal investigations of the Detroit Police Department, the Michigan State Police, Mayor Edward J. Jeffries, and other municipal officials.

The reports of his own policemen, Edward M. Butler and Emanuel Kline, who had been sent to observe the Detroit riot, placed more blame on blacks for having caused that disorder than did observers like White, but they gave La Guardia a candid account of the overt cause for riot and the police reaction to it. Butler and Kline had also conferred with Mayor Jeffries, Police Commissioner John H. Witherspoon, and various high-ranking local and state police officials (which doubtless accounts in part for their interpretation of the riot's causes). Detroit's police department, Butler had reported on June 23, "was not ready" for the riot and subsequently it spread out of control.[10] Most important was the absence of superior officers to coordinate police activities. "Due to the lack of leadership," the officers reported, "the patrolmen may not have used the best judgment in certain instances."[11] Although Butler and Kline had hesitated to criticize Detroit's police, Wilkins and White had not.

Butler and Kline recommended police action if a similar disorder occurred in New York City. Probably at the Gracie Mansion conference of June 28, La Guardia and black leaders had expanded the seventeen suggestions to twenty-four.[12] The more important of these related to the method and the spirit of police action.[13] Superior officers would accompany patrolmen, who would operate in numbers, at least in twos. If possible, they would arrest looters, but use force only "when necessary," and shoot only as "the last resort." Tear gas would not be used except as a last measure. In order to control and contain the rioting, bars would be closed, the sale of intoxicants prohibited, the weapons in pawnshops and gunstores guarded, as would be fire-alarm boxes and schools, and traffic diverted around the disorder. Remembering the wanton mob attacks on black persons in Detroit, police would protect passengers of buses, cars, and trolleys. When riot came on August 1, these recommendations were implemented quickly and efficiently.

There is no way of knowing how often, between late June and early August, policemen had been told that if riot came restraint was both expected and necessary. No doubt, five weeks of preparation had influenced police action considerably. Knowing what to expect and how to react, New York patrolmen on the riot scene suppressed personal feelings that prompted indiscriminate and undisciplined action. Unlike Detroit's patrolmen, they knew emphatically that neither La Guardia nor Valentine would tolerate brutality and that human life held priority over property and law and order. Upon Detroit's tragedy La Guardia laid the foundation that precluded disgraceful police action in the Harlem riot.

Insensitive and irresponsible police action did occur, but on a comparatively small scale. As a black man attempted to cross Seventh Avenue during the riot, a mounted policeman lunged in front of his car. "Do I have to get out of the way for you? You black bastard," snapped the officer.[14] In the slaying of two black looters, it is unclear whether Patrolman Benjamin Wallace acted irresponsibly, but his actions seem contrary to departmental orders; the looters had been attempting to escape and had not threatened his personal safety or that of others. And in the riot's aftermath, at least one black resident accused detectives of confiscating for themselves the stolen goods recovered from looters and charged patrolmen with brutality.[15] No doubt, there were several similar incidents of indiscriminate police behavior that should not be dismissed lightly. As a unit, however, the NYPD had been exemplary in its handling of the riot and deserved acknowledgment as "New York's Finest."

The disorder was handled so well that La Guardia did not request assistance from the State Guard. More than twenty black citizens, whom Herbert L. Bruce called together during the riot, urged Governor Thomas E. Dewey to send troops into Harlem.[16] Perhaps in response to their telegram, Dewey offered La Guardia such assistance. The Mayor requested only that they be mobilized and held in reserve.[17] In the event they were needed, their arrival would be immediate. Meanwhile, La Guardia placed full confidence in Valentine and the police department. The State Guard was moved into municipal armories, but it was never ordered into the streets.

In addition to the overwhelming praise for La Guardia and the police department, most New Yorkers agreed on the nature of the riot. Reiterating La Guardia's radio statement of August 2, blacks and whites insisted that "this was not a race riot."[18] According to Adam Clayton Powell, Jr., who accurately reflected the leadership and press of both races, the disturbance in Harlem could not "by any stretch of the imagination nor distortion of the fact be called a race riot."[19] This conviction was based on two premises. One was a narrow definition of what constitutes a race riot: compared with the riots in Detroit and elsewhere, the one in Harlem was largely free of physical violence between blacks and whites. Second was the belief that Harlem's disorder was the work of hoodlums, who destroyed black as well as white property. In La Guardia's words, "the thoughtless hoodlums had no one to fight with"; rather they stole from and injured "their own people."

La Guardia, Powell, and numerous others may have had two other reasons for insisting that Harlem's riot was not racial. For one thing, cognizant of the inflammatory effect that rumor and race had played in Detroit, La Guardia sought to minimize disunity in New York City. "Misrepresenting the situation as a race riot," he informed the Newspaper Guild's president on August 2, "may have a serious effect in inciting disturbances in other mixed areas in Greater New York."[20] La Guardia's effort to manage the news probably succeeded not only because the press, too, considered a race riot one in which large numbers of both races fought one another, but also because newspaper reporters also wanted to prevent further disorder.

Secondly, others, black leaders in particular, were doubtless concerned about future racial harmony and the struggle for equality. A "race" riot could increase tensions and turn sympathetic whites away from the struggle for civil rights. State official and Urban Leaguer Elmer A. Carter, for example, contended that the disorder would make it "infinitely more difficult for colored people to live in decent neighborhoods and to secure improvements in Harlem."[21]

A handful of perceptive observers, however, realized that Harlem's disorder was fraught with racial implications. One correspondent contended that although blacks did not attack whites directly, "it was a RACE RIOT."[22] The actions and motivations of the rioters supported a racial interpretation of the disorder. Even some of those who charged hoodlums with igniting the riot observed its racial character. Warren Brown, whom La Guardia commended for the accuracy of his observations, reported that many rioters resented foreigners, who received opportunities that were denied them, and "complained about whites not being fair to Negroes."[23] More overtly, blacks had told a white reporter to leave the riot vicinity; after having been clouted on the back, he raced down Eighth Avenue.[24] Certainly the pattern of blacks destroying white property, as Lester B. Granger and others noted, reflected racial tensions.[25] The looting had begun spontaneously and as "an afterthought"—several hours after the riot's destruction of store windows had begun.[26] If the riot was caused solely by hoodlums, why had they waited so long before looting and why had they looted white stores predominantly?

The rioters' motivations were also directly associated with race and racism. Several observers, like Roy Wilkins, interpreted Harlem's disturbance as "the boiling over of pent-up resentment in the breasts of millions of American Negroes all over this country."[27] A white resident perhaps most eloquently expressed an understanding of AfroAmerican frustration and resentment: Harry Shatsky asked La Guardia to imagine himself black.[28] How would he feel if he had met with constant discrimination in employment, if he was charged exorbitant prices for inferior goods and unreasonable rents for filthy, rat-infested apartments, if he had a son in the army and heard how many black soldiers were beaten and slain by white mobs for no other reason than the blackness of their skins? If black children, Shatsky elaborated, did not have "to watch their parents suffer and struggle to keep their families together," live in unhealthy tenements, work rather than attend school, "if they weren't called 'Nigger bastard' or cursed," few would have engaged in disorder. To use an anonymous columnist's words, Shatsky was accurately contending that hoodlum activity "may be reflecting racial frustrations."[29]

This important point was completely disregarded by most New Yorkers, who attributed the riot to Harlem's less respectable elements or, according to La Guardia, "thoughtless hoodlums." Both races, but especially blacks, advanced this thesis. W. E. B. DuBois' observation about Detroit and New York was typical: "The black folk in this land have developed a dangerous criminal class."[30] Black residents stressed their own innocence. One advised La Guardia that Harlem's "self-respecting and law-abiding citizens" opposed the disorder; others blamed it on "the unthinking and lawless element."[31] White officials and the daily press also placed the guilt squarely on the community's baser residents.[32]

If not hoodlums, then uneducated black southern migrants were responsible for the riot. Again, more blacks than whites seemed to express this belief. Some black correspondents attributed the disorder to the southern system, which fostered in blacks "a deep-rooted hatred for white people."[33] In part, they believed that the liberal northern atmosphere accounted for the misbehavior of migrants. Whatever the reasons for misbehavior, an elderly AfroAmerican woman, herself a relocated Mississippian, advised La Guardia to return the troublemakers to the south.[34]

According to a black pastor, riot participants were also few in number, "didn't know any better and are to be pitied."[35] Perhaps because riots, like crime, only made the struggle for equality more difficult, most AfroAmericans refused to recognize the participation of law-abiding citizens in the disorder. To the Reverend John H. Johnson, who represented the feelings of many blacks, the riot was "another black eye" for Harlem.[36] Rowdies and hoodlums, he lamented, "will never win one battle for us." Acceptance of the hoodlum-migrant thesis also reflected the classes and tensions within black society. The rioters were described as "people who had not been oriented into the ways of our community."[37] Their appearance, behavior, and "illiterate, frustrated condition" indicated that they were "newcomers."

The hoodlum or riffraff thesis, however, oversimplfies the very complex process of riot participation. Most observers based their interpretation on the behavior of rioters, all of whom appeared to have been engaged in vandalism and looting. From this, they assumed that the motivation of all riot participants must have been criminal. In fact, while it was relatively easy to make descriptive generalizations about the behavior being observed, it was impossible to identify accurately the motivations that prompted such behavior. It was, therefore, extremely risky to attribute motivations simply on the basis of behavior; every act of destruction and theft was not necessarily motivated by maliciousness and greed. Most interpreters also seemed to associate the hoodlum-riffraff thesis with lower-class culture; since rioters stole, they must have been poor. This association between socioeconomic status and criminal behavior was made without objective data. The lower class was distinguished by substandard educational and economic levels rather than by specific behavior traits. The lower-class context may have promoted violence and crime, yet lower-class segments also opposed such activity. Black welfare recipient Dorothy Simons had advocated punishment for hoodlums before the riot, and there is no reason to believe that she felt otherwise afterward.[38] Moreover, once disorder occurred, class differences collapsed as rioters shared the overwhelming commonality of being black in a white society. And as the relative socioeconomic differences between lower-class and middle-class participants melted in the face of their frustrations and resentment, they behaved identically. Rather than merely "the malicious and mischievous misdoings of imprudent youth," several black organizations led by the National Council of Negro Women understood that riot was "an echo of what lies in the hearts and minds of millions of American Negroes whose customary restraint, patience, and good will is all that has stood between them and racial outbreaks."[39] Most public, official evaluations of the riot were made by persons who did not represent the participants and who possessed an ideological orientation that judged social upheaval both disgraceful and counterproductive. In fact, some like La Guardia and Walter White, were predisposed to the hoodlum thesis. "We have," White contended in the original draft of his June 28th letter to black leaders, "too large an amount of lawlessness by irresponsible Negroes particularly in their late teens."[40] But in urging that efforts be made to prevent their behavior from igniting "the spark" that would "set off trouble here," even he recognized the underlying universality of black grievances that could erupt in riot at any moment.

Other advocates of the hoodlum thesis were influenced by Harlem's reputation for juvenile delinquency and crime, which was sometimes reinforced by personal experience. Whenever a rash of muggings involving white victims broke out in and around lower Harlem, white dailies sensationalized a "crime wave." This adverse publicity irritated blacks because it reinforced racial stereotypes and because equivalent attention was not given to crimes against black citizens. Individuals living and working in Harlem knew the situation firsthand. During late 1941, C. M. Hall, who had been held up twice, complained that "every street corner is full of bums, either shooting crap or lounging around waiting for someone they can rob."[41] Other residents informed La Guardia of similar robberies, drunkenness, prostitution, gambling, narcotics, and general lawlessness throughout the community.[42] "Harlem," wrote one of many whites who observed the neighborhood, "is rapidly becoming a sort of jungle, much to the distress of the great majority of decent colored people."[43] Black leaders, too, who clearly understood that crime was largely caused by social disorganization resulting from poverty, periodically acknowledged the presence of "an unhealthy situation."[44]

When riot came, its origin and pattern reinforced the negative feelings that segments of the Harlem community had toward migrants, the lower class, and, particularly, hoodlums. Located on West 126th Street, the Braddock Hotel, known for its traffic in prostitution and narcotics, had been, for over a year, at the time of the disorder a "raided premise" under police surveillance. A black correspondent later asked La Guardia to close down the hotel, "for it is ruination to our young girls."[45] The crowds that

formed outside the Braddock, the 28th precinct headquarters, and especially Sydenham Hospital represented
every segment of black society, but the lower class constituted the majority.[46] The vandalism and looting was
largely undertaken by male teenagers and young adults.
Of the 590 persons arrested during the riot, 129 were
males between the ages of 16 and 20, and 353 were adult
males, mostly young.[47] These participants, assisted by
young women, adolescent girls, and children, appeared to
fit the general concept of lower-class types and hoodlums.
One high-ranking police officer spoke for many citizens
when he characterized the rioters as "ignorant and irresponsible," whose "rebellion against lawful authority"
was matched by "the inherent trait to steal."[48] The riot's
circus atmosphere, especially evident in the slum sections,
reinforced the hoodlum thesis.

Certainly, some hoodlums—meaning individuals who
indulged in delinquent or criminal activities regularly—
participated in the upheaval. In Walter White's words,
they "seized the occasion to pillage and destroy."[49] Jack
Reed, whose father had a long police record, was one of
these; he came from the Bronx to participate in disorder and
receive stolen property.[50] Yet the riot was not centered in
lower Harlem along West 110th Street, where, according to
then hustler Malcolm Little, the most criminal-prone population lived.[51] Nor were those who initially gathered to protest Bandy's alleged death necessarily the ones who later
looted. Often a breakdown in social order promotes uninhi-
bited, even hostile actions that may be unrelated to "the
conditions giving rise to the initial outburst."[52] Even White
realized that the outburst triggered by rumors of Bandy's
death involved ordinary citizens, who were replaced by
"hoodlums" when looting started. In other words, more
than hoodlums rioted.

In fact, rioters represented various socioeconomic back-
grounds. Well-dressed members of the middle class were
among the original protesters at Sydenham Hospital, and
some took part in the vandalism and looting.[53] Although it

is difficult to determine the social strata of soldiers, some of them also participated in various stages of riot. Private James Logwood was charged with "inciting a riot," while eleven other servicemen were arrested for unlawful entry or burglary.[54] While a few servicemen protected whites from rioters, many more of the five hundred soldiers in Harlem might have participated in the riot if they had not been evacuated by military police.[55] Several observers recalled seeing "solid citizens," women, housewives, and children looting.[56] Some were "gainfully employed and financially able to purchase any of the articles" they stole.[57] Even a police commander acknowledged that rioters were "of a general type of person . . . from varied occupations."[58] Facts like these prompted a black editor to contend that the majority of those rioting "hardly represented criminal tendencies."[59]

It is difficult to develop a profile of the average rioter. None of the proponents of the hoodlum thesis, La Guardia included, defined "hoodlum." That catch-all term described rioters without providing vital information on age, sex, socioeconomic status, or educational level. Who at the Braddock Hotel "pummelled, kicked, and punched" patrolman Collins in protest of Polite's arrest?[60] Which members of society were concerned enough about Bandy's condition to congregate outside the hospital and police station? Who exactly ignited the rumors of Bandy's death? Were they agitators, as the police reported, whose propaganda changed "the crowd into a mob"?[61] Which persons in the crowd recruited others from the street and protested by destroying store windows along St. Nicholas Avenue and 125th Street?[62] Were these the same individuals who later, almost as "an afterthought," looted the stores? Who assaulted the handful of whites in the area? What of the numerous children like Claude, Danny, Butch, and Kid, who scavenged grocery stores for food?[63]

Answers to these questions are found in the varying motivations of the participants rather than in their homogeneous behavior. Clearly, those at the Braddock resented being pushed around. For six weeks before August 1, a series of "petty brawls" had occurred in the hotel's vicinity. According to one commentator, the police "seemingly strained neighborhood feelings" by barring racially mixed couples from the Braddock, regardless of their marital status, and by entering their rooms to eject the white person forcibly.[64] Vandals and looters were present in various classes, but R., an anonymous eighteen-year-old participant, may have been typical of lower-class rioters. R., who had dropped out of vocational high school in order to "have some fun" before his induction into the army, ran out of a theater to participate in the riot.[65] He then joined other youths in vandalism, looting, and confrontations with the police. Although articulate and intelligent, R. consciously called attention to himself by strutting, swearing, and using slang. This so-called "zoot effect" is often associated with social isolation, rejection, discrimination, and chronic humiliation, which nurtures protest against society. Hence R. possessed no sympathy for injury inflicted on other individuals, no respect for private property, and no guilt feelings for his behavior. Attacking symbols of white property and authority reflected both a desire for revenge against larger society and a drive for ego-security. "Do not," R. admonished, "attempt to fuck with me." Since his parents were separated and he lived in a boarding-house, R. had few responsibilities or checks on his behavior. Since most males lived outside the home, rioters were generally young men.

Middle-class participants, however, were more accepting of the dominant societal values and, therefore, more inhibited by them. Frustrated by similar rejection and, paradoxically, by the rising expectations of a war atmosphere, many protested for more clearly identifiable and political reasons: the abuse of black people collectively— as symbolized by Bandy—in a war being fought for democracy. Others who temporarily lost their middle-class inhibitions and rioted may have been like A., an anonymous teenage girl, who, returning from a theater, "ran right into the disturbances."[66] Opposed to the destruction of other people's property, she did not steal, but walked through the streets and "sort of got into the spirit of the thing." People began giving her stolen items, which she in turn passed on to others. In the process, she encouraged bystanders to participate. A. had "never stolen anything in [her] life," and eventually regretted her behavior and urged La Guardia to designate places where people could return articles without getting into trouble. "Temptation is tempestuous," she wrote in the urgent, special-delivery letter to the Mayor, "but conscience is more." Educated and religious, A. lived at home and was urged by her mother to return the fur coat she had acquired in the riot. Most middle-class participants, except for the soldiers who were trained in violence, found it difficult, though not impossible, to engage in destruction and theft.

No doubt numerous participants felt what sociologist Robert K. Merton has called the strain toward normlessness.[67] In the United States, emphasis has been placed on goals rather than on the means by which to achieve them, thereby creating needs for immediate gratification. Inferior education and limited job opportunities have reduced the legitimate means for goal-achievement among blacks, nurturing frustration in some blacks who were constantly confronted with the symbols of "success" and told that achieving such "success" was tantamount to personal dignity. This goal-emphasis and uneven distribution of legitimate means fostered deviance among the most frustrated individuals. Thus, rioters feeling the greatest strain were least inhibited and most destructive, but they were not alone. Sociologist Harold Orlansky correctly interpreted the Bandy-Collins incident as being "sufficiently close to the frustrations of all Negroes to unite them in mass protest."[68] As this homogenizing effect produced hostile outburst, openings occurred in the social order, drawing in participants with varying motivations.[69] This explains why targets of attack shifted throughout the disorder. First the crowds gathered in protest; then spontaneous, intense outbreaks of window-smashing aimed at symbols of oppression occurred, followed by large-scale looting. Those who deliberately attacked the handful of black-owned stores were undoubtedly alienated by the black as well as the white establishment. Targets were primarily determined by the riot area's ecology. The targets, therefore, were white policemen—of whom more than sixty were injured—and white-owned property.[70] In the outlying areas of the riot, most notably at West 125th Street and St. Nicholas Avenue, a small number of white pedestrians and trolley passengers were attacked by black youths.[71] This was at the far western border of Harlem, a contested neighborhood that the Young Citizens' Committee on Race Relations identified as a spawning ground for white 'conflict gangs.'[72] Although the NYPD and ecological factors contained interracial clashes during the riot, more would have occurred had white people been more accessible. The circus atmosphere was generated by the gratification of releasing pent-up emotions, the reaction to expected behavior and boredom in a war-regulated society.[73] Perhaps among those looting, it also represented collective support for a redefinition of property rights.[74] To a perceptive resident, the disorder was much more than "just pure 'Hoodlumism.' "[75]

Nevertheless, most black citizens accepted the thesis and regretted the riot's occurrence. Odell Clark was reluctant to claim Harlem as his home, while others felt shame for being black.[76] That black society might be judged by the lawlessness of a few concerned some correspondents, of whom at least three informed on looters.[77] Minnie P. Littlejohn experienced all of these feelings. For the first time in forty-two years of life, she was sorry "to be a Negro."[78] Informing La Guardia of an address where stolen merchandise could be found, she asked him not to think "all Negroes are alike." As for La Guardia, a few residents "shed tears" knowing that the people of Harlem had "let you down."[79]

Certainly many, but not all, blacks were ashamed of the riot. Columnist M. Moran Weston considered it a tragedy, but found whites guiltier than blacks and those blacks who felt shame "stupid."[80] A survey undertaken by psychologist Kenneth B. Clark of CCNY indicated that twenty blacks, 30 percent of those interviewed, accepted or justified the riot as a form of group violence.[81] Although some respondents regretted the suffering of innocent people and the looting, they neither felt shame nor considered the rioters hoodlums. No doubt, some riot participants, like R., experienced no feelings of guilt for their activities. There is, of course, no way of knowing how many AfroAmericans shared Weston's feelings, those of the survey, and R's attitude. Those who agreed with them were not likely to express their feelings to La Guardia. Given the available evidence, the temper of the times, the outlook of black leadership, and the apparent belief among blacks that they could achieve equality by operating within the system, the majority probably considered the riot shameful. Most of them were sincere. Nevertheless, a certain amount of role-playing cannot be dismissed. Although in the minority, Weston and those who thought like him reveal the rage that was present among segments of black society. "The Negro has lost confidence in the white man," a black New Yorker informed Roosevelt in December 1943.[82] As "a rebellious Negro," Thomas L. Mason was determined to fight anyone who would deprive his people of "human rights." Clearly, the origins of the postwar struggle were emerging.

So, too, were the positive racial attitudes of numerous whites. Some correspondents informed La Guardia of their efforts to bring the disorder to an end. In the immediate wake of upheaval, Councilman Cacchione, for example, had black political supporters circulate through the riot district "trying to pacify the people."[83] Individuals and groups, particularly teachers and union members, offered La Guardia their cooperation and services. Evidently a meaningful number of residents felt the same reaction as the Transportation Workers Union, which pledged "the fullest cooperation in any program designed to strengthen the unity and constructive working together of all New Yorkers."[84] In part they may have been influenced by the white press, which covered the riot with a sensitivity that amazed most AfroAmericans. "I cannot," Powell commended, "sing too highly the praises of excellent, sound and democratic treatment of the outbreak by the Metropolitan press."[85]

Another indication of public concern was the number of suggestions La Guardia received from members of both races. During the riot some correspondents recommended the immediate use of additional police force, particularly state or extralegal units. Perhaps a 9:00 P.M. curfew or a blackout, the assignment of biracial troops or an all-black unit would bring the riot to an end.[86] Questionable motives may have prompted some of these white requests, but for the most part they do not appear to have been made by racists seeking violent repression; "war necessities," a white shop steward wired, "demand [the] fullest protection for Negroes in the war effort."[87] Some blacks advised additional police force and suggested, among other measures, a curfew on saloons and the prevention of liquor sales to minors.[88] There was humor, unintended to be sure, in some proposals. One resident urged the closing of all pawnshops, saloons, and liquor stores, with a few of the latter left open for dispensing alcohol for medicinal purposes.[89]

Other suggestions were both impractical and, in some cases, idealistic. "Have Bill Robinson talk to his people," J. Henricks advised somewhat impatiently.[90] A black woman advanced the idea of broadcasting spirituals as a means of quelling riot should it recur.[91] Although a few of the recommendations, like Henricks', smacked of negative racial attitudes, most of them seem to have been well-meaning. Both races, of course, were offering suggestions they believed would improve relations as well as thwart disorder.

The war's emphasis on democracy seems to have been the main factor in fostering a better understanding of race relations in white New Yorkers. The totalitarian racism of the Axis and the Allied propaganda against it made many whites more conscious of their own beliefs and the inequities in society. "We expect . . . Negroes to fight for democracy," Cecil Shapiro reasoned logically. "Let's give them a share in it."[92]

Their concern for national unity and the war effort led a few correspondents to attribute the riot to fifth columnists, "Nazis," or even Communists who aimed to disrupt morale and production.[93] Others realized the presence of racial inequality but were also concerned for the war effort. One hundred black and white workers considered the riot a "terrible blow to national unity, [the] war effort and reputation of our city."[94]

Nevertheless, not all whites were concerned about either democratic principles or national unity. Some simply wanted racial peace for its own sake. Although New York City escaped the interracial clashes that occurred in Beaumont, Los Angeles, and Detroit, a large portion of its white population was actively or passively racist. One bus driver glared at a black passenger and complained about Harlem's disorder.[95] Often letters to La Guardia were more direct: "Black savages," "niggers," or "negroes" should be sent to Africa, "an island in the Pacific," or kept in Harlem.[96] An anonymous correspondent castigated AfroAmericans for ruining "nice middle-class neighborhoods" and La Guardia for allowing it in return for their votes.[97] "When you can sit down . . . with a black wife . . . and a black, kinky-haired son . . . on your lap," he declared, "then you can say you are not race prejudiced." Passive racism was even more widespread; while most white New Yorkers may not have practiced overt discrimination, they possessed beliefs that fostered such discrimination. In one white man's "humble" opinion, "it will never do to mix the races."[98]

Nevertheless, the war and competent leadership seem to have made many white New Yorkers more tolerant. La Guardia's mail clearly reveals that of those whites corresponding on the riot, the overwhelming majority were sympathetic to black residents. This is supported by the unity pledges and rallies of numerous citizens, the press coverage of the riot, and the efforts of most community leaders. More important, once disorder began no whites attempted to enter Harlem or other ghettos to assail black residents.[99]

Having made serious efforts to maintain racial peace, New Yorkers of both races responded to the Harlem riot with restraint. Together they deluded themselves into believing "hoodlums" or "migrants" were responsible for the disorder. Together they set out to rebuild mutual understanding. Perhaps the biracial cooperation and competent handling of the riot fostered such delusion and unity. In reality, the riot's causes were more complex. No doubt individuals seeking loot or escape from the boredom of a war-regulated society played meaningful roles in the disorder. But without the presence of more deep-seated grievances and the participation of law-abiding citizens, it might never have developed. The rioters, hoodlum or not, were fully aware of their plight as black people. Although not in the sense of blacks fighting whites, the riot contained definite racial overtones. The "hoodlum—no race riot" theory was, in fact, only a theory.

8

Conditions for Riot

It is very difficult to identify the causes of riot. Individuals and cultures respond differently to strain induced by oppression, and, even in a violence-prone society like that of the United States, aggression stemming from it may be inwardly directed or displaced in alcoholism, crime, or other asocial activities.[1] Since social disorder is one of many possible reactions to strain, pinpointing exact causes for disorder is risky.[2] In contrast, the conditions that promoted racial upheaval in Harlem in 1943 are readily identifiable. Long before August 1943, black residents had grievances directly related to the war effort as well as the perennial distresses of ghetto living. The combination of new and old grievances fed frustration and resentment that culminated in riot. The Bandy-Collins altercation touched off an already strained situation.

At the center of wartime grievances were the inflationary economy and the absence of rent control and price regulation in New York City. The riot, Richard Wright contended, stemmed primarily "from the economic pinch."[3] While the war provided blacks with more and better jobs, it also spawned inflation and thereby limited their economic gains. High rents and outlandish prices irked blacks who had been denied admittance to the war effort until after the exhaustion of white manpower. Before 1943 they had experienced nearly three years of inflation as menial laborers and relief recipients. Among the grievances that bothered Matilda B. Vasquez and numerous other blacks, exorbitant rents, high food prices, and inferior products headed the list.[4] Many blacks told of flagrant OPA violations, which they did not report for fear of economic reprisals.[5] Others were unfamiliar with the process of complaint. Economic injustice was a spur to participation in the riot. Urban Leaguer Lester B. Granger recalled the riot as one "against white-owned property and white-owned businesses."[6] It was, the *Amsterdam News* concurred, vandalism against businessmen who insisted on following the "white is right" line.[7]

A few blacks expressed anti-Semitic feelings toward Harlem's Jewish merchants. Lee Allan attributed the riot to "hate for the Jew, who charges high rent and gives nothing in return but fairy tales."[8] Indeed, throughout the 1930s and 1940s anti-Semitism surfaced in Harlem. As late as April 1943, Roy Wilkins acknowledged its presence, and a week before the Harlem riot the Reverend Ben Richards began a newspaper series designed to promote tolerance between blacks and Jews.[9] While it is difficult to estimate the depth of anti-Semitism among the rioters, numerous Jewish-owned shops in Harlem were destroyed. Even the store of a Russian Jew who had been "very helpful to the Negro population for twenty years" was plundered.[10] Not doctrinaire anti-Semites, many rioters probably resented the role of Jewish merchants in the ghetto.

Some whites, although ignoring the ethnic composition of Harlem's merchants, clearly understood that economics played an important part in creating riot. Segregation and exploitation "due to exorbitant prices and rents," contended an official of a local Book and Magazine Union, were "bound to produce an explosive situation."[11] This contention was common among those whites corresponding with La Guardia. Of all the conditions that needed improvement, Kay Margolis singled out the application and enforcement of OPA price regulations.[12] But not all whites were sympathetic to the economic plight of black people. "A Group of White People" noted that they paid "the same high prices for rent and food on much less than what a great percentage of niggers are making."[13] How come "the nigger can afford to dress (and strut) far better than a lot of whites?" Although an extremely small number of those whites corresponding with La Guardia expressed this view, no doubt other New Yorkers, particularly those living close to black communities, agreed with them.

Throughout the spring of 1943, interracial clashes and muggings of whites occurred periodically in several interracial neighborhoods. Those involved in these incidents drew rigid racial lines of right and wrong. Some blacks would blame the muggings of whites on "hate for the many unjust things" that had been done to AfroAmericans.[14] Others, even more sensitive, would defend a black youth before determining whether he was innocent of a specific white allegation.[15] Similarly, some whites overreacted to muggings and categorized all blacks as criminals. Others predicted racial conflict if black encroachment into white neighborhoods continued. If attacks against whites continued, a "Citizen" informed La Guardia in June, there would be a race riot "in your own back yard."[16] Although neither muggings nor border incidents were major causes of the Harlem riot, the discord involved in them did make riot more possible.

So did war-related events that dampened AfroAmerican morale. In the seven months before the Harlem riot, New York City's black population was embittered by three events. First, Hunter College was rented by the United States Navy, then the Savoy Ballroom was closed by the NYPD, and, most disturbing, the city approved plans to construct a segregated quasi-public housing unit called Stuyvesant Town. In each case, La Guardia—whom blacks genuinely respected—aligned himself against the interests of black people.

Late in 1942, the Navy requested La Guardia's permission to use Hunter College and Walton High School, both in the Bronx, as part of a training center for enlisted women. The racial segregation policy of the Women's Reserve of the United States Naval Reserve (WAVES) was well known, but was not mentioned in the request or ensuing negotiations. The Mayor offered his full cooperation.[17] On January 11, 1943, a scant three weeks later, Under Secretary James Forrestal thanked La Guardia for "the speed and accommodating spirit" that enabled the Navy to bring "this matter to a prompt conclusion."[18]

Before January ended, a few New Yorkers protested the Navy's use of municipal facilities for a segregated unit. The logic of a local spokesman for the March on Washington movement previewed the arguments eventually applied to Stuyvesant Town. Since the WAVES refused to admit black women for training or service, its use of Hunter gave "the sanction of the public to a policy of discrimination."[19] This obviously violated both municipal regulations and "democratic principles." Pressure mounted in early February as the City Council unanimously approved a resolution calling on La Guardia, the Board of Estimates, and the Board of Education to request Navy officials to end discrimination, particularly at Hunter College. The measure, introduced by Adam Clayton Powell, Jr., during the previous month, emphasized the hypocrisy of a public facility openly supporting racism.[20] The war had forced several organizations, such as municipal hospitals, to abandon long-standing discriminatory practices, and the breakdown of these, Powell stressed, should be continued.

La Guardia willingly had accepted the plans for Hunter College. As an intimate friend and staunch supporter of the President, as well as being a mayor who had benefited from generous New Deal funds and programs, he now, as so many times before, returned the favor. You "must," the Mayor ordered his Housing and Building Commissioner, "cooperate with the U.S. Navy in every possible way."[21] As former Civilian Defense Director and chairman of the United States Section of the Joint Defense Board, he knew firsthand the difficult task of mobilization. Like Roosevelt, he believed that democracy had to be saved before its flaws could be corrected. New York in 1943 was neither the place nor the time to protest military segregation. More specifically, La Guardia denied having authority over "any activity of the United States Navy."[22] Hunter's buildings, he informed a dissenter, were "requisitioned" by a federal agency, and under the War Powers Act, "the property must be turned over to the requesting authority." Protest, therefore, should be directed to the Navy.

In fact, protest was relatively small and the Hunter College episode was far removed from the riot of August. It was, however, part of a larger sequence of mayoral decisions that made the war for democracy appear increasingly hypocritical. Officially closing the Savoy Ballroom in late April for alleged prostitution was another such event. In time, the decision to revoke the nationally famous dance hall's license was affirmed by the Supreme Court's appellate division.[23] New York City's black residents were irate. Closing the Savoy seemed to have been prompted by race-mixing on the dance floor rather than by sexual solicitation in the men's room. This was the contention of fair-minded Roy Wilkins, who dubbed the closing "an ugly discrimination strictly on the color line."[24] An unknown poet satirized the Savoy's guilt in the context of Allied war aims. Yes, the Savoy was guilty:

> Guilty of national unity,
> Of practising real Democracy,
> By allowing the races, openly
> To dance and mingle in harmony.

But mostly, the Savoy was guilty "of being in Harlem."[25]

Blacks asked several pertinent questions: If the Savoy was so immoral, why had it done everything possible—including the termination of liquor sales and the discharge of hostesses—to operate a legitimate business?[26] And why did the most conservative and religious of Harlem's organizations, such as St. Ambrose's Roman Catholic Church, use it?[27] More specifically, Roy Wilkins asked, why was the management not given a formal hearing and why were similar rules not applied to big dance halls downtown?[28] Why, some must have queried, was the Savoy closed if at one point the appellate division justice considered the evidence "incompetent"?[29] The answer to all of these questions, of course, was racial discrimination.

In response to the closing of the Harlem landmark and the implication that black people were immoral, the *People's Voice* investigated several white dance halls. An anonymously printed article, introduced by the headline "PV Exposes Vice and Filth in Downtown Dance Halls," asserted that prostitution was widespread in eight of the city's "better" dancing establishments.[30] Having been propositioned at several of these "meat-centers," the reporter contended that "after hours" dates were prevalent and that dancing was "an excuse for a degenerate form of fornication right on the floor." Compared to these "flesh joints," he concluded bitterly, "the Savoy is a Christian Youth Center." Obviously, this was overstatement, but the Savoy was no different from many other night spots that remained open. What disturbed blacks most was that the incident served to perpetuate the smear that black people were less decent than white people.

Soon the Mayor came under severe criticism. When asked to investigate the incident, La Guardia told Walter White that he was "helpless" because the appellate division affirmed the revocation of Savoy's license.[31] According to Roy Wilkins, La Guardia "ought to get some of the bile out of his system" and become "the square shooter" that he had once been.[32] Readers of the *People's Voice* were reminded that the Savoy's closing happened in "the New York of that arch 'liberal,' Fiorello H. La Guardia."[33] There was no mayoral investigation and the Savoy remained closed for six months. Blacks viewed the closing as an unjust racist act and as a sellout by La Guardia, although his role is not clear. Their views were supported by considerable evidence. Like that of Hunter College,

the Savoy Ballroom incident added to the deterioration of
black morale, but neither had the impact of the Stuyvesant
Town controversy.

Between the Savoy's closing in May and the Detroit riot
in June, the administration contracted the Metropolitan
Life Insurance Company to build a quasi-public housing
project in Manhattan's lower east side. In return for tax
exemptions and eminent domain powers, the Metropolitan
agreed to construct Stuyvesant Town. Since the company
was given control of tenant selection and since its usual
policy was one of residential segregation, the contract
came under increasing public criticism. La Guardia, nevertheless, supported the contract, which was eventually
promulgated without a nondiscriminatory tenant clause.
His action upset numerous black and some white New
Yorkers. Black parents told La Guardia their sons had volunteered "to help all people to be free," and pleaded not
to let them return and find "Hitler's policies right here in
dear old New York."[34] One correspondent urged La Guardia not to "sow the seeds of a future revolution for space to
live and the right to be free."[35] Perceiving the demoraliz-
ing effect of Stuyvesant Town on black residents, a white
Brooklyn correspondent contended that it was a racial slur
and would convince "many Negroes that this is not their
war."[36] No protest, however, altered La Guardia's position.

After the Detroit riot in late June, La Guardia suddenly
gave race relations top priority and quickly moved to cool
the tension that it had created in New York City. Some
white residents clearly realized the inconsistency between
the Mayor's appeal for unity and his position on Stuyvesant Town. A mayor "who has wisely claimed 'No Detroit
Here,'" criticized one correspondent, "should not permit
the seeds for just such riots . . . to be planted."[37] After the
Harlem riot some black residents attributed the disorder to
anger at such discriminatory incidents. Stuyvesant Town,
chided the City-Wide Citizens' Committee on Harlem,
"has caused deep resentment among Negroes."[38] White
residents, too, recognized the connection between the

housing project, black resentment, and the Harlem riot: to a Long Island City resident, Stuyvesant Town led to such "occurrences."[39]

When the formal contract for Stuyvesant Town was finally signed on August 4, three days after the riot, La Guardia made it clear that he would implement a judicial decision against discriminatory tenant selection if a decision (as he expected) was forthcoming. Although he had decided this before the riot,[40] instead of publicizing his position and thereby reducing resentment, he remained silent in order not to jeopardize the commitment of private enterprise, which the Metropolitan symbolized, to public housing.

The exact effect of the incidents at Hunter College, the Savoy Ballroom, and Stuyvesant Town on the Harlem riot cannot be measured. Each seems to have increased the overall frustration and, in the minds of some rioters, justified lawlessness. Occurring in 1943, these incidents were additional evidence of national racial injustice, climaxing in the spring riots in other cities.

Partly because of the riots, black morale was low. The Detroit riot particularly incensed black Harlem. Pictures of that disorder showed black victims at the mercy of vicious citizen and police attacks, clearly indicating even to a special assistant of the United States Attorney General that police protection was "in many cases no protection at all."[41] When James Baldwin returned to Harlem in July, resentment filled the air and there was "a new stillness in the streets."[42]

While the resentment did not pertain solely to the treatment of blacks in the Detroit riot, it is difficult not to assume that the most infamous and recent disorder was significant in shaping the attitudes of black New Yorkers. For them, the spring riots—particularly Detroit's—began a racist program and symbolized all the degredation (including Hunter College, the Savoy Ballroom and Stuyvesant Town) that had been heaped upon black society since the war's beginning. A limited survey made after the Harlem riot indicated that both respondents who "accepted" and those who "rejected" that upheaval considered "generalized racial tensions and resentment of injustices" its underlying cause.[43]

Against the background of tensions created by these various grievances, the Bandy-Collins altercation precipitated riot. It is significant that the interaction of a white patrolman and a black soldier was the spark. In part, it confirmed the belief among black people that policemen were brutal and unjust. At the time of the Bandy-Collins fight, Marjorie Polite's alleged reference to Collins as a "mother fucker" and the beating he received from bystanders reflected the contempt of some blacks for the police.[44] Interviewing Harlem residents after the riot, a *PM* reporter heard two statements repeated constantly: "A white cop shot a Negro soldier."[45] "Them cops got it coming to them." According to a black district leader, La Guardia could avert future riots by making the police "stay sober."[46] And Eleanor Roosevelt was told by the "plain, colored citizens" that white policemen were "unnecessarily harsh to young colored people."[47] Advice that black men be used to restore order in Harlem also indicated the community's feeling toward white policemen. Walter White, among others, had urged La Guardia to request the assignment of black military policemen to evacuate the area of soldiers.[48] Black patrolmen, another observer had advised, should cover the principal streets, encouraging rioters to go home.[49] The situation would not be eased by assigning more white policemen to the riot scene.

In spite of the police department's responsible handling of the riot, blacks continued to believe that the police were sometimes brutal. Ten days after the disorder a Harlem resident reported police brutality toward a black youth who was having a mock fight with a friend.[50] By the end of August, an *Amsterdam News* editorial probably reflected a majority view. Lawbreakers should be punished and laws should be enforced, but Harlem would not be "bullied, brow-beaten, or bull-dozed."[51]

Some blacks, the minority to be sure, did not fully agree with the view of police brutality. "I do hope," Ashley L. Totten wrote to La Guardia after the riot, "that you will . . . do all that you possibly can to drive all the hoodlums out of Harlem."[52] Another correspondent was concerned because black youngsters were boasting about the police having been afraid of them during the riot.[53] Other blacks temporarily reconsidered their view of the police. On August 6, for example, a crowd of blacks applauded Patrolman Joseph Cavano for arresting an elderly man who smashed a store window in Harlem. "Take him away," shouted a bystander.[54] "The likes of him caused enough trouble up here." This response, nevertheless, must be considered in the context of the riot's aftermath: the belief that hoodlums caused the riot, the realization that policemen acted responsibly, and the regret that blacks felt together explain the applause for Cavano, but this does not mean that blacks ceased to believe in police brutality.

As most blacks believed in police brutality, some whites believed in police leniency. "The riots," a white attorney criticized La Guardia, ". . . could have been quelled in their inception by stern and direct action."[55] Columnist Westbrook Pegler was the harshest critic, accusing the Mayor of appeasing Harlem's hoodlums and handcuffing police efforts against them.[56] The charge was as old as La Guardia's denunciation of it.

La Guardia publicly dismissed the seemingly contradictory charges of police brutality and police leniency, but privately he was sensitive to them. Many critics could be dismissed, but respected friends like Eleanor Roosevelt had to be taken more seriously. Although she had not criticized La Guardia, black residents had told her that poor police-community relations and future riots could be prevented by increasing the number of black policemen and their opportunities for advancement. If such was done, she advised La Guardia, "there might not be such instances as the past regrettable one."[57] La Guardia's response indicated that, as he often felt when criticized, he was feeling abused "by agitators and selfish people or by thoughtless and well-meaning people."[58] Together, they presented "nothing but lies, lies, lies and more lies." In between the charges of brutality and leniency, La Guardia wrote on August 6, "I must gather that we are trying to do a good job and are keeping a wholesome attitude and conduct toward these unfortunate people." Efforts were constantly being made to recruit black policemen, and no brutality existed. La Guardia hoped the First Lady would not believe "the Peglers."

The following day, La Guardia felt compelled to explain to Mrs. Roosevelt why so few policemen were black. He had already admitted that black members of the NYPD numbered only twenty-two more than they had a decade earlier. Of the 155 black policemen, six were sergeants, one a parole commissioner, and one a surgeon.[59] La Guardia stressed that the shortage of black policemen was due to the war and the lack of black applicants to the police force. "Commissioner Valentine," he contended rather unconvincingly, "would take one hundred right now if he could only get them."[60] Furthermore, he recalled that, not too long before, Harlem residents complained about black policemen, whom they did not want around, for being "too rough."

La Guardia believed in his position, but it missed the point entirely. Police brutality and police leniency are not mutually exclusive; police can treat individuals brutally and at the same time be lax in enforcement throughout a community, as had been the case in Harlem. To La Guardia, the charges were contradictory, and as such he took neither of them seriously. Instead he defended the NYPD just as he defended all the municipal departments. After all, he had hand-picked Valentine and, of course, to admit that racial discrimination in the police force existed was to criticize the most progressive administration in the history of New York City. It was much easier to attribute the shortage of black policemen to inadequate funds and manpower shortages due to the war, and their token upgrading to the fair but competitive civil service system.[61] Or everything could be explained by black indifference to police work, for La Guardia did not seem to understand that the police reputation among blacks might have been an important impediment to their taking police recruitment seriously. Moreover, since it was common for ghetto youths to attain police records early in life, most black men could not qualify for the NYPD. The complaint that AfroAmerican policemen treated blacks "too rough" certainly did not represent the consensus of blacks. Although some critics were too harsh on La Guardia, he was much too easy on himself. Certainly, the NYPD handled the riot excellently, but that did not erase the years of poor police-community relations, which were a factor contributing to the disruption.

The AfroAmerican view of police brutality was not, however, the only reason why the Bandy-Collins incident led to disorder. Of equal importance was the resentment of blacks toward the abuse at home of their men in the armed services. According to columnist M. Moran Weston, the riot occurred because it was believed that a black soldier had been killed by a white policeman: the rioters "had lost all confidence in the willingness or ability of the government to do anything about the outrages which have been happening daily to Negro soldiers."[62]

Weston's contention, shared by many leading blacks, was accurate. From the time that blacks were admitted into the army, they encountered verbal harassment and physical abuse from white citizens, officials, and soldiers. Afro-American servicemen had undergone similar treatment in World War I, but twenty-five years later black protest was more articulate and black soldiers even less willing to be denied the very democratic principles which they were being trained to protect. The most serious racial confrontations involving black soldiers occurred in southern states, where most military training camps were located.

A year before the riots, black people had already become concerned about the abuse of their soldiers. In early 1942, several servicemen from Harlem were involved in racial clashes that took the lives of six blacks at camps Claiborne and Livingston in Louisiana.[63] Later, in April, when the *People's Voice* asked five Harlem residents if "the growing conflicts between Negro and white soldiers" would reach "national proportions" unless something were done immediately, they all responded in the affirmative.[64] Nor could all black New Yorkers have overlooked the racial disorder in nearby Hempstead, Long Island, after a confrontation between a black soldier and a white policeman. For three hours on May 7, the entire black community rampaged before a "riot force" restored order.[65] Despite black protest, the abuse of servicemen continued into 1943. Harlem draftees trained in southern camps informed their relatives of experiencing "vicious prejudice."[66] In fact, two hundred members of New York's all-black 369th Infantry were treated as inferiors by southern whites and at least two German-born soldiers at Camp Stewart, Georgia.[67] By the time riots had swept through the nation later in the year, most blacks deeply resented the numerous stories of maltreatment. Following the Detroit riot, a headline in the *Amsterdam News* revealed the apprehension: "Widespread Race Riots Feared Over Abuse of Negro Troops."[68]

Because the abuse of soldiers prompted deep resentment, many people attributed the Harlem riots simply to the fact that Bandy was a soldier. The rumor of his death, Walter White wrote, "fell like a torch into dry summer grass."[69] If Bandy had been a civilian, the NAACP official contended, no disorder would have resulted from the shooting. "It was," White informed Secretary of War Henry L. Stimson, "born of repeated, unchecked, unpunished, and often unrebuked shooting, maiming, and insulting of Negro troops."[70] Less well-known blacks expressed similar beliefs. According to Helen Coleman, decent black citizens felt the riot was "born out of resentment of the evil treatment given our men in the service."[71] Typical of perceptive white citizens, Frank Monters realized that behind the disorder lay "a story of the resentment of the

Negro people against the treatment of Negro soldiers, especially in the South."[72] *PM* accurately reported that the Harlem upheaval was related to those of Mobile, Beaumont, and Detroit.

While the conditions underlying riot are clear, it is more difficult to determine why disorder came in August rather than late June or early July. Since tension appeared to have been highest immediately after the Detroit riot, it might be assumed that upheaval should have come then, or not at all. Such an assumption wrongly establishes the Detroit riot as "the" cause for tension. That disorder certainly heightened existing tension and, more than any other single event, incensed Harlemites, and revealed the crisis situation of race relations. It was not, however, the sole cause for creating tension among Harlemites, but rather the most recent and worst of a long series of attacks on black Americans. Moreover, tension in Harlem did not subside with the passing of time, but carried into July.

Mayoral and public concern was also extended into that month. But mayoral leadership was neither as visible nor as assertive as it had been in the immediate wake of the Detroit riot. Indeed, La Guardia seems to have believed that by mid-July the danger period for a possible disorder in New York City had passed. It was at this time that he backed away from creating a committee on race relations. La Guardia's efforts to ease tensions in the wake of the spring riots were exemplary but not sufficient to end the numerous injustices that had for some time assaulted the dignity of black New Yorkers. The Bandy-Collins incident was—in Benjamin J. Davis, Jr.'s apt phrase—"made to order."[73] Coming when it did, the riot-prone incident opened wounds that mayoral efforts had never healed completely. The resulting strain erupted into riot.

9
Aftermath: Official Response and Local Programs

To concerned citizens, Harlem's disorder had dangerous national implications. It broke the six-week peace after the Detroit riot and, appearing to be a continuation of the nation's racial crisis, increased the anxiety spawned by the earlier riots. Looking to President Roosevelt for leadership, New York City residents urged him "to go on the air immediately" and to investigate those "inciting racial hatreds and violence."[1] Roosevelt's response to Harlem's disorder, however, was similar to his position on the Detroit riot, which a Harlem columnist dubbed the "Ostrich Policy."[2] Having given up on Roosevelt, an Indiana resident suggested that La Guardia provide the leadership. Americans, he wrote, were "badly in need of a chief" in the area of race relations.[3]

Aside from a plea for tolerance by Eleanor Roosevelt, no meaningful public action was taken in August by the Administration. Roosevelt was absorbed with foreign affairs. Jonathan Daniels—officially designated the President's special assistant on race relations barely a week before Harlem erupted—and his small staff were only beginning to correlate and synthesize the material. Daniels, nonetheless, had thought about the problem of race relations since June and had already received several suggestions from cooperative administrative personnel. On August 2, the day after the Harlem riot and at a time when "dangerous inter-racial situations" were evident elsewhere, he recommended that the President issue a "direct and disciplinary" statement to the nation.[4] In fact, it should demand "civil obedience from all groups" and promise "to suppress violence anywhere." Daniels prepared a "militant" statement. As he awaited Roosevelt's reply, he pursued other possibilities for executive action and informed a concerned Brooklyn resident that the riots were receiving "thoughtful consideration."[5]

By August 10, Daniels had passed on further recommendations to the President. In addition to a "straight line" public statement, federal, state, and municipal officials should collaborate on the use of federal troops and encourage the creation of local race-relations committees.[6] Careful study needed to be given the Army's handling of black soldiers, "an increasingly dangerous disciplinary problem," and the enlistment of black leaders in postwar plans for "human security." Daniels finally suggested that old promises be fulfilled "as steadily as possible." He began consideration of another, more comprehensive proposal for presidential attention.

In his recommendation of August 2, Daniels had advised Roosevelt against creating a special committee on the racial crisis (which "would only serve as a new ground for controversy"); but gradually he began to reconsider that position.[7] He no doubt knew of Attorney General Francis Biddle's July recommendation for a private national committee to educate the public on "the race problem."[8] Before and since then Interior Secretary Harold L. Ickes had repeatedly suggested a commission and "a permanent government agency" on race relations.[9] Daniels had also received separate reports from two administrative officials, each suggesting that permanent local comittees be established to develop programs for the particular problems of their communities and that a national committee serve as a model for the betterment of race relations.[10] Neither report considered the federal government completely responsible or singularly capable of checking racial violence.

It was a private citizen, however, who submitted a plan that most interested Daniels. On August 11, Howard Odum, of the University of North Carolina's Institute for Research in Social Science, sent Daniels a plan that the Continuing Committees of the Durham and Atlanta Conferences had recommended to the President.[11] A national committee on "racial and regional development" would be appointed by Roosevelt to study all aspects of the crisis, advise him on racial matters, and undertake special assignments in related emergencies. Accordingly, a committe of forty distinguished persons, a director of research, and a staff, to be supported by private donations, was recommended. Since the Southern Regional Council had conceived the general idea, Odum expected it would participate in the overall operation as a permanent action agency endowed with adequate financial support rather than as "an advisory committee." Earlier in the racial crisis, he had advised Roosevelt to remain silent. Now, he contended, the time was "ripe for a major, composite gesture," which would be "more than gesture."[12]

Seeking to prepare a race-relations program that would meet with presidential approval, Daniels conferred with Odum throughout August. He proceeded cautiously, knowing Roosevelt's desires and concerned that the committee "succeed in a way creditable to the President and commensurate with the problem involved."[13] Odum agreed, but urged Daniels to go "a little further and explore the plan which I had in mind." Whatever their disagreement, tentative plans were made to get together with a "preliminary, exploratory committee." Although different from Odum's original recommendation, a national committee for race relations was definitely under consideration.

By August 23, Odum presented Daniels with additional suggestions. First, a preliminary committee of eminent individuals would be asked to participate in a conference that would recommend Roosevelt's appointment of a president's committee on race and minority groups. The committee, a revision of Odum's earlier proposal, would then study the racial situation, coordinate local efforts, and publish its findings. Financing could be public or private, but if it was private—Daniels added—no single organization would be granted special influence. Odum's previous suggestions for a separate research unit and the Southern Regional Council's favored position were conspicuously omitted. Familiar with Roosevelt's thinking, Daniels vetoed the questionable items in order to give the general proposals a chance for approval. Odum and Daniels agreed that a preliminary committee would be beneficial, perhaps because it was the only way to goad Roosevelt into action. Odum also sent Daniels a list of twenty-one names, mostly of prominent educators, that they had agreed upon as a "nucleus" for the preliminary committee. Penciled notations by Daniels clearly indicated his concern for the project and attempts to anticipate Roosevelt's questions. But there were no questions.[14]

The President refused. "I am sorry," Daniels informed Odum on September 1, ". . . that at the present time my boss does not think well of the idea."[15] Odum commented that Roosevelt acted "wisely in going slowly on this Committee."[16] Instead of expressing discouragement, he explained why he had pressed for a preliminary conference. "Our haste," he told Daniels, who needed no explanation, resulted from the hope that "a permanent committee might go to work" immediately. Expressing appreciation and perceiving Odum's dejection—and probably his own—Daniels urged Odum to send him further suggestions on race relations.[17]

What caused the President to disapprove such an ambitious proposal? Of course, it was the war, not race relations, that concerned Roosevelt. "Just another case of lack of interest in domestic affairs," remarked Ickes.[18] Indeed, throughout August Roosevelt concentrated on the invasion of Sicily and the Quebec Conference. Daniels' memoranda on the racial crisis, dated August 2 and August 10, were returned fourteen and seven days later without decisions, but with instructions to see Roosevelt upon his return.[19] In essence, Roosevelt's decision in regard to the Detroit riot became the decision for all riots: since presidential interference might alienate more white workers and spark additional racial conflict, inaction best served the war effort. Both the calm that existed throughout July and the mildness of the Harlem disorder, which in comparison to Detroit's was not a race riot, probably encouraged Roosevelt to continue his policy of inaction. When he finally returned from Quebec to consider the Odum-Daniels proposal, the racial crisis had cooled, and that may have served to convince him of the rightness of his earlier position on the Detroit riot.

Biddle, who had always opposed a presidentially appointed committee, influenced Roosevelt's decision. Roosevelt had asked Biddle to read Daniels' memorandum of August 2 calling for a presidential address.[20] Perhaps in reference to that request, Biddle indirectly advised Daniels not to expect presidential action in race relations. On August 27, he forwarded a letter from Lester B. Granger, parts of which were carefully marked for Daniels' attention: "The President," Granger contended, "can do little more at this time than stress the point that racial conflict is a deterrent to victory, and that sacrifice of racial prejudice by both whites and Negroes is as important in winning the war as sacrifice of weekend driving, butter, and scrap metal."[21] Although a presidential address would be beneficial, Granger asserted that it would not "automatically and of itself make bad matters better." The real need was for "improving local interracial situations." If Roosevelt had any doubts about vigorous action, Biddle's urgings and Granger's letter probably convinced him that anything more than an indirect statement (which was even less than what Granger suggested) would be detrimental to the war effort.

Daniels, as administrative assistant, had little influence: he was to gather and synthesize information for Roosevelt, but was without real authority and was not among the President's intimate advisers. Roosevelt relied on seasoned members of his administration, such as Biddle, to evaluate Daniels' proposals, and they were more concerned with the larger issue of the war than the specific one of race relations. In addition, Daniels' original position of August 2 opposed the naming of a special committee. As a result, the Odum-Daniels plan never really had a chance of adoption. By this late date in the crisis, presidential action was doubtless less significant than it would have been in the spring when it might have dampened the resentments that led to the Harlem riot. Granger was also correct in emphasizing the need for local rather than federal action. Nevertheless, he clearly called for a presidential address. Eventually Roosevelt would give one, evasive and token, but significantly he used Granger's letter to absolve himself from any meaningful action. In this way, he appears to have justified his earlier decision to ignore the racial crisis.

Regardless of Biddle's advice or Granger's letter, Roosevelt also disapproved the Odum-Daniels plan on the basis of his experience with the Fair Employment Practices Committee. Since southern whites were alienated by the FEPC's activities and since the State Department argued that the FEPC's public hearings provided Axis agents with information for their propaganda, Roosevelt felt the FEPC could disrupt the war effort at home and abroad.[22] What, he must have thought, would be the reaction to a national committee on race relations? How, moreover, would such a body affect his leadership? Odum had told Daniels that the committee should have "a very definite function over a definite period of years with definite [presidential] support," and it should be "so strong that its purpose and its capacity would not be questioned."[23] Like La Guardia, Roosevelt had decided that public committees, particularly those dealing with race relations, presented the issues too forcefully and the recommendations too idealistically.

Roosevelt, furthermore, believed that racial conflicts were primarily local issues requiring local leadership. This, of course, was Granger's point, and it countered Ickes' earlier advice that the issue "cannot be handled except on a comprehensive national scale."[24] Roosevelt knew that local committees for the improvement of race relations were being created across the nation. From mid-July through September, Ickes informed him of "the latest" municipal and state organizations.[25] Most attractive to Roosevelt, they offered a means for dealing with the racial crisis without jeopardizing national unity or presidential leadership (as he believed a national committee would have done).

Certainly, Roosevelt was correct in believing that the improvement of race relations was very much dependent on local leadership and that without it presidential leadership was meaningless. He had little control over the local circumstances that fostered riot. Nevertheless, it was incorrect to assume that local leadership and local circumstances alone were responsible for either racial crisis or racial harmony. Exactly because national policies were partly responsible for black resentment and local organizations on race relations were, according to Ickes, "only pulling and hauling and overlapping," the President and the federal government had a responsibility to unify local efforts.[26] Local leaders could focus their attention on racial problems peculiar to their communities, but only Roosevelt could deal with the national problems affecting every locale.

Roosevelt's disapproval of the Odum-Daniels plan was also prompted by his racial attitudes. Roosevelt, like most white Americans, believed that progress in race relations could not be forced, but required a gradual process of education. For this reason, he favored the more moderate, usually southern, leadership of black and white civil rights advocates. Similarly, he disapproved of a national committee on race relations that might alienate whites. Ironically, Roosevelt did not seem to realize that such a body would

foster the education that he judged so important. Slowly
and reluctantly, Roosevelt responded to the racial crisis. In
reply to Granger's invitation, he sent a message to the
National Urban League's annual convention. In part,
Granger's views on the President's role in the racial crisis
account for Roosevelt's decision. More important, Roosevelt was provided a forum from which to deliver a public
statement on the racial crisis, but one that would permit
his words to be heard or read by the majority of blacks
while remaining relatively unpublicized to whites. Since
Roosevelt's message was not delivered in person or over
radio, white coverage was minimal. In short, he was afforded the chance to pacify one race without alienating the
other.

On September 7, Granger received the presidential message. It had been drafted by Elmer Davis, and Roosevelt
softened the language but retained the spirit of the message, which resembled Granger's earlier letter to Biddle.[27]
Racial cooperation was stressed as being necessary for the
war effort and the war aims. "We cannot," Roosevelt admonished, "stand before the world as a champion of op-
pressed peoples unless we practice as well as preach the
principles of democracy for all men." Racial conflict de-
terred war production, increased Allied casualties, destroyed national unity, and rendered us "suspect abroad."
In addition, Roosevelt imparted a special, though indirect,
admonition to resentful blacks: as well as protecting "the
inalienable rights of all men," true citizens must accept
"the responsibilities that go with democratic privileges."

Clearly, Roosevelt attempted to lift black morale, but to
avoid alienating the white majority, he had carefully re-
worded some of the more cogent and explosive passages in
Davis' original draft. "Principles of equality of all men"
was changed to "principles of democracy for all men."[28]
He also deleted some passages completely, such as, "The
extent of which Negroes and other racial groups are included in our way of life becomes a test of the sincerity of
our belief in the principles of democracy."

As Roosevelt expected, his message was well received by the black press. It was the strongest appeal for racial unity he had made to date. "After months and years of tomb-like silence," the *Amsterdam News* editorialized, "President Roosevelt . . . gave the Negro . . . some heart."[29] The editor did express the reservation of many blacks, however, when he called upon Roosevelt to back up his words with deeds. On this issue, the President was probably satisfied with the year-end summary of an aide. Discrimination continued to exist throughout the nation, but "undeniably" progress was being made in every field.[30]

Although understandable, Roosevelt's inaction in the racial crisis of 1943 was unfortunate. Admittedly, the era's racism, the lack of precedents and uncertainty of the government's role in race relations, Roosevelt's ambivalence toward civil rights, his physical incapacity, and his single-minded concern for the war were barriers to any sweeping progress regardless of presidential action. Nevertheless, Roosevelt's inaction depressed black morale and threatened the gains that had been made as a result of the war. It, in fact, made the existing formidable barriers greater. Roosevelt's stature, influence, and impact among white Americans could have done much to reduce, though not eradicate, those barriers.

Roosevelt's decision to leave race relations to local authorities meant that New Yorkers would confront the aftermath of the Harlem riot without federal assistance. This task would not be easy, for racial harmony and racial antagonism existed side by side. Concerned citizens strove to improve race relations and La Guardia provided leadership, though not as effectively as during the riot. From August to December, he stressed education as the vehicle—in his mind the only vehicle—by which racial harmony could be achieved.

As usual, La Guardia was at his best before a radio or live audience. On August 14, he introduced the radio series "Unity at Home—Victory Abroad," which ran for five weeks. He acknowledged that the city was still learning the lessons of tolerance, understanding, and good will, but stressed its racial harmony as "a working model of democracy."[31] Whether New Yorkers were black or white, native or immigrant, Catholic, Protestant, or Jew, "we have learned to get along together." America's existence and the United Nations' future depended on "the spread . . . of tolerance." New York, he asserted, must join in the struggle against bigotry. Such was "the true spirit of America."

Accordingly, Eleanor Roosevelt, Pearl Buck, Senator Robert Wagner, and Charles Colman of "Porgy and Bess" fame appeared on the series. La Guardia considered their performances "a real contribution to the cause of maintaining racial and religious tranquillity here at home."[32] In another address, he associated unity at home with victory abroad and called on New Yorkers to remember that they had built a great city "by rising above prejudices."[33]

The Board of Superintendents also undertook efforts to increase tolerance among New York's schoolteachers and school children. Beginning September 21, "Intercultural Relations," a course that emphasized AfroAmerican contributions to society and suggested the application of democratic principles in and out of the classroom, was offered to all teachers.[34] Programs begun before the riot were expanded. The New York Foundation and the Board of Education, for example, united in an experiment to reduce juvenile delinquency by developing racial pride. Many schools were working on individual projects, while others joined with settlement houses to develop better race relations.

In addition, La Guardia moved to eradicate some of the more pressing causes for black resentment. Immediately after the riot, he announced that discrimination in tenant selection was unlawful and that he would implement whatever judicial decision emerged from the controversy over Stuyvesant Town. Later, at the Interracial Unity Conference at Hunter College, La Guardia spoke for a Double V. Perhaps he intended to remind everyone of his progressivism and thereby offset the criticism he had incurred for permitting segregated WAVE units to train on campus. Reopening the Savoy Ballroom in October was, in the partisan words of co-owner Charles Buchanan, "a four-freedomed victory for the people of Harlem."[35] While these acts probably were not contrived specifically for this purpose, they enhanced La Guardia's postriot attempts to achieve racial harmony.

In areas of long-standing grievances, La Guardia realized that the financial, material, and manpower needs of war prevented any meaningful action. Still, he put in motion plans to be implemented after the war. Postwar housing plans for Harlem had been decided upon before the riot. In response to charges of the Kings County Grand Jury, La Guardia also considered similar, federal plans for black communities in Kingsboro, Brooklyn, and South Jamaica, Queens.[36] After careful study, he announced on November 21 plans for each of those areas and for the Bronx.[37] In essence, he held out promise for meaningful progress in the immediate future.

La Guardia was able to take more positive action in price regulation and rent control, areas less directly affected by war exigencies. Within one week of the riot, the Office of Price Administration announced plans to open an office in Harlem and to appoint black administrative assistants and food price specialists.[38] Shortly thereafter, La Guardia declared that the Commissioner of Markets was conducting "an intensive drive in Harlem against price ceiling violators."[39] To the black press, these actions were directly related to the riot.[40] So, too, was the OPA's mid-September announcement that a special study was being made of the possibility of establishing rent control in New York City.[41]

Progress seemed instantaneous, and only businessmen bothered to ask why the Mayor or the OPA had not acted with equal vigor before the riot. Between August 1 and August 15, the Department of Markets issued fifty-five court and ten departmental summonses and fifty-one warnings to Harlem merchants.[42] On the latter date, La Guardia announced that in addition to the regular departmental inspections "special drives" would be conducted periodically. OPA activities were assisted by publication of the names of violators in the AfroAmerican press.[43] By September, OPA officials considered their campaign in Harlem very effective.[44] Federal rent control was also implemented before the year ended, making New York the last major city to be regulated.[45]

Some critics believed more could be done. Roy Wilkins contended that prices were still too high.[46] Others complained that more investigators and an educational program in OPA regulations were needed, as well as the use of trained volunteers on price and ration boards. Many were concerned because cooperation between the Harlem Advisory Committee and the OPA had subsided. Hence, council candidate Benjamin J. Davis, Jr., led a delegation to meet with OPA officials, and the City-Wide Citizens' Committee on Harlem formed a subcommitee on consumer problems.[47] The district OPA spokesman acknowledged the validity of AfroAmerican complaints, suggesting that plans were under way to correct them.[48]

Government officials were not alone in their efforts to improve race relations. The most ambitious and substantial program was undertaken by the Emergency Conference for Interracial Unity. Chaired by Marian Anderson and Dr. William Jay Schieffelin, the conference's initiators, executive committee members and sponsors were more than two hundred prominent clergymen, community and union leaders, educators, entertainers, and liberal politicians—including Archbishop William Ernst, Adam Clayton Powell, Jr., Michael J. Quill, Ruth Benedict, Duke Ellington, and Stanley M. Isaacs. The executive committee, under Channing Tobias, planned the conference for September 25 at Hunter College. For maximum effect, La Guardia opened the conference by receiving the 100,000 "Pledges of Unity" that Jean Muir had collected since July.[49] More than 2,000 persons representing 350 organizations attended panel discussions on employment, housing, education, armed services, and "organized racial antagonisms," seeking action at "the root of the problem."[50] They drew up a series of resolutions designed to improve black morale and living conditions as well as promote racial harmony. The first of seventeen resolutions called on La Guardia to appoint a committee to identify both opportunities for interracial cooperation and conditions contributing to racial antagonisms, recommending "immediate remedial action in such matters."[51] Others called for more mayoral appointments of blacks on policy-making bodies, stepped-up activity by state and national committees against discrimination in employment, rigid enforcement of OPA regulations, creation of a state department on consumer affairs, abrogation of the Stuyvesant Town contract, integration of the armed services, and federal investigation of fifth-column forces. In closing, the participants requested all organizations to take "parallel action" for implementing the resolutions. By any standard the conference succeeded in publicizing the problems confronting black and white society. Those who attended committed themselves to continuous action.

Several organizations, such as the Citizens Committee on Better Race Relations, assembled to discuss the riot. Others sponsored unity gatherings. In August, residents of Manhattan's upper west side coordinated a People's Unity Festival that pledged "to cement the solidarity" of all racial, religious, and ethnic groups.[52] As late as December, community efforts to improve race relations continued.[53] Concerned individuals also moved to improve race relations. A Brooklyn teacher, for example, informed her pupils that responsibility for the riot must be shared by both races.[54] Mrs. Ligne Michelesen was typical of some black and white parents. In her Midwood neighborhood of Brooklyn, the school children formed an organization "to help do away with Negro discrimination."[55] Introduced to the organization by her daughter, Mrs. Michelesen was told that "it may take fifty years" before any good would come from her work. Accordingly, she asked President Roosevelt for a letter so "we may work faster."

Probably the best overall indication of racial tolerance was the election of Benjamin J. Davis, Jr., to the City Council. Davis, an avowed Communist and a black man, could not have been elected without white support. His election proved to one black editor that whites would vote "for qualified Negroes."[56] The election of other blacks also confirmed that an important number of whites did not harbor deep-seated racist feelings.

Although the efforts made to promote racial harmony should not be overstated, they were meaningful. By no means the majority of black and white New Yorkers, those working to improve race relations represented thousands of residents. That a Jewish newsdealer, several black air raid wardens, an Irish storekeeper, and an Italian shoemaker could, in the wake of the Harlem riot, present La Guardia with a pledge from the People's Unity Festival is almost as important as the tensions that caused the riot.[57] They helped to stabilize the immediate situation. The numbers of people involved, their intent, and their positive influence at a crucial period cannot be dismissed as a footnote.

Racial tension, of course, was still high in parts of New York City. Interracial clashes continued in neighborhoods on the verge of integration. In the Washington Heights area, a continual racial battleground during the war, apartment houses opened to black tenants were vandalized by white youths. Despite La Guardia's orders to increase protection in the area, the incidents recurred. Buildings that housed black residents were disfigured by red paint and crude swastikas. In fact, white parents encouraged their children to commit these acts.[58]

Nor was everyone satisfied with La Guardia's handling of the riot. Harlem's white businessmen were particularly displeased. To offset the financial losses from looting and vandalism, a committee representing several local business organizations sought mayoral assistance in areas of rent moratoriums, bank loans, financial credit, and building materials.[59] What appeared to be a routine request for municipal aid soon became a verbal and, eventually, a legal contest between Harlem's white merchants and La Guardia. On August 9, Colonel Leopold Philipp, the president of the Uptown Chamber of Commerce and the man who would represent the businessmen, contacted La Guardia. "The policy of sparing lives and sacrificing property [during the riot] had been vindicated," but businessmen now feared for their personal safety and property.[60] Many of them, Philipp contended, might leave Harlem. That action would undermine the community's entire economic structure, strain race relations, and deprive the city of substantial tax revenue. Therefore, "drastic steps" were needed to reassure businessmen "that their investments will be better safeguarded." Philipp also asserted that La Guardia's "policy of sacrificing property" placed the city under "a *moral* obligation to compensate those who sustained losses." As a result, he requested a mayoral conference to discuss municipal liability for riot losses. "Unless we can bring them some reassuring word from you," he predicted, "you may be sure that these people will take matters into their own hands, with possible embarrassment to you."

La Guardia ignored Philipp's request, perhaps because it smacked of intimidation. Always suspicious, the Mayor had Philipp investigated, only to find that he was a sound businessman, allegedly "well liked by the Negroes of Harlem."[61] The Mayor, of course, did not believe that the city was legally or morally responsible for the merchants' losses. The New York State Emergency War Act made the general municipal law inapplicable "to property destroyed or injured by mobs or riots."[62] Moreover, to have paid for such losses without also providing the necessary funds to improve living conditions in Harlem would have been politically and morally unacceptable to black New Yorkers. The scarcity of municipal funds, no doubt, would permit neither.

Ignored by La Guardia, Philipp prepared the business community for action. On September 1, at a meeting of Harlem merchants Philipp and his supporters revealed their strategy for collecting four million dollars' worth of damages from the riot.[63] La Guardia was singled out as the adversary responsible for inadequate police protection. Those members of the police department regularly assigned to Harlem were praised. Nor were black citizens criticized collectively, although Powell and the AfroAmerican press were censured for attributing the riot to high costs of rent, food, and clothing. La Guardia was the culprit, and the courts were the battleground; instructions were given on how to sue the city.

Several articles in *Uptown New York*, the official publication of the Uptown Chamber of Commerce, clarified Philipp's strategy. In order to hold the city morally responsible for business losses, it was necessary to emphasize police toleration of looters, play down economics as a cause for riot, and underline the hoodlum thesis. To believe that resentment against alleged rent-gouging and high food costs sparked the upheaval was "to charge that the decent respectable people of Harlem inspired the plundering."[64] Such a charge was considered "unthinkable" by the diplomatic merchants, who blamed "gangsters" for the disorder.

Philipp hoped the courts would take issue with the New York State War Emergency Act: did the legislature intend "to relieve municipalities of all responsibility for property damaged by riot . . . or simply to release the cities from responsibility if the riot grew out of the war?"[65] Ruben A. Lazarus, mayoral representative at the state legislature, had participated in the final drafting of the War Emergency Act and was confident that no court would challenge the legislature's intentions.[66] But if a legal contest materialized, the administration would be ready. Lazarus forwarded information to Corporation Counselor Ignatius M. Wilkinson, believing it would be of interest in defending the city against the businessmen.[67]

In early November, La Guardia began to reconsider his position. The riot was three months past and his handling of it had proven to be just. Negotiation with the merchants would prevent litigation. Knowing that the city would probably be involved in court cases concerning Stuyvesant Town and the Kings County Grand Jury, perhaps La Guardia sought to avoid involving the city in a third case. Therefore, he consulted with James W. Danahy, spokesman for the West Side's Association of Commerce, about giving serious consideration to a meeting with the Uptown Chamber of Commerce.[68]

The Kings County Grand Jury controversy revived La Guardia's relationship with black leaders, which had been elusive since the riot. In August, the grand jury investigated crime in Bedford Stuyvesant, criticizing the administration and, some thought, black residents by implying that collectively they were criminal-prone. La Guardia vigorously opposed these findings and their implications.[69] By late autumn, Walter White, A. Philip Randolph, and Channing Tobias, among others, closed ranks with La Guardia as they had done before on this very same issue.[70] It was no surprise, then, for La Guardia to call on White to inquire about Philipp, the Uptown Chamber of Commerce, and several businessmen whom he was considering for a conference. According to White's findings, black opinion of the exclusively white organization was "not too favorable."[71] Nevertheless, White believed, "it would be well" to receive its delegation. Before La Guardia conferred with them, however, he should "see representatives of infinitely more representative groups." Specifically, the City-Wide Citizens' Committee on Harlem and the Citizens Emergency Conference for Interracial Unity had been seeking mayoral appointments since the riot. The latter group had been trying to place its September 25 recommendations for improved race relations before the Mayor. By seeing them, La Guardia could receive sound advice as well as lessen their disappointment at having been ignored so long.

La Guardia followed White's suggestion. He invited Algernon Black and Channing Tobias, who were specifically named by White and who represented the organizations he cited, to a mayoral conference on December 10.[72] By then the merchants were definitely engaging in court action.[73] The impasse between them and the Mayor would continue into the new year.

Also by December, La Guardia began to consider racial antagonism in a broader context, seeking more effective and lasting measures to end it. Accordingly, he created a biracial committee on race relations. He had considered such a committee immediately after the Detroit riot, and he knew of similar committees that had been formed as a result of that disorder. Following the Harlem riot, private residents, as well as influential leaders of both races, again urged La Guardia to appoint an interracial body that would promote unity, investigate black neighborhoods, and recommend "a constructive social and welfare program."[74] At first, La Guardia gave little consideration to these urgings. Perhaps he was smarting from Channing Tobias' implication that failure to carry out mayoral plans for an interracial committee before August 1 could have been a cause for riot.[75] Others had accused him of not implementing the recommendations of the Mayor's Commission.[76] Equally important, his municipal and defense duties had been interrupted. "Do," he replied to A. Philip Randolph's request for a conference on the disorder, " . . . give me a chance to get all caught up with my work."[77] La Guardia's dislike for committees that operated outside mayoral authority and that could embarrass the administration probably most prevented him from seriously considering such a body during the riot's early aftermath. In fact, he deliberately avoided meeting with Randolph's Citizens' Committee on Better Race Relations, which had recommended the appointment of a commission on race relations "to coordinate, promote, and recommend for execution the report of the Mayor's own Committee of 1935."[78]

As the Harlem riot became history and as racial tensions

eased, however, La Guardia began to consider a long-range program. Not only did the explosive summer, interested residents and black leaders, local and national urgencies demand it, but so did his humanitarian instincts. He later informed John D. Rockefeller that a major national problem was that "of the Negroes."[79] Recalling World War I, he feared a critical period for postwar race relations and "repercussions following demobilization." But La Guardia was slow to move. As late as November 30, Walter White advised him on the Uptown Chamber of Commerce and black leaders without mention of an interracial committee. If anyone would have been informed about mayoral plans for race relations, it would have been La Guardia's close friend. When La Guardia followed White's advice and met with Black, Tobias, and their colleagues on December 10, he had already decided on a committee and probably so informed them.[80] For that reason, black leaders who had been seeking such a committee for months found the meeting "satisfactory."[81] Soon La Guardia was conferring with White about the Mayor's Committee on Unity.[82]

The Mayor's Committee on Unity was not to be just another blue-ribbon panel on race relations. La Guardia informed Rockefeller that he had "something entirely different" in mind: more than a committee, he envisioned an "institution" to study "the causes of discrimination, prejudice and exploitation" with such accuracy and thoroughness that it would be considered "authoritative," and perhaps serve as a beginning for a permanent investigation of race relations.[83] To achieve this purpose, the fifteen committee members would be individuals commanding confidence and respect, while receiving the assistance of advisory committees in fields of specialization and "a staff of experts" to conduct the necessary research. It is unclear whether La Guardia contemplated or foresaw a determined postwar civil rights drive, in which his committee's "authoritative" work would be utilized. Certainly he imagined the Mayor's Committee on Unity as providing the educational process through which racial harmony could ultimately be achieved.

Although the Mayor's plan was commendable, it was somewhat idealistic. Similar local and state studies, such as the Mayor's Commission on Conditions in Harlem and the New York State Commission on the Condition of the Urban Colored Population, had already done on a smaller scale what La Guardia was proposing. Since their findings, which pertained to a more homogeneous and controlled situation, were unable to bring about major reform, there was no reason to believe that a more far-reaching committee would present any new information or promise any better results. The plight of black Americans and the reasons for it had been well established for some time. Most puzzling was La Guardia's apparent ignorance of the monumental study of Gunnar Myrdal and his associates, sponsored by the Carnegie Corporation of New York City, and soon to be published as *An American Dilemma*.[84] It undertook exactly what the Mayor's unity committee was designed to do.

Whatever the plan's limitations, La Guardia moved to create the committee. When eminent businessman Beardsley Ruml declined the chairmanship, he approached Rockefeller.[85] Like Ruml, Rockefeller was too busy for the demanding role of chairman.[86] Conversations with Court of Appeals Justice Irving Lehman and Charles Evans Hughes, Jr., who did become the committee's chairman, lifted the Mayor's "pretty low" spirits.[87] Finally on February 27, more than two months after La Guardia had decided to appoint the committee, it was created and by summer involved in research and study.[88]

One of the committee's first assignments was to work with an ad hoc group formed by Walter White for the purpose of "preventing another riot this summer."[89] In the postwar years, it considered recommendations for reducing race tensions in New York City, and some credited it with arousing support for the establishment of the State Commission Against Discrimination and passage of the

Fair Employment Practices Act.[90] These achievements were significant, but did not approach what La Guardia had hoped for. Perhaps the most important contribution of the Mayor's Committee in late 1943 and early 1944 was to give hope for the improvement of race relations. Coming on the heels of a year marked by ominous racial violence, that contribution should not be overlooked.

Side by side, then, there existed in New York City hope and despair. In spite of the Harlem riot, the tensions that caused it, the resentment and discrimination that remained after it, La Guardia was optimistic because he believed that his administration, the city, and its residents were the most progressive in the United States. Black residents, however, continued to experience abject ghetto conditions and ingrained racial prejudice. Since World War II the dichotomy has continued finding expression in the hope of civil rights legislation and in the despair of race riots.

10

The Riot in Historical Perspective

Historians and sociologists identify shifting patterns and periods of urban racial violence in the twentieth century.[1] Riots in which blacks were victimized by one-sided white attacks became increasingly rare as the century wore on. Most disorders of the World War I period were relatively more evenly matched interracial clashes, while those of the 1960s depicted black outbursts against symbols of white society. The riots of World War II represent a transition from the interracial or communal riots of earlier years to the property-oriented or commodity upheavals of recent times. Nowhere was the emergence of the contemporary pattern of race riots more clearly revealed than in the Harlem riot of 1943.

During World War I, riots grew out of interracial competition that threatened white economic, political, and social positions. Opportunities generated by migration and war intensified the rivalry and raised expectations. As a result, white-initiated violence was met with a heightened black militancy and retaliation. Often the disorders began in a public place and then spread to the borders of black neighborhoods. At every stage blacks were generally on the defensive, though whites made few attempts to invade the ghetto. Much of this pattern was made possible by undermanned police forces, racist attitudes, and an ecology characterized by relatively small black populations and close interracial contacts.

Gradually, racial disturbances emerged from continuous blocked opportunities for blacks and their unfulfilled expectations, as well as their increasing awareness of deprivation in comparison with opportunities and benefits afforded whites. Hence, in the 1960s, postwar socioeconomic developments, civil rights gains, and supportive white attitudes raised expectations but the progress paradoxically lagged behind the pace of improvement desired by the black working class and poor. The hostile outbursts that resulted were marked by black destruction of predominantly white-owned property and confrontations with white police officers. These commodity riots occurred in an atmosphere of militancy and rhetorical violence, confined to black communities. Blacks were now on the offensive, but they did not have institutional power. Certainly, blacks were more assertive and whites more understanding than ever before in the nation's history, and numerous whites appeared to be less threatened economically, politically, and socially. But police forces were stronger than during earlier periods and, therefore, more capable of protecting white physical and psychological needs. Demographic shifts, most notably the formation of large black ghettos and white suburbs, fostered relatively secure areas for black-initiated violence and fewer circumstances for interracial contact.

The riots tended to occur in clusters around the two world wars and the 1960s, with less severe clashes occurring between these periods. Black society was less dependent on white people as opportunities increased and, thereby, became more assertive and politically aware in each era of racial conflict. Nevertheless, the transition from the communal to the commodity type of riot did not alter the sociological factors or underlying conditions necessary for a hostile outburst to occur. The Detroit riot of 1943 demonstrated characteristics of each type of disturbance,[2] but it was the Harlem upheavals of 1935 (which needs further study) and 1943 that ushered in Watts, Newark, and the second Detroit.

In several ways, nevertheless, both Harlem riots were similar to the communal disorders. Elliot M. Rudwick and William M. Tuttle, Jr., have documented the underlying causes, precipitating incidents, contributing factors, and ecological patterns of the riots in East St. Louis (1917), Chicago (1919), and Detroit (1943).[3] All occurred during a period of war when migration increased expectations, competition, and tension, and were preceded by a series of conflicts that escalated racial antagonisms. Moreover, the precipitating incidents involved both races at the close of hot summer weekends when multitudes converged in public. Rumors—partly fed by newspapers—swept through black and white neighborhoods, exaggerating and distorting the incidents, and intensified each situation. Prejudiced, incompetent, and unprepared public officials and policemen contributed to the carnage, which resulted in the death and injury of many more blacks than whites. Interracial clashes occurred in downtown areas where whites were in the vast majority, in hostile neighborhoods where victims were caught unexpectedly or that they had to traverse in order to get to and from work, and along contested borders, in pitched battles. Blacks fought whites, in Tuttle's phrase, over "gut-level issues." Racial antagonisms were reinforced and carried after the riots, when token reforms were shortlived. Occurring in clusters, the riots reflected deep-seated national crises that spanned a generation.

The two Harlem riots were similar in some respects. Each took place during a period of crisis—the Depression and war respectively—when expectations were raised somewhat by New Deal and war programs.[4] Neither riot was preceded by the substantial kinds of antagonizing incidents that marked East St. Louis, Chicago, and Detroit; militant black rhetroic and leadership were nevertheless present in Harlem. Both riots were sparked by clashes involving the police and spread by inflammatory rumors. Police activity had contributed significantly to the resentment that produced upheaval in 1935 and 1943, even though it did not result in the disgraceful assault of black participants and bystanders that accounted for the large number killed and injured in the other upheavals. These numbers were also reduced in Harlem, where riot was confined and interracial clashes largely limited to participants and police. Formed in the aftermath of riot, the Mayor's Commission on Conditions in Harlem and, to a much lesser degree, the Mayor's Committee on Unity brought more lasting reforms than those found in other cities. These improvements in socioeconomic conditions and race relations, nevertheless, were not enough to prevent future disorder.

The Harlem riots, nevertheless, were not identical to one another. The riot in 1935 occurred on March 19, neither in hot weather nor on a Sunday. Migration had increased Harlem's population during the Depression, and the riot of 1935, when compared with those of World War II, was more or less isolated. Although rising expectations had been generated by New Deal programs, the period was marked by economic hardship. The greatest source of resentment was discrimination in employment, especially on 125th Street, Harlem's main thoroughfare; according to Adam Clayton Powell, Jr., of 5,000 store employees, scarcely a hundred were black (mostly porters and maids).[5] This situation had led to the formation of boycott activities, which in some cases were accompanied by militant rhetoric. Like other communities at this time, Harlem was a hotbed for leftist organizations. Although riot erupted spontaneously, the Young Liberators distributed leaflets urging protest after it had begun. Several persons believed that this contributed to the tension, but in itself it could not have sparked disorder.[6] Few of these factors were present in 1943, when a booming war economy and patriotic impulses created strain in areas less directly associated with bread and butter issues. In 1935, three were killed, more than two hundred injured and more than one hundred arrested, with damages estimated at two million dollars.[7] In all categories the figures were below those for 1943, yet Allen D. Grimshaw and Robert M. Fogelson have shown the riots were more alike than dissimilar.

Despite these meaningful comparisons, Harlem's riots, particularly that of 1943, were different from earlier disorders like Detroit. Max Yergan rightly contended that all the racial upheavals of 1943 were "the direct result of continued discrimination" at a time when the country was engaged in "a great democratic war for freedom."[8] In Detroit, this was played out in traditional interracial competition for socioeconomic services. Certainly some of this occurred in New York City, but there the underlying cause for riot resulted from more of an interlocking of local and national issues. New York registered no large permanent in-migration and, therefore, experienced less racial competition for living facilities and social services. While neither city received adequate federal assistance to improve these fields, Detroit suffered more because of its phenomenal growth as a war industries center. Similarly, intolerance was present among northern white residents of both cities, but New York contained few white southern migrants whom some held responsible for the Detroit riot.[9] As a result, Harlem did not experience the numerous, increasingly intense interracial clashes that climaxed in predictable riot at Detroit. Interracial clashes were on the rise during the war in New York, and many, like La Guardia, were concerned, but the issues generating most resentment were more directly related to the national racial situation. Inflation augmented by the absence of price and rent controls and the training of WAVES at Hunter College were local issues resulting from a war atmosphere. These heightened resentment, as did the Savoy's closing and Stuyvesant Town. Nevertheless, it was, in Lester B. Granger's phrase,[10] largely the "unforgivably timid" position of Roosevelt's administration on the role of blacks in the war effort that lowered morale, while the spring riots—

especially in Detroit—and the abuse of black soldiers more than anything changed a Harlem crowd into a mob. As economic and civil rights inroads elevated prospects, racial indignities and white violence compounded existing strain.

All the discrimination and violence that had been heaped on AfroAmericans since the beginning of the war-preparedness program culminated in the spring of 1943 in what appeared to be a racial pogrom. The Detroit riot, in which twenty-five blacks were killed, most by policemen, climaxed a series of smaller disorders that had occurred throughout the nation and stood as a harbinger of what many blacks feared could occur elsewhere. Black New Yorkers were incensed, and against this background, the Bandy-Collins incident brought black resentment to the surface. To a perceptive editor, the Harlem riot was a crusade for the Four Freedoms. A few more schools, playgrounds, and jobs would not solve the problem, which was more psychological than tangible; "the brutal Nazi-like policy of hatred and arrogance on the part of a large element of white Americans" gave black citizens "a complete feeling of not belonging."[11]

Harlem in 1943 differed from Detroit in significant ways. Unlike Mayor Edward J. Jeffries, La Guardia was not indifferent to the plight of black residents and responded magnificently to the racial crisis. Similar to police departments in most of the earlier riot cities, those of Detroit and New York were understaffed during the summer of 1943. Fiscal limitations, selective service, and industrial employment reduced police forces and lowered standards, often resulting in the recruitment of inadequate personnel. Despite Detroit's population increase of almost 500,000 since 1940, its police were 280 men short of budget allotment when the riot occurred.[12] "There can be no doubt," a special assistant to the attorney general remarked, "that the Police Department does not have sufficient numbers of men to handle a major extraordinary crisis like this riot."[13] New York's police department was also understaffed by several hundred men.[14] The difference—a very crucial one—was that La Guardia had prepared the NYPD psychologically and physically in riot control, something that no other mayor had done before the late 1960s. In the earlier riots, writes Rudwick, "the more basic problem involved not the numbers but rather the unpreparedness, corruption, and prejudicial attitudes of the police officers."[15]

Unlike Detroit, New York City did not contain notable race-baiters like Father Charles F. Coughlin.[16] As we have seen, leaders and interested citizens of both races endeavored to maintain a racially tolerant atmosphere. In Detroit, for example, the majority of white residents protested against blacks being housed in the Sojourner Truth project; in New York, black and white residents together objected when blacks were barred from tenancy in Stuyvesant Town. Partly because of this positive climate, destruction and death in the Harlem riot were minimal, and the communal desire for improved race relations continued in the wake of disorder. Compared to other riots, interracial fighting between black and white citizens in Harlem was minimal. Undoubtedly this was the result of ecology and a social structure characterized by strong police and government controls that checked extreme interracial clashes and reinforced relatively peaceful, though not harmonious, racial coexistence. In every major previous riot, including that of Detroit, the communities' external controls had been weak.[17]

According to a National Urban Leaguer the New York disturbance was "a new and entirely different kind of riot."[18] Although this was not true—given the Harlem riot of 1935 and aspects of the Detroit Riot of 1943—the statement was perceptive. A comparison of the Harlem disorder and those of the 1960s suggests more similarities than differences in underlying causes, preconditions, and aftermaths, and provides insights into the evolution of race relations since World War II.

In a general sense, conditions in Harlem in 1943 and the

riot cities of the 1960s promoted resentment over relative deprivation caused by rising expectations, blocked opportunities, and, in the postwar period, increased political awareness. World War II and the civil rights movement elevated black prospects. The ultimate inclusion of blacks in defense industries, the creation of the Governor's Commission on Discrimination in Employment and of the FEPC, the civil rights legislation enacted in New York City, and the leadership of La Guardia and blacks who played up progress quickened the demand for more black socioeconomic and political participation in the earlier period. Similarly, the Supreme Court cases, federal legislation, presidential leadership, and civil rights activists led many blacks to expect more immediate benefits in the 1960s. Both periods were also characterized by articulate spokesmen, such as Adam Clayton Powell, Jr., Martin Luther King, Jr., and later Stokely Carmichael, who projected a new militancy. As some opportunities were blocked by continued white resistance and as blacks began to perceive that they were not receiving the treatment they deserved, hostile outbursts erupted. This deprivation manifested itself in the belief among Harlemites that black society collectively had not been treated fairly by white people during a war that was being fought for democratic principles. Throughout the 1950s and 1960s, blacks of the working and lower middle class experienced an alarming housing squeeze at the very time they expected their lot to improve. Disorder erupted in their neighborhoods in the 1960s.[19] Rioters of both periods seemed to express anger and hope, and a desire "to participate in and transform the larger society."[20] Riots of both periods reflected the progress made thus far as well as the distance that remained to be traveled before the achievement of full equality.

Invariably the hostile outbursts that occurred involved some confrontation in which deeply held beliefs of one race were transgressed by the other.[21] In the Harlem riot of 1943 and in most of those in the 1960s, the precipitating incident and accompanying rumor involved police activity.

These incidents and rumors channeled general beliefs into concrete antagonisms, which sharpened and intensified strain, thus providing justification for mob action.[22] Rumor of Bandy's death spread rapidly exactly because it reinforced the existing value conflicts, hostile beliefs, and community concern of blacks in regard to the NYPD.[23] Because of the communication breakdown between black society and traditional sources of information, rumor continued to spread. After the riot, a white reporter informed black youths that Bandy had only been wounded; it was not believed: shouted one of the teenagers, "Mayor La Guardier [sic] is lying."[24]

Once mob actions emerged, they followed similar ecological patterns and riot stages. Enough has already been said about the historical transformation of cities that isolated black communities and reduced interracial contacts, thereby limiting the chances for communal riots. As Allen D. Grimshaw has pointed out, the sheer size of Harlem's black population in 1943 pre-empted an invasion by white residents and dictated that only policemen were adequately equipped to cope with the riot.[25] Essentially this demographic fact marked the shift from earlier interracial disorders to the commodity disturbances of the 1960s. In both 1943 and the 1960s, the stages of riot were also similar. An analysis of seventy-five riots during 1965–1967 suggested three stages of commodity-riot development, each increasing in intensity.[26] Crowds formed in response to a precipitating incident; window-smashing occurred, followed by looting; some rioters engaged in arson and sniping, then police countered them (at times terminating disorder, other times escalating it). Within the second stage additional patterns have been identified. Initial looting, often symbolic acts of defiance, was followed by more economically motivated theft.[27] Finally, looting became normative as participants redefined property rights. This, of course, was exactly what evolved in the Harlem riot of 1943. For the first three or four hours, Walter White informed Secretary of War Henry L. Stimson, infuriated rioters smashed store windows "for no other reason than that they symbolized a bitterness which has grown among Negroes all over the country."[28] Later, "looters took advantage of the disorder to pillage." Indeed as looting became the norm, even A., who was described earlier as having been taught to respect other people's property, participated. Harlem also experienced arson and participant-police confrontations, although sniping was not characteristic as it was in the 1960s. In fact, few instances of shooting were reported in the Harlem upheaval and fewer than ten persons were arrested for possession of firearms.[29] Undoubtedly, the accessibility of weapons in recent years had escalated racial conflict.[30] Police counteraction in Harlem, unlike that in many of the contemporary riots, was firm but restrained, resulting in an end to hostilities.

The targets of attack were almost identical in 1943 and in the 1960s. Even though white motorists and pedestrians passing through the riot zone or along its fringe were in some cases assaulted, policemen and white-owned stores were singled out as the main symbols of white oppression. Despite deep-seated black resentment toward the police in both periods and even after guardsmen and local police killed many blacks in the more recent disorders, riot participants did not concentrate on taking white lives.[31] Nor did they focus on institutions—libraries, schools, hospitals—that render needed services.[32] Looters worked over small and large businesses, taking furniture, groceries, liquor, and other items of symbolic value.[33] Establishments that were believed to sell inferior goods and charge exorbitant prices seem to have been singled out for attack. Some rioters, perhaps still psychologically dependent on white society and aware of police firepower and repression, chose their targets realistically. Psychologist John P. Spiegel observed "an intense ambivalence" among riot participants toward white society: "Its hated stores and their beloved contents, its despised police and their admired weaponry, its unregenerate bigots and its exemplary civil rights advocates."[34] Not all participants felt these tensions, but A. was typical of some in the Harlem riot who did.

Throughout the riots of both periods, particularly during the initial stages, a frivolous atmosphere prevailed. In addition to representing gratification for the emotional release of frustrations, it revealed a commonality of purpose. In 1943, "law-abiding" citizens, reported a police official, "aided and abetted" the disorder "by their presence."[35] Perhaps because of this commonality or, in Joseph Boskin's phrase, "urban-ethnic group consciousness" and because violence was black-initiated, some interpreters saw the recent upheavals as revolts.[36] One hypothesis proposed that disorder in the 1960s was brought about less by "impersonal, anomic, or psychologically stressful conditions of urban life" than by "the emergence of group political identity," which sought to reclaim authority over ghetto areas.[37] Other commentators considered them riots because they were spontaneous, disorganized, and, at least in the earlier stages, not aimed at seizing or overthrowing the government.[38] Almost everyone, however, agreed that the disorders were not merely criminal acts and that many participants, like revolutionaries, were rejecting the legitimacy of the system in which they found themselves. A similar attitude, though much less pronounced, was present in some participants in the Harlem riot. An attack on white-owned stores, commented a sociologist in 1943, was a blow "at the very heart of . . . American economic and social systems" and, therefore, "a revolutionary act."[39] Apparently, rioters in both periods used revolutionary means, but not for "truly revolutionary ends."[40] It was the Harlem riot of 1964, however, rather than that of 1943, that began the prolonged urban black protest throughout the nation.[41]

While more persons participated in the riots of the 1960s than in that of Harlem in 1943, the composition of rioters in both eras appears to have been similar. In the most violent recent disorders, about 15 percent of a given city's total black population became involved. Similar statistics do not exist for the Harlem upheaval of 1943, but clearly a similar percentage of that community's population—approximately 24,000 persons—did not riot.[42] Rioters in the 1960s, according to the National Advisory Commission on Civil Disorders, were generally single males, ranging in ages from fifteen to twenty-four, northern-born and life-long residents of the riot city.[43] Under- and unemployed in menial and unskilled jobs, they believed themselves deprived of better employment because of racial discrimination. They were better educated than the average ghetto resident and, most significantly, they were politically aware, racially proud, hostile to whites and middle-class blacks, and actively involved in civil rights. Although they were drawn from all social strata, evidence indicates that participants were predominantly of the lower and working class.[44] The greatest majority of rioters, however, were not hoodlums. Sketchier data indicated that Harlem rioters in 1943 possessed some of these characteristics.

The large proportion of lower- and working-class participants in commodity riots of 1943 and the late 1960s probably reflected increasing group awareness and dissatisfaction with the goals and middle-class leadership of the civil rights movement.[45] Black leaders cooperated with municipal authorities to quell the disturbances and initially denounced them as lawless, unrepresentative of black society, detrimental to the civil rights movement, and unrelated to conscious protest.[46] Lesser known black counterrioters were better-educated and earned higher incomes than those rioting.[47] A similar though less well-documented schism between classes was present in the Harlem riot of 1943. As Walter White and other black leaders toured the riot zone in an effort to stop the upheaval, they were met with obscene language, bottles and bricks.[48] White assured the public, as did many civil rights leaders in the 1960s, that "irresponsible persons" dominated the riot, while "the overwhelming majority" of Harlem residents were "at home asleep during the trouble."[49] The "crimes," of course, were neither excused nor condoned. Harlem's leaders and citizens, summarized the Citizens' Emergency Conference for Interracial Unity, "took second place to none in their condemnation of what had occurred."[50] Counterrioters were probably from higher educational and economic strata than the majority of riot participants, although no concrete data confirmed this point. Nevertheless, divisions between classes were perceived by some Harlem leaders and residents. Lester B. Granger implied this, as did John N. Griggs who told La Guardia to restrain "the class of people engaged in these disorders."[51] Of course, the Harlem riot of 1943 and those of the 1960s were forms of protest, a fact even White conceded in 1943, as did most interpreters of the recent upheavals who considered them part of the civil rights struggle.[52]

Riot participants, including those in the earlier communal disorders, have traditionally reflected some satisfaction with their activity.[53] In the 1960s, rioters and significant numbers of nonparticipants considered the upheaval purposeful, justifiable protest.[54] Somewhat similar, although certainly much less widespread feelings emerged among the active and uninvolved populations of Harlem in 1943. For example, twenty of sixty-seven black residents interviewed in a survey conducted by Kenneth B. Clark after the riot considered it an instrument for establishing "a specific socially desirable and ethical end."[55] This evidence is admittedly very sketchy, but it accurately indicated future attitudes of urban black residents.

Once riots began, regardless of type or era, identical tactics were employed to stop them. Police cordons were set up in and around the riot zone, curfews established, alcohol sales prohibited, and, in the commodity disorders, black leaders and celebrities urged rioters to disband.[56] Such measures contained many riots, but were not necessarily responsible for curtailing them. Skillful mayoral leadership, police performance, and black cooperation clearly were largely responsible for controlling and terminating the Harlem riot of 1943, but sociologist Alfred McClung Lee contended that "a great many major riots terminate through exhaustion rather than effective strategy."[57] In all riot situations, however, the kind of police tactics used was crucial in escalating or checking violence. La Guardia and the NYPD's riot control actions were exemplary.

In the aftermath, segments of black communities that experienced riot were optimistic about the future. A majority of Clark's extremely small sample of Harlem residents who accepted the riot of 1943 believed that some good would come from it, and a significant percentage of both those who accepted and those who opposed the disturbance were hopeful for what lay ahead.[58] Seven months later Lester B. Granter admitted that Harlem's disorder had some positive effects on New York City, for it called attention to a lack of necessary facilities in black communities.[59] Of course, others like Walter White stressed "the harm done to the Negro" by riot.[60] In the 1960s, these attitudes, especially optimism, again surfaced, as blacks sensed a oneness and as private and federal monies began to pour into their neighborhoods.[61] Despite some meaningful efforts, the National Advisory Commission on Civil Disorders reported "little basic change took place in the conditions underlying . . . disorder."[62] In both periods, white officials wrongly blamed riots on hoodlums, militants, or outsiders and contended that the majority of black residents considered them purposeless criminal acts, destroying their community and civil rights efforts. Certainly La Guardia's interpretation was adopted by later mayors and presidents. During the disorders of World War II President Roosevelt remained outwardly unconcerned. Such was not the case in the 1960s, for President Lyndon B. Johnson demonstrated relative concern for civil rights, racial disorder, and poverty. Unfortunately, the Vietnam war's inflationary and divisive impact increasingly absorbed the attention of Johnson and white America. Unlike the feeling in some cities in the 1960s, however, the postriot atmosphere in New York in 1943 was not marked by diminished interracial communication or increased racial distrust and extremism. Efforts by the Citizens' Emergency Conference for Interracial Unity, City-Wide Citizens' Committee on Harlem, NAACP, Urban League, and Mayor's Committee on Unity worked to improve race relations.

The Harlem riot of 1943, then, was a harbinger of the 1960s' urban black protest. It reflected in microcosm the shifts in racial attitudes and demography that were occurring under the transforming process of urbanization. Tendencies toward less interracial contact, increased black assertiveness, and white tolerance crystallized in postwar decades.[63] More sophisticated mass media, especially television, reinforced black commonality and perceptions of deprivation. Paradoxically, in the 1960s it played an important role in breaking down racial stereotypes and, through coverage of disorders, alerting white society of a basic social problem, but it possibly encouraged riot behavior in some viewers.[64] Although attitudes have changed since World War II, socioeconomic conditions that made riots probable remain. Harlem, for example, experienced another riot in 1964, and received model cities planning grants from the federal government in 1968 because its residents suffered "from every illness of slum life."[65] Nevertheless, Milton Bloombaum has suggested that future racial disturbances may result more from militant ideology than from institutional breakdowns in the economic, political, and social order.[66] Similarly, strong external controls may no longer prevent disorder (although undoubtedly they will be important in riot control). If black perceptions of deprivation develop enough strain, especially in a cultural and historical context that assumes oppression inevitably leads to riot, sympathetic mayors and prepared police forces may not be sufficient to avert riot. Indeed, Harlem in 1943 exploded despite a relatively tolerant atmosphere, an enlightened mayor, and a trained police department. Whatever the specific physical, psychological, and political conditions causing riots and whatever form future urban racial discord takes—creative disorder, collective revolt, or individual guerilla activity—more violence is certain so long as black Americans experience strain and powerlessness. "All of this is known to students of Harlem," Leopold Philipp informed Governor Lehman of that community's needs in 1941, but until the job is undertaken by public officials, social-minded citizens, and community leaders, "we shall have no peace here."[67] Much the same can be said about the future of race relations throughout the United States.

Abbreviations

COHC	Columbia Oral History Collection, Columbia University, New York, New York
JDP	Jonathan W. Daniels Papers, Southern Historical Collection, University of North Carolina, Chapel Hill, North Carolina
FHLP	Fiorello H. La Guardia Papers, Municipal Archives and Records Center, New York, New York
HIP	Harold L. Ickes Papers, Manuscript Division, Library of Congress, Washington, D.C.
HHLP	Herbert H. Lehman Papers, Columbia University, New York, New York
MRL	Municipal Reference Library, New York, New York
NA	National Archives, Washington, D.C.
NAACP	National Association for the Advancement of Colored People Papers (1940–1955, General Office), Manuscript Collection, Library of Congress, Washington, D.C.
NULP	National Urban League Papers, Manuscript Collection, Library of Congress, Washington, D.C.

FDRP	Franklin D. Roosevelt Papers, Roosevelt Library, Hyde Park, New York
SCNLH	Schomburg Collection of Negro Literature and History, New York, New York

Notes

Introduction

1. Alex Haley and Malcolm X, *The Autobiography of Malcolm X* (New York, 1964), p. 102.

2. Elliot M. Rudwick, *Race Riot at East St. Louis, July 2, 1917* (Carbondale, Ill., 1964), p. 3.

3. William Muraskin, "The Harlem Boycott of 1934: Black Nationalism and the Rise of Labor-Union Consciousness, *Labor History,* 13 (Summer 1972), 361–373.

Chapter 1. The Mayor and the Councilman

1. Arthur Mann, *La Guardia: A Fighter against His Times, 1882–1923* (New York, 1959), for information in this paragraph.

2. Arthur Mann, *La Guardia Comes to Power: 1933* (New York, 1965), pp. 153, 161: La Guardia's opponents were Democrat John P. O'Brien, Democrat-Fusionist Joseph V. McKee, and Socialist Charles Solomon.

3. "The Reminiscences of Benjamin McLaurin" (COHC), 1:18.

4. Mayor's Commission on Conditions in Harlem, "The Negro in Harlem: A Report on Social and Economic Conditions Responsible for the Outbreak of March 19, 1935," pp. 13–15 and 18, Box 2550, FHLP (hereafter cited as Mayor's Commission, "The Negro in Harlem").

5. Ibid., pp. 116–118.

6. La Guardia to Paul Kellog, April 27, 1936, Box 2550, FHLP.

7. Alain Locke to La Guardia, June 12, 1936, Box 2550, FHLP, for a synopsis of the reports filed by the Municipal Commissioners.

8. Oswald Garrison Villard telegram to La Guardia, Sept. 26, 1936, and La Guardia telegram to Villard, Sept. 29, 1936, Box 2550, FHLP, for charges by the vice chairman of the Mayor's Commission that La Guardia suppressed the report.

9. La Guardia to Paul Kellog, April 27, 1936, Box 2550, FHLP.

10. Mayor's Commission, "The Negro in Harlem," foreword.

11. Ibid., p. 107.

12. Valentine to La Guardia, April 30, 1936, Box 2550, FHLP.

13. Locke to La Guardia, June 12, 1936, Box 2550, FHLP.

14. Alain Locke, "Harlem: Dark Weather-Vane," Survey Graphic, Aug. 1936, p. 458.

15. Alain Locke, "La Guardia and Harlem" and "Forward with La Guardia for a Better Harlem" (MS, c. 1937), Box 2549, FHLP, for information in this paragraph.

16. Locke, "La Guardia and Harlem," p. 2.

17. *Amsterdam News*, Jan. 6, 1940, pp. 1 and 19.

18. Ibid., p. 8.

19. Lester B. Stone to Locke, Dec. 9, 1937, Box 2549, FHLP; see note 15 above for Locke's material, which was not used because Tammany Hall "decided to ignore Harlem."

20. Ernest E. Johnson, "Five Times a 'First,'" *Crisis*, Oct. 1942, p. 316.

21. *New York Times*, Feb. 14, 1940, p. 13.

22. White to La Guardia, Dec. 5, 1940, Box 2693, FHLP.

23. *New York Times*, Nov. 4, 1941, p. 19, for quotations and information in this paragraph.

24. Stephen S. Jackson, "Plan for Prevention of Juvenile Delinquency in the City of New York," and La Guardia to John Warren Hill, May 29, 1940, Box 771, FHLP.

25. *New York Times*, Nov. 7, 1941, pp. 1, 18, and 23.

26. Jackson to La Guardia, Nov. 17, 1941, Box 752, FHLP.

27. La Guardia to Robert Moses, Nov. 13, 1941, Box 752, FHLP.

28. *Herald Tribune*, Nov. 30, 1942, "Scrap Book," 299:72, FHLP.

29. Correspondence between La Guardia and his commissioners, Box 2534, FHLP.

30. La Guardia to W. W. Kellett, Feb. 13, 1941, Box 2546, FHLP, for an example.

31. Collier to La Guardia, May 9, 1941, Box 808, FHLP.

32. Stephen Early to Wayne Coy, June 6, 1941, OF 391, FDRP.

33. Memorandum for the President (from E.M.W. [Edwin M. Watson]), June 14, 1941, OF 391, FDRP; La Guardia, Randolph, Walter White, Eleanor Roosevelt, Anna Rosenburg, and Aubrey Williams attended the conference of June 13.

34. Randolph telegram to Roosevelt, June 16, 1941, OF 391, FDRP; "The Reminiscences of Lester B. Granger" (COHC), 2:306.

35. Herbert Garfinkle, *When Negroes March* (Glencoe, Ill., 1959), p. 61. The committee included Randolph, White, Layle Lane, Frank Crosswaith, and Aubrey Williams.

36. It appears as if La Guardia's committee drew up a proposal which the Administration then passed on to Joseph L. Rauh of the Office for Emergency Management for consideration. Rauh reworked the proposal in accordance with the positions of Randolph and Roosevelt. Roosevelt procrastinated a bit before finally signing the order on June 25, 1943: Memorandum for the Files (by hm [Helen Manns, secretarial clerk?]), June 24, 1941, and "Executive Order Reaffirming Policy of Full Participation in the Defense Program by All Persons, Regardless of Race, Creed, Color or National Origin," OF 4245-G, FDRP; Jervis Anderson, *A. Philip Randolph: A Biographical Portrait* (New York, 1973), pp. 258–259, for Rauh's role; Joseph P. Lash, *Eleanor and Franklin: The Story of Their Relationship, Based on Eleanor Roosevelt's Private Papers* (New York, 1971), p. 535, for Roosevelt's procrastination; Executive Order 8802, *Federal Register*, 6 (June 27, 1941), 3109.

37. White telegram to Stephen Early, July 14, 1941, OF 4245-G, FDRP.

38. Memorandum: Committee to Enforce Executive Order against Discrimination to the President (from La Guardia), July 18, 1941, OF 4245-G FDRP.

39. Bernard Rosenberg to Lester B. Stone, Sept. 10, 1941, Box 808, FHLP; Ethel S. Epstein to Bledsoe, Jan. 5, 1941, Box 774, FHLP, for an example.

40. William Meyers to La Guardia, May 17, 1942, and Edmond B. Butler to La Guardia, June 26, 1942, Box 809, FHLP, for an example.

41. Quoted in *Amsterdam News*, Feb. 21, 1942, p. 2.

42. City Council of New York, "Local Laws of New York City, 1942–43," n.p. Nor was it lawful for any person contracted by New York City to request or reveal the race, color, creed, or religion of any person he employed or who sought employment. These provisions were to be written into all city contracts, and their violation was punishable "by a fine of not more than one hundred dollars or by imprisonment for not more than thirty days, or both." On March 24, 1942, Di Giovanna's bill was unanimously adopted by all council members present, but La Guardia did not sign it into law until September 9, 1942, and then with less stringent penalties.

43. La Guardia to Carrie Brown Shaskan, Dec. 14, 1943, Box 2546, FHLP.

44. La Guardia to Higgins, Aug. 29, 1941, Box 2683, FHLP.

45. Correspondence between La Guardia and Moss, Boxes 2546 and 808, FHLP.

46. City Council of New York, "Local Laws of New York City, 1942–43," n.p.

47. *Daily Worker*, Oct. 12, 1941, "Scrap Book," 199:175, FHLP; correspondence related to the Spring Products Corporation, Box 778, FHLP.

48. City Planning Commission, "Proposed Postwar Works Program" (unpublished report, 1942), p. 1, Box 800, FHLP.

49. La Guardia to Dewey, Feb. 20, 1943, Box 2565, FHLP; *Age*, July 10, 1943, p. 1.

50. Arthur Simon, *Stuyvesant Town, U.S.A.: Pattern for Two Americas* (New York, 1970), for a history of Stuyvesant Town from its inception to 1970.

51. La Guardia to Moses, April 21, 1944, Box 2554, FHLP.

52. La Guardia to Roosevelt, March 28, 1940, Box 2572, FHLP; La Guardia to Mrs. Ogden Reid, May 6, 1942, Box 2669, FHLP.

53. Simon, *Stuyvesant Town*, pp. 46–48, 57–69, 83–91 and 106, for information in this paragraph.

54. Mrs. B. Fishman to La Guardia, June 14, 1943, Box 762, FHLP.

55. La Guradia to Dorothy Clement, Jan. 20, 1941, Box 2671, FHLP.

56. Fiorello H. La Guardia, "Harlem: Homelike and Hopeful" (typewritten, 1944), p. 17, Box 2549, FHLP.

57. La Guardia to August B. Rechholtz, Oct. 17, 1941, Box 2546, FHLP, for this and the following quotation.

58. Quoted in *Herald Tribune*, Nov. 30, 1942, "Scrap Book," 299:72, FHLP.

59. *Crisis*, March, 1940, p. 84; La Guardia to A. Philip Randolph, Sept. 15, 1941, Box 2546, FHLP.

60. *Amsterdam News*, Feb. 24, 1940, p. 11, and March 13, 1943, p. 3; White to La Guardia, June 16, 1943, Box 762, FHLP, and *Crisis*, Nov., 1942, p. 334.

61. Memo for the Mayor (from Anonymous), Nov. 18, 1941, Box 2633, FHLP, for an example: Battle's role in the "Harlem Crime Wave."

62. In the summer of 1940, La Guardia was appointed chairman of the American section of the Joint Permanent Defense Board. In May 1941, he became Civilian Defense Director, but resigned in February 1942 as a result of having too much to do and of clashing with other officials: Charles Garrett, *The La Guardia Years: Machine and Reform Politics in New York City* (New Brunswick, N.J., 1961), p. 268.

63. "Reminiscences of Newbold Morris" (COHC), p. 68.

64. La Guardia to Angelo J. Rossi, June 19, 1942, Box 2546, FHLP. Given Powell's relentless charges of discrimination and his consistent harassment of La Guardia in the *People's Voice*, I assume he was clearly on the Mayor's mind.

65. La Guardia's address in "A Digest of Proceedings: The Negro Press Conference, May 7–8, 1943," p. 34, OF 4245-G, FDRP.

66. "The Reminiscences of Samuel J. Battle" (COHC), p. 46.

67. Roi Ottley, *'New World A-Coming'* (New York, 1945), pp. 220–235, for a perceptive contemporary view of Powell.

68. Adam Clayton Powell, Jr., *Adam by Adam: The Autobiography of Adam Clayton Powell, Jr.* (New York, 1971), pp. 14, 24, and 32.

69. Adam Clayton Powell, Jr., *Marching Blacks: An Interpretive History of the Rise of the Common Man* (rev.; New York, 1973), p. 30.

70. Quoted in Dan Wakefield, "Adam Clayton Powell, Jr.: The Angry Voice of Harlem," *Esquire*, Nov. 1959, p. 120.

71. Powell, *Marching Blacks*, p. 92.

72. In 1939, the Abyssinian Baptist Church membership was given at 8,000 persons: Gunnar Myrdal et al., *An American Dilemma: The Negro Problem and Modern Democracy* (2 vols.; New York, 1944), 2:863, n. a.

73. Powell, *Marching Blacks*, pp. 86 and 101 for the quotations in this paragraph.

74. Office of Facts and Figures, "The Negro Looks at the War: Attitudes of New York Negroes towards Discrimination against Negroes and a Comparison of Negro and Poor White Attitudes toward War-Related Issues" (mimeo., SCNLH, 1942), p. 19, Table 40.

75. Lee A. Daniels, "The Political Career of Adam Clayton Powell: Paradigm and Paradox," *Journal of Black Studies*, 4 (Dec. 1973), 135, n. 1, and 120.

76. James Q. Wilson, "The Negro in Politics," in *The Negro in America*, ed. Talcott Parsons and Kenneth B. Clark (New York, 1966), pp. 435, 438.

77. *Age*, Nov. 15, 1941, p. 1.

78. *The City Record: Official Canvass of the Votes Cast in the Counties of New York, Bronx, Kings, Queens and Richmond at the General Election Held November 4, 1941*, 69:79.

79. *People's Voice*, July 11, 1942, p. 5.

80. Ibid., Feb. 21, 1942, p. 5.

81. Quoted in *Age*, Oct. 25, 1941, p. 1.

82. *Amsterdam News*, Oct. 25, 1941, p. 7, and Nov. 15, 1941, p. 8.

83. Powell to La Guardia, Feb. 4, 1942, Box 2614, FHLP.

84. Quoted in *Amsterdam News*, Oct. 25, 1941, p. 7.

85. *People's Voice*, July 17, 1943, p. 15. The emphasis is Powell's.

86. *People's Voice*, May 2, 1942, p. 5.

87. Ibid., Aug. 1, 1942, p. 20, and *Amsterdam News*, June 12, 1943, p. 1.

88. *Amsterdam News*, Jan. 6, 1940, p. 9.

89. *People's Voice*, Feb. 14, 1942, p. 5.

90. Powell, *Marching Blacks*, p. 92.

91. *People's Voice*, March 28, 1942, p. 5.

92. Quoted in Neil Hickey and Ed Edwin, *Adam Clayton Powell and the Politics of Race* (New York, 1965), p. 57.

93. Powell, *Marching Blacks*, p. 98.

94. Powell to La Guardia, Jan. 21, 1942, Box 2614, FHLP.

95. Confidential Memorandum to La Guardia (from Powell), n.d., Box 752, FHLP, for this and the following quotations; La Guardia's remarks are scribbled on an unidentified and undated sheet of paper attached to Confidential Memorandum: the emphasis is La Guardia's.

96. The Rapp-Coudert Committee was named after its co-chairmen Senator Frederick R. Coudert, Jr., and Assemblyman Herbert A. Rapp.

97. *Amsterdam News*, May 3, 1941, pp. 1 and 17.

98. *Age*, May 3, 1941, p. 1.

99. Resolution No. 31 in City Council of New York, *Proceedings, 1942*, 1:265.

100. City Council of New York, *Proceedings, 1942*, 1:287. In the City Council vote to table Powell's resolution, two abstained and five were not present.

101. *Amsterdam News*, Feb. 21, 1942, p. 24. The Council members were Louis Cohen, Joseph E. Kingsley and Gertrude Klein.

102. *Age*, Feb. 28, 1942, p. 6.

103. *Amsterdam News*, March 7, 1942, p. 6.

104. Memorandum for the Mayor (from Florence P. Shientag), Jan. 28, 1941, Box 2672, FHLP.

105. William H. Dean, Jr., to Walter White, Feb. 1, 1941, Box 2672, FHLP.

106. Quoted in *Amsterdam News*, March 14, 1942, p. 10.

107. *People's Voice*, Nov. 21, 1942, p. 8.

108. This handbill is in Box 752, FHLP.

109. Lewis J. Valentine to La Guardia, May 15, 1942, Box 752, FHLP.

110. Memorandum: Clayton Powell, n.d., Box 752, FHLP.

111. Memorandum: Mass Meeting Protesting the Killing of One Wallace Armstrong by a Patrolman of This Department to Commanding Officer, Criminal Alien Squad (from Frank M. Schilbersky), May 17, 1942, Box 752, FHLP (hereafter cited as Schilbersky, "Mass Meeting").

112. *People's Voice*, May 23, 1942, p. 20.

113. La Guardia to S. W. Garlington, Jan. 28, 1943, Box 2671, FHLP.

114. "The Reminiscences of Genevieve Earle" (COHC), p. 102.

115. Powell, *Marching Blacks*, p. 153, and for an overview of his councilmanic efforts, pp. 152–155.

116. Resolution No. 240, City Council of New York, *Proceedings, 1943*, 1:134.

117. Claude Lewis, *Adam Clayton Powell* (New York, 1963), p. 55.

118. Quoted in Ernest Dunbar, "The Audacious World of Adam Powell," *Look*, May 7, 1963, p. 39.

119. Powell, *Marching Blacks*, p. 153.

120. Adam Clayton Powell, Jr., "The Duties and Responsibilities of a Congressman to the United States," *Esquire*, Sept. 1963, p. 111.

121. Powell, *Marching Blacks*, pp. 25, 29, 49.

122. James Q. Wilson, "Two Negro Politicians: An Interpretation," *Midwest Journal of Political Science*, 4 (Nov., 1960), 351–352, provides the best, recent interpretation of Powell's political style.

Chapter 2. Ghetto Life during the Depression

1. James Weldon Johnson, *Black Manhattan* (New York, 1930), pp. 281, 284, for this and the following quotation.

2. New York State Temporary Commission against Discrimination, *Report of the New York State Temporary Commission against Discrimination* (Albany, N.Y., 1945), p. 16 (hereafter cited as State Commission against Discrimination, *Report*).

3. *Pittsburgh Courier*, March 2, 1940, p. 4.

4. Welfare Council of New York City, *Census Tract Data on Population and Housing, New York City: 1940* (New York, 1941), p. 5.

5. Florence Murray, ed., *The Negro Handbook* (New York, 1942), pp. 188–190.

6. Welfare Council, *Census Tract*, p. 5, table 1.

7. Claude McKay, *Harlem: Negro Metropolis* (New York, 1940), p. 16.

8. William Wilson to La Guardia, Oct. 6, 1944, Box 2549, FHLP; Olivia P. Frost, *An Analysis of the Characteristics of the Population in Central Harlem* (New York, 1946), p. 5; E. Franklin Frazier, "Negro Harlem: An Ecological Study," *American Journal of Sociology*, 43 (July, 1937), 72–88, for the pattern of settlement in Harlem.

9. Gardner Jones, "Pilgrimage to Freedom" (WPA, Research Paper, SCNLH, c. 1939–1940), pp. 37, 39; Wilfred R. Bain, "Negroes in Queensboro," (WPA, Research Paper, SCNLH, c. 1939), p. 4.

10. Sub-Committee of the Committee on the Domestic Relations Court of the New York County Lawyers' Association, "Report of the Sub-Committee on Negro Child Problem," April 1, 1935, p. 12, reel 66, Governorship Papers, HHLP.

11. New York State Temporary Commission on the Condition of the Urban Colored Population, *Report of the New York State*

Temporary Commission on the Condition of the Urban Colored Population to the Legislature of the State of New York (Albany, N.Y., 1938), p. 5 (hereafter cited as State Commission, *Report to the Legislature*).

12. Lehman to Homer Folks, Dec. 24, 1934, reel 71, Governorship Papers, HHLP.

13. New York State Temporary Commission on the Condition of the Urban Colored Population, "Public Hearings" (9 vols., SCNLH; hereafter cited as "Public Hearings"); Gilbert Osofsky, "The Enduring Ghetto," *Journal of American History*, 55 (Sept. 1968), 243–255.

14. For an important account of the vicious cycle today, see Kenneth B. Clark, *Dark Ghetto: Dilemmas of Social Power* (New York, 1965).

15. State Commission, *Report to the Legislature*, p. 12.

16. Mayor's Commission, "The Negro in Harlem," p. 36.

17. New York State Temporary Commission on the Condition of the Urban Colored Population, *Second Report of the New York State Temporary Commission on the Urban Colored Population to the Legislature* (New York, 1939), p. 35 (hereafter cited as State Commission, *Second Report*).

18. Quoted in ibid., p. 36.

19. State Commission, *Second Report*, pp. 34, 40; the Mayor's Commission had found identical patterns of occupation in Harlem, "The Negro in Harlem," pp. 21–22.

20. Testimony of Manning A. Johnson, "Public Hearings," 9:1608.

21. Mayor's Commission, "The Negro in Harlem," pp. 30–31.

22. State Commission, *Second Report*, p. 64.

23. Mayor's Commission, "The Negro in Harlem," p. 23.

24. Testimony of Robert W. Boyd, "Public Hearings," 9:1624, 1626, 1633.

25. State Commission, *Report to the Legislature*, p. 58.

26. State Commission, *Second Report*, p. 54.

27. Testimony of James P. Allen, president of a local NAACP branch, "Public Hearings," 6:1211, for an example.

28. Testimony of A. Philip Randolph, "Public Hearings," 8:1538, 1940.

29. Testimony of J. Pollard, secretary-treasurer-manager of Local 272, Garage Workers Union, "Public Hearings," 8:1487–1488.

30. Mayor's Commission, "The Negro in Harlem," pp. 22–23.

31. Carl Offord, "Negro Business" (WPA, Research Paper, SCNLH, c. 1936–1940), p. 8.

32. Mayor's Commission, "The Negro in Harlem," pp. 25–26.

33. State Commission, *Report to the Legislature*, p. 18.

34. Testimony of Walter Williams, "Public Hearings," 8:1513 for the quote, 1514, 1522.

35. State Commission, *Second Report*, p. 38.

36. Ibid., p. 74.

37. State Commission, *Report to the Legislature*, p. 50. Other neighborhoods, notably East Harlem, were deteriorated more than black Harlem, but in comparison to the city as a whole, most black sections were among those dilapidated: Franklin O. Nichols, *Harlem Housing* (New York, 1939), pp. 10 and 19.

38. Gilbert Osofsky, *Harlem: The Making of a Ghetto* (New York, 1966), pp. 127–149, for the deterioration of Harlem in the 1920s.

39. Nichols, *Harlem Housing*, p. 14.

40. Testimony of Morris Hubbard, a Harlem tenant, "Public Hearings," 7:1318.

41. State Commission, *Second Report*, p. 81.

42. Testimony of Langdon Post, "Public Hearings," 7:1329.

43. Testimony of Morris Hubbard, "Public Hearings," 7:1317.

44. Mayor's Commission, "The Negro in Harlem," p. 61.

45. Dr. John L. Rice, New York City Health Commissioner, "Twelve Months of Health Defense," *Herald Tribune*, Oct. 6, 1941, Box 2736, FHLP.

46. Louis B. Bryan, "Visiting Nurses Services of Harlem" (WPA, Research Paper, SCNLH, 1937), p. 1.

47. Testimony of Dr. Peter Marshall Murray, "Public Hearings," 6:1174.

48. Mayor's Commission, "The Negro in Harlem," p. 67.

49. Testimony of Reverend John W. Robinson, "Public Hearings," 6:1054.

50. Testimony of Emmet M. May, "Public Hearings," 6:1077.

51. [Unknown] Clarke, "Impressions of New York" (WPA, Research Paper, SCNLH, c. 1938–1940), n.p.

52. Nichols, *Harlem Housing*, p. 18.

53. Mayor's Commission, "The Negro in Harlem," pp. 95, 97.

54. In 1936, blacks constituted 43 percent of all female and 15 percent of all male offenders in New York State: State Commission, *Second Report*, p. 143, table XVIII.

55. Mayor's Commission, "The Negro in Harlem," p. 98.

56. Ibid., pp. 1–12, 100–108.

57. Testimony of Andrew R. Newhoff, secretary of the New York State International Labor Defense, "Public Hearings," 9:1703–1704.

58. Alvin Moses, "Description of Harlem from 110th to 135th Streets" (WPA, Research Paper, SCNLH, c. 1938–1940), p. 11.

59. Reverend John H. Johnson, *Harlem, the War and Other Addresses* (New York, 1942), p. 68.

60. Quoted in Stanley High, "Black Omens," *Saturday Evening Post*, May 21, 1938, p. 66.

61. Allen F. Kifer, "The Negro under the New Deal, 1933–1941" (Ph.D. diss., University of Wisconsin, 1961), p. 75, for the percentage; John A. Salmond, "The Civilian Conservation Corps and the Negro," *Journal of American History*, 52 (June 1965), pp. 85 and 87, for FDR's political concerns.

62. Robert C. Weaver, "Negro Labor since 1919," *Journal of Negro History*, 35 (Jan. 1950), 25.

63. *Amsterdam News*, Oct. 12, 1940, p. 12.

64. *The City Record: Official Canvass of the Votes Cast in the Counties of New York, Bronx, Kings, Queens and Richmond at the General Election Held November 5, 1940*, 68: 7, 73, 115, 190, and 222.

65. John A. Davis, "The Negro Outlook Today," *Survey Graphic*, Nov. 1942, p. 500.

66. Floyd Snelson, "Occupations from Which Negroes Are Barred" (WPA, Research Paper, SCNLH, 1938), p. 5.

67. Mayor's Commission, "The Negro in Harlem," p. 1.

68. Carlton Moss, "The 'People's Court' " (WPA, Research Paper, SCNLH, 1939), p. 2.

69. Office of Facts and Figures, "The Negro Looks at the War," p. 1.

70. *Amsterdam News*, Jan. 27, 1940, p. 15.

71. Howard H. Long, "The Position of the Negro in the American Social Order: A Forecast," *Journal of Negro Education*, 8 (July, 1939), 616.

72. The letterhead, Walter White to La Guardia, March 21, 1940, Box 2693, FHLP.

73. National Association for the Advancement of Colored People, *Youth Bulletin*, Nov. 1940, p. 2.

74. State Commission against Discrimination, *Report*, p. 21.

75. "The Reminiscences of Lester B. Granger" (COHC), 1:137; Jay Anders Higbee, *Development and Administration of the New York State Law against Discrimination* (University, Ala., 1966), for the impact of the State Commission's efforts on the postwar period.

Chapter 3. Black Response to World War II

1. Alfred A. Duckett, "Uncensored," *Age,* Jan. 18, 1941, p. 7.

2. A. P. Johnson to Hilman [sic], June 5, 1940, Box 69, Record Group 228, NA.

3. *Age,* June 28, 1941, p. 1; *Amsterdam News,* July 12, 1941, p. 14.

4. *Age,* Dec. 13, 1941, p. 1.

5. *Amsterdam News,* Dec. 20, 1941, p. 9.

6. Quoted in *Amsterdam News,* April 26, 1941, p. 13.

7. *Amsterdam News,* Oct. 16, 1943, p. 13-A.

8. Richard M. Dalfiume, *Desegregation of the U.S. Armed Forces: Fighting on Two Fronts, 1939–1953* (Columbia, Mo., 1969), and Ulysses Lee, *The Employment of Negro Troops* (Washington, D.C., 1966), for the role of black servicemen in World War II.

9. *Amsterdam News,* Dec. 19, 1942, p. 1, reported that over a million black men were in the service, which was the number that served during the entire war.

10. Bethune to Sidney Hillman, June 6, 1940, Box 69, Record Group 228, NA.

11. *Amsterdam News,* Jan. 9, 1943, p. 1; Roi Ottley, *'New World A-Coming'* (New York, 1945), pp. 335–338 and *Age, Amsterdam News,* and *People's Voice,* Feb.–Dec. 1942, for background and details of this case.

12. A. M. Wendell Malliet, "The World Fronts," *Amsterdam News,* Dec. 26, 1942, p. 9.

13. *Amsterdam News,* May 31, 1941, p. 3, for the view of Roy Wilkins, Lester B. Granger, James H. Hubert, William T. Andrews, and others.

14. Quoted in *Pittsburgh Courier,* July 26, 1941, p. 19.

15. *Amsterdam News,* Jan. 17, 1942, pp. 1 for the quotation, 4 for the vote. Of the nineteen delegates who abstained from voting, several agreed with the resolution but feared it would hurt the drive for racial justice.

16. Collier Anderson to Roosevelt, Aug. 16, 1940, OF 93, FDRP.

17. American Negro to Roosevelt, March 1, 1942, OF 93, FDRP.

18. *People's Voice*, Feb. 21, 1943, p. 4, for an example.

19. Alex Haley and Malcolm X, *The Autobiography of Malcolm X* (New York, 1964), pp. 104–107, for this incident.

20. Quoted in Kenneth B. Clark and James Barker, "The Zoot Effect in Personality: A Race Riot Participant," *Journal of Abnormal and Social Psychology*, 40 (1965), 145.

21. Office of Facts and Figures, "The Negro Looks at the War," intro.

22. *Amsterdam News*, Sept. 28, 1940, p. 6; *Pittsburgh Courier*, Jan. 4, 1941, p. 12; *New York Times*, Dec. 19, 1940, p. 28, for respective examples.

23. *Age*, Jan. 25, 1941, p. 1.

24. Carl Lawrence, "On the Level," *Amsterdam News*, Nov. 14, 1942, p. 9.

25. Henry K. Craft to David Stentner, April 15, 1941, Box 808, FHLP.

26. Olzaria Blackburn to La Guardia, Oct. 16, 1942, Box 2546, FHLP.

27. Jessie P. Guzman and W. Hardin Hughes, "Lynching—Crime," *Negro Year Book: A Review of Events Affecting Negro Life, 1941–1946*, ed. Jessie P. Guzman (Atlanta, Ga., 1947), pp. 302–311, records 16 known lynchings for 1940–1943.

28. *Age*, July 25, 1942, p. 1, and *Amsterdam News*, July 25, 1942, p. 13.

29. *Amsterdam News*, June 21, 1941, p. 14.

30. Many of New York City's black leaders, like the black population generally, had been newcomers: James S. Watson came from Jamaica and Frank Crosswaith from the Virgin Islands; Myles Paige and Charles E. Toney journeyed from Alabama; Ferdinand Q. Morton, A. Philip Randolph, and Walter White came from Mississippi, Florida, and Georgia respectively.

31. *Amsterdam News*, March 9, 1940, p. 15.

32. *Age*, March 8, 1941, p. 6.

33. *Pittsburgh Courier*, March 9, 1940, p. 6, for alleged mistreatment of a black migrant family by the New York City Welfare Department.

34. *Amsterdam News*, Jan. 17, 1942, p. 7.

35. Quoted in Sterling A. Brown, "Out of Their Mouths," *Survey Graphic*, Nov. 1942, p. 482.

36. *Amsterdam News*, Feb. 8, 1941, pp. 1 and 7.

37. *People's Voice*, Feb. 14, 1942, p. 3.

38. Malcolm S. MacLean to Roosevelt, Oct. 15, 1940, PPF 682, FDRP.

39. Ludlow Werner, "Across the Desk," *Age*, May 29, 1943, p. 6.

40. "Example for America," *Crisis*, June 1940, p. 179.

41. Quoted in Brown, "Out of Their Mouths," p. 482.

42. Quoted in *Amsterdam News*, May 23, 1942, p. 3.

43. *Black Worker*, Sept., 1940, p. 8.

44. G. G. M. James, *The Fate of Black People under Germany* (New York, 1941), which Ebenezer Ray publicized in "Dottings," *Age*, June 21, 1941, p. 6; Hans Habe, "The Nazi Plan for Negroes," *Nation*, March 1, 1941, pp. 232–235, which was reprinted in condensed version in the *Age*, Nov. 22, 1941, p. 2; columnists also warned of Nazism: Frank Crosswaith, "Around and Beyond," *Amsterdam News*, Nov. 1, 1941, p. 13, Nov. 8, 1941, p. 9, Nov. 15, 1941, p. 9, and Nov. 22, 1941, p. 9.

45. Quoted in *Amsterdam News*, Sept. 20, 1941, p. 3.

46. "The Reminiscences of George S. Schuyler" (COHC), 2:324.

47. Office of Facts and Figures, "The Negro Looks at the War," p. 111. To black interviewers, 22% of the respondents believed that they would have been treated the same as under American rule, 63% worse and 14% did not know; the corresponding figures for responses to white interviewers were 12%, 71%, and 16%. White respondents replying to white interviewers registered 11%, 76%, and 12%, respectively.

48. George W. Harris, "Where Would Colored Americans Come In Should Japan, Hitler and Italy Win?" *Amsterdam News*, Jan. 31, 1942, p. 12, for an example.

49. Ottley, '*New World A-Coming*,' pp. 327–342, for Japanese propaganda.

50. Office of Facts and Figures, "The Negro Looks at the War," pp. 4, 5, and 111, for the information in the remainder of this paragraph: when questioned by white interviewers, 8, 30, 29, and 33 were the respective percentages as blacks were less candid, perhaps because they feared being considered unpatriotic.

51. J. Saunders Redding, "I Believe in This War," *Negro Digest*, Dec. 1942, p. 8.

52. *Amsterdam News,* Feb. 6, 1943, p. 9; *Age,* May 8, 1943, p. 6; "Program of the Eastern Seaboard Conference on the Problems of the War and the Negro People," April 10–11, 1942 (mimeo. copy), Box 2670, FHLP (hereafter cited as "Program of the Eastern Seaboard Conference").

53. Harvard Sitkoff, "Racial Militancy and Interracial Violence in the Second World War," *Journal of American History,* 58 (Dec. 1971), 661–681, and Lee Finkle, "The Conservative Aims of Militant Rhetoric: Black Protest during World War II," *Journal of American History,* 60 (Dec. 1973), 692–713, for an overview of black protest in World War II and the controversy over how militant it was.

54. Quoted in Charles Williams, "Harlem at War," *Nation,* Jan. 16, 1943, p. 88.

55. *Amsterdam News,* Nov. 23, 1940, p. 8.

56. Quoted in *Age,* Dec. 20, 1941, p. 1.

57. *People's Voice,* May 2, 1941, p. 5; Langston Hughes, "How About It?" *Journal and Guide* (Norfolk, Va.), Jan. 30, 1943, p. 8.

58. "Program of the Eastern Seaboard Conference," n.p.; Resolution No. 37, City Council of New York, *Proceedings, 1942,* 1:267; *Amsterdam News,* Feb. 14, 1942, p. 7, and July 18, 1942, p. 1.

59. A. M. Wendell Malliet's series on Ethiopian history, for example, begins in *Amsterdam News,* March 15, 1941, p. 13.

60. *Age,* June 7, 1941, p. 6.

61. Ibid., March 7, 1942, p. 6.

62. William Henry Huff, "When This War Is Over," *Age,* April 4, 1942, p. 6.

63. Roosevelt to Sumner Welles, March 5, 1943, OF 93, FDRP. Welles was instructed to inform White that consideration would be given to including at least one black among American delegates to the peace conference. However, no formal peace conference emerged. Instead, the terms of peace were established in a series of summit meetings between leaders and officials of the Allies that occurred during and after the war. Black Americans did attend the United Nations' organization meeting in San Francisco in 1944 as observers and staff. John Hope Franklin, *From Slavery to Freedom* (New York, 1967), pp. 600–607.

64. Eugene Kinckle Jones to Mrs. Samuel I. Rosenman, Feb. 8, 1943, OF 93, FDRP.

65. Anonymous, "Negro Organizations and the War Effort" (unpub. memorandum, 1942), p. 3, Box 427, Record Group 228, NA (hereafter cited as "Negro Organizations and the War Effort").

66. Walter White, "What the Negro Thinks of the Army," *Annals*, 223 (Sept., 1942), 70.

67. "Should Negroes Demand Equality Now?" *Negro Digest*, Jan. 1943, pp. 49–51, for white liberal views. Although black leaders were unified on the Double V campaign, they sometimes differed on strategy. In New York City, for example, they split over whether or not an all black State Guard Unit would assist black people by preparing soldiers for an integrated armed forces in the future or, by the very nature of its segregation, retard that integration. The unit was created: *Age*, Nov. 7, 1942, p. 6 and Walter White to Lehman, Dec. 4, 1942, Special File, HHLP, for opposing views.

68. The Harlem Labor Committee, the Greater New York Coordinating Committee for Employment and the National Negro Congress comprised the coalition: *New York Times*, April 20, 1941, p. 35, for the agreement.

69. Powell, *Marching Blacks*, p. 128.

70. Finkle, "The Conservative Aims of Militant Rhetoric," pp. 692–713, is correct in arguing that the rhetoric of black protest was far more militant than the aims and actions of black leadership. Yet many blacks and the majority of whites considered black rhetoric, aims and action—or threat of action—to be militant for that period; Russ McFarland to Stephen Early, July 7, 1943, OF 93, FDRP, for an example of white concern.

71. Quoted in *Amsterdam News*, April 5, 1941, p. 9.

72. "Negro Organizations and the War Effort," p. 3.

73. "The Case against the Negro Press," *Negro Digest*, Feb. 1943, pp. 44–53, and W. E. B. DuBois, "The American Negro Press," *Negro Digest*, April 1943, pp. 33–36, for the controversy over the role the black press should play in the war.

74. *Opportunity*, April 1943, p. 63.

75. Office of Facts and Figures, "The Negro Looks at the War," p. 1; Hampton Institute, "Findings," p. 52, for the quote.

76. *People's Voice*, Nov. 14, 1942, p. 5.

77. National Urban League, *Racial Aspects of Reconversion* (New York, 1945), p. 4.

78. Ira De A. Reid, "Special Problems of Negro Migration

during the War," *Postwar Problems of Migration* (New York, 1947), p. 152.

79. "Negro Internal Migration, 1940–1943," *Monthly Summary of the Events and Trends of Race Relations*, 1 (Sept. 1943), 11.

80. *Age*, March 8, 1941, p. 6.

81. Lorenzo F. Davis, Jr., in *Amsterdam News*, May 29, 1943, p. 18.

82. Warren M. Banner, "Profiles: New York," *Journal of Educational Sociology*, 17 (Jan. 1944), 273.

83. Lorenzo F. Davis, Jr., "Semi-Annual Report: Negro War Worker—Asset or Liability? America Must Decide Now" (mimeo. copy, 1943), OF 93-C, FDRP (hereafter cited as "Semi-Annual Report, 1943").

84. *New York Post*, Oct. 18, 1943, "Scrap Book," 255:122, FHLP, for an example.

85. *Amsterdam News*, July 24, 1943, p. 3, for estimates by the National Urban League and local politicians.

86. Walter R. Thomas to La Guardia, Aug. 4, 1943, Box 752, FHLP.

87. Mildred I. Yemmans to La Guardia, Jan. 21, 1942, Box 809, FHLP, for an example.

88. Negro Employees (14 and 15 Manhattan Districts) to La Guardia, Oct. 4, 1942, Box 809, FHLP.

89. City-Wide Citizens' Committee on Harlem, reports on employment, education, health, housing, and recreation (mimeo. copies, 1942–1945), SCNLH.

90. New York Urban League, *Annual Report for 1940* (New York, 1941), p. 1, for this percentage and the following quotation.

91. *Age*, May 17, 1941, p. 6, for an example.

92. Walter White to La Guardia, March 5 and March 21, 1940, Box 2693, FHLP; *Crisis*, May 1940, p. 150.

93. National Association for the Advancement of Colored People, *Annual Report, 1940* (New York, 1941), p. 7.

94. *New York Times,* Jan. 22, 1941, p. 14.

95. *Crisis*, March 1941, p. 84. Senators W. Warren Barbour of New Jersey, Prentiss Brown of Michigan, and Arthur Capper of Kansas were co-sponsors.

96. *New York Times*, May 7, 1941, p. 19.

97. Address to the State Legislature, "Recommending Methods of Advancing the Social and Economic Welfare of the People

of the State," Jan. 14, 1941, in *Public Papers of Herbert H. Lehman, 1941* (New York, 1946), p. 26.

98. Memorandum, March 20, 1941, reel 25, Governorship Papers, HHLP.

99. Interview with Roy Wilkins, New York City, Jan. 29, 1968; interview with Charles Poletti, New York City, March 8, 1968.

100. Lehman to Roosevelt, June 9, 1941, OF 4245, FDRP; Mr. [Stephen] Early (from Anonymous), June 18, 1941, OF 91, FDRP, especially the marginal note.

101. *Herald Tribune,* Sept. 1, 1941, "Clippings," 94:11540, HHLP.

102. Charter Meeting Address to the City Council, Jan. 7, 1942, City Council of New York, *Proceedings, 1942,* 1:10.

103. *Age,* May 9, 1942, p. 7. The official was Charles C. Berkley, industrial secretary.

104. Roosevelt telegram to La Guardia, June 11, 1942, Box 2572, FHLP. The other officials included Jesse Jones, Robert Patterson, James V. Forrestal, and Admiral [Emory S.?] Land, Maritime Commissioner.

105. Memorandum: Statistics on Unemployment in New York City for P. M. McCullough (from Shelby C. Davis), Aug. 20, 1942, Box 778, FHLP.

106. Roosevelt to La Guardia, July 22, 1942, Box 2599, FHLP.

107. Correspondence related to the Smaller War Plants Corporation, especially between La Guardia, Paul V. McNutt, and Donald Nelson, Box 2599, FHLP.

108. *New York Times,* Nov. 10, 1942, "Clippings," 103:13356, HHLP. Anna Rosenburg is the director.

109. John A. Kennedy, Memorandum: Progress Report, New York City Unemployment, Oct. 16, 1942, Box 2599, FHLP. These figures excluded commitments made by the Brooklyn Navy Yard and "some other items."

110. Forrestal to La Guardia, Oct. 20, 1942, Box 2599, FHLP.

111. *New York Times,* Nov. 11, 1942, "Clippings," 103:13358, HHLP.

112. Memorandum to Niles (from FDR), Nov. 16, 1942, in *F.D.R.: His Personal Letters, 1928–1945,* ed. Elliot Roosevelt (4 vols.; New York, 1950), 4:1368.

113. "Employment Conditions, January-March, 1943," *Employment Review,* 5 (April, 1943), 84.

114. "On the Level," *Amsterdam News,* Jan. 2, 1943, p. 7.

115. Davis, "Semi-Annual Report, 1943," p. 8.

116. *Amsterdam News,* Dec. 11, 1943, p. 11-B.

117. Banner, "Profile: New York," p. 273.

118. "Placement of Negroes in the State," *Employment Review,* 5 (May, 1942), 235.

119. James A. Davis, *How Management Can Integrate Negroes in War Industries* (New York, 1942), p. 4.

120. M. Moran Weston, "Labor Forum," *Amsterdam News,* Sept. 4, 1943, p. 13.

121. Anonymous, "Compliance Data: Firms Involved in Old [FEPC] Hearings" (mimeo. copy, n.d.), Box 546, Record Group 228, NA; American Management Association, *The Negro Worker* (New York, 1942), p. 7.

122. Lester B. Granger, "Report to the Annual Conference of the National Urban League," Sept. 28, 1943 (typewritten copy), p. 8, Series 1, Box 169, NULP, for a summation of Urban League activities; Committee on Discrimination in Employment, "History of the Committee on Discrimination in Employment" (unpub. report, n.d.), reel 54, Governorship Papers, HHLP; Louis Ruchames, *Race, Jobs and Politics* (New York, 1953), p. 2. President's Committee on Fair Employment Practices, Memorandum, n.d., p. 4, Box 547, Record Group 228, NA, reveals that a regional office was not opened in NYC until over a year after Executive Order 8802 was issued.

123. President's Committee on Fair Employment Practices, Press Release: Case No. 2-BR-232, n.d. (attached to Memorandum, Dec. 4, 1943), Box 547, Record Group 228, NA.

124. John J. Slocum to Daphne King, Jan. 14, 1942, Box 809, FHLP.

125. Jonathan Daniels to Monsignor Francis J. Hass, Sept. 8, 1943, OF 4245-G, FDRP.

126. La Guardia to Grace Aviles, Nov. 14, 1941, Box 2672, FHLP, for the limits of mayoral authority in this area; La Guardia to Thomas C. Desmond, March 13, 1941, Box 2566, FHLP; Resolution No. 206, City Council of New York, *Proceedings, 1941,* 1:522 and 523.

127. *New York Sun,* April 15, 1942, "Scrap Book," 215: 4, FHLP.

128. Joanne Otte, *Food Costs More in Harlem* (New York, 1943).

129. Memorandum for Leon Henderson (from M. H. McIntyre), Oct. 5, 1942, OF 93, FDRP.

130. La Guardia to Helen Hoerber, May 4, 1942, Box 2553, FHLP.

131. New York City Housing Authority, *Tenth Annual Report: 1944* (New York, 1945), pp. 10–11.

132. *Amsterdam News,* June 6, 1942, pp. 1 and 5.

133. *Amsterdam News,* March 14, 1942, p. 13; *People's Voice,* Jan. 30, 1943, p. 3.

134. Anne L. Bloch, "Syndenham Hospital: Harlem, New York," *A Monthly Summary of Events and Trends in Race Relations,* 3 (April 1946), 281–282.

135. *Amsterdam News,* Dec. 5, 1942, p. 1.

136. *Age,* July 10, 1943, p. 1.

137. *Amsterdam News,* Nov. 16, 1940, p. 2; Thomas B. Dyett to La Guardia, Aug. 6, 1942, Box 2671, FHLP, presents a different view.

138. *Herald Tribune,* June 3, 1942, "Scrap Book," 217:130, FHLP.

139. *Age,* November 28, 1942, p. 1.

140. *Amsterdam News,* Aug. 23, 1941, p. 16, for an example.

141. "The Story of the City-Wide Citizens' Committee on Harlem" (mimeo. copy, 1943), pp. 3, 4, and 8, Series 1, Box 38, NULP, for the information in this paragraph.

Chapter 4. New Yorkers' Response to the Detroit Riot

1. Charles R. Lawrence, Jr., "Race Riots in the United States, 1942–1946," in *Negro Year Book, 1941–1946,* ed. Jessie P. Guzman (Atlanta, 1947), pp. 232–257, for a synopsis of these riots.

2. Walter White, "What Caused the Detroit Riots?" Box 2574, FHLP, part two of White and Thurgood Marshall, *What Caused the Detroit Riot?* (New York, 1943).

3. Louis E. Martin, "The Truth about Sojourner Truth," *Crisis,* April 1942, pp. 112–113+, for the information in this paragraph.

4. Quoted in Alfred McClung Lee and Norman Daymond Humphrey, *Race Riot* (New York, 1967), p. 74.

5. "Erasing Color Lines," *Negro Digest,* Dec. 1942, p. 75.

6. Harvard Sitkoff, "The Detroit Riot of 1943," *Michigan History,* 53 (Fall 1969), 318–322, for the information in this paragraph.

7. Walter White, *A Man Called White* (New York, 1945), p. 225.

8. White telegram to Roosevelt, June 21, 1943, OF 93-C, FDRP.

9. Michael Carter to Roosevelt, June 25, 1943, OF 93, FDRP.

10. *Amsterdam News*, June 26, 1943, p. 1, refers to the cities of Chicago, Beaumont, El Paso, Inkster (Michigan), Detroit, Chester (Pennsylvania), Collins (Mississippi), and Camp Steward (Georgia); *Age*, June 26, 1943, p. 1.

11. *Age*, June 26, 1943, p. 6.

12. *Amsterdam News*, June 26, 1943, p. 10.

13. Stephen H. Bronz, *Roots of Negro Racial Consciousness: The 1920's* (New York, 1964), pp. 74–75.

14. Powell telegram to La Guardia, June 22, 1943, Box 2574, FHLP.

15. Powell to "My dear Fellow Citizens," June 23, 1943, Box 2574, FHLP.

16. City-Wide Citizens' Committee on Harlem telegram to La Guardia, June 23, 1943, Box 2574, FHLP, the marginal note.

17. Transcript of Adam Clayton Powell's Remarks to the City Council, June 24, 1943, pp. 1–4, Box 2574, FHLP.

18. Anonymous, "A Report on Adam C. Powell, Jr.'s Citizens' Emergency Meeting," June 24, 1943, Box 2574, FHLP, for the information in this paragraph. Julius Holland was the third leader.

19. Donald Lovell to La Guardia, June 25, 1943, Box 810, FHLP.

20. Bedford to La Guardia, June 25, 1943, Box 2574, FHLP; Bedford to La Guardia, Nov. 14, and Nov. 27, 1941, Box 752, FHLP, for Bedford's racial views, which did not represent the Roman Catholic Church or Roman Catholics collectively (although they probably were shared by a portion of his congregation at the Church of the Nativity in Brooklyn).

21. "A Former Associate of Powell," Confidential Letter to the Members of the City Council, July 3, 1943, Box 810, FHLP.

22. *People's Voice*, July 3, 1943, p. 5.

23. Ibid., July 10, 1943, p. 15.

24. Ibid., July 24, 1943, pp. 1 and 2, for the following quotation.

25. Ibid., July 31, 1943, p. 5.

26. Crosswaith to La Guardia, July 24, 1943, Box 809, FHLP.

27. The marginal note on "Digest" of Crosswaith's letter, Box 809, FHLP.

28. Lewis J. Valentine to La Guardia, June 26, 1943, Box 2574, FHLP.

29. Report: Councilman Powell's Statement Regarding a Complaint Filed by Him with the Department of Investigation to La Guardia (from Herlands), June 26, 1943, pp. 1–5, Box 2574, FHLP.

30. *Amsterdam News,* July 3, 1943, p. 10, for the number of blacks killed by policemen, which varied in press reports but was always in double figures.

31. *Amsterdam News,* July 3, 1943, p. 11.

32. Julius J. Adams, "Other Riots Will Strike Unless America Wakes Up," *Amsterdam News,* July 3, 1943, p. 21.

33. *People's Voice,* July 3, 1943, p. 1.

34. Langston Hughes, "Beaumont to Detroit, 1943," *Common Ground,* Winter 1943, p. 104.

35. *Amsterdam News,* July 10, 1943, p. 10.

36. Kenneth B. Clark, "Group Violence: A Preliminary Study of the Attitudinal Pattern of Its Acceptance and Rejection: A Study of the 1943 Harlem Race Riot," *Journal of Social Psychology,* 19 (May, 1944), 328 for the quotation, 335, concluded that blacks who condemned the riot read black newspapers more habitually than blacks who condoned disorder.

37. *New York Times,* June 25, 1943, p. 8.

38. Bonnie Robinson to La Guardia, n.d., Box 810, FHLP.

39. Stephanie S. Altan to La Guardia, July 7, 1943, Box 2574, FHLP.

40. *New York Times,* June 27, 1943, p. 13.

41. Teachers of the History and Civics Department of Boys High (Brooklyn) to La Guardia, June 30, 1943, Box 810, FHLP.

42. *People's Voice,* July 10, 1943, p. 15.

43. L. C. Barrow to Walter White, July 1, 1943, "Racial Situation Inquiries" folder, NAACP; Edward S. Lewis to Lester B. Granger, June 25, 1943, Series 1, Box 14, NULP.

44. Messages for [Lester B.] Stone, June 29, 1943, Box 809, FHLP.

45. *Amsterdam News,* July 24, 1943, p. 2.

46. *People's Voice,* July 31, 1943, p. 3.

47. Quoted in *New York Times,* July 7, 1943, p. 21.

48. Ibid., July 12, 1943, p. 31.

49. *Amsterdam News,* July 10, 1943, p. 10.

50. *Age,* July 24, 1943, p. 7.

51. O'Hara to La Guardia, June 23, 1943, Box 2574, FHLP.

52. Martin A. Remer to La Guardia, June 28, 1943 (rec'd), and Milton Bass to La Guardia, June 28, 1943, Box 810, FHLP.

53. C. T. Nesbitt to La Guardia, June 24, 1943, Box 810, FHLP, for an example; Mrs. Anna Lion to La Guardia, June 29, 1943, Box 2574, FHLP.

54. Lawrence J. Seco to La Guardia, June 25, 1943, Box 810, FHLP; Young Communist League and Citizens of Astoria to La Guardia, June 30, 1943, Box 2574, FHLP.

55. *Amsterdam News*, July 10, 1943, p. 3.

56. Homer A. Tomlinson to La Guardia, July 10, 1943, Box 2574, FHLP.

57. *Amsterdam News*, July 31, 1943, p. 2. Hawkins was pastor of St. Augustine's Presbyterian Church.

58. Allen D. Grimshaw, "Government and Social Violence: The Complexity of Guilt," in his *Racial Violence in the United States* (Chicago, 1969), p. 519, contends that violence does not always occur when tension is high, for "when government officials have taken strong stands, social violence has been prevented."

Chapter 5. Official Response to the Detroit Riot

1. Message for LBS [Lester B. Stone], June 22, 1943, Box 810, FHLP.

2. Fiorello H. La Guardia, "Statement," June 22, 1943, Box 2574, FHLP.

3. Ibid.

4. La Guardia telegram to White, June 22, 1943, Box 2574, FHLP.

5. Lewis J. Valentine to La Guardia, June 23, 1943, Box 2574, FHLP.

6. Memorandum: Information Received Regarding Racial Trouble in Detroit to the Police Commissioner (from Edward M. Butler and Emanuel Kline), June 28, 1943, p. 1, Box 2574, FHLP; White to La Guardia, July 13, 1943, Box 2574, FHLP.

7. Walter White, *A Man Called White* (New York, 1945), p. 230.

8. Edith Kaplan to La Guardia, June 14, 1943, Box 762, FHLP.

9. Official Communication to Valentine, June 23, 1943, Box 762, FHLP.

10. Memo to Stone (from Eileen [?]), n.d., Box 2574, FHLP.

11. La Guardia, "Directive," June 25, 1943, Box 2574, FHLP.

12. Jean Muir to La Guardia, July 19, 1943, Box 2574, FHLP.

13. *New York Times,* June 28, 1943, p. 23.

14. Rabbi Alexander Segal telegram to La Guardia, July 2, 1943, Box 810, FHLP.

15. White to La Guardia, June 29, 1943, Box 2574, FHLP.

16. White to Ministers, Club Presidents, Labor Organizations in Harlem and Brooklyn, June 30, 1943, Box 2574, FHLP.

17. La Guardia to Roosevelt, June 27, 1943, OF 93-C, FDRP.

18. Issues of *PM* featured detachable copies of the oath, and form post cards were circulated: "A New Yorker's Pledge," n.d., Box 809, FHLP.

19. Beecher to La Guardia, July 4, 1943 (postmark), Box 2574, FHLP.

20. Muir to La Guardia, July 19, 1943, Box 2574, FHLP.

21. La Guardia to the Clergy of New York City, n.d., Box 810, FHLP.

22. Memo to Harten (from Stone), July 13, 1943, Box 771, FHLP.

23. Siegel to Stone, July 16, 1943, Box 771, FHLP.

24. Memorandum: Complaints Received ... on Racial Incidents Referred to Police Department during ... July, on Which No Report Has Been Submitted, n.d., Box 752, FHLP.

25. *Amsterdam News,* July 17, 1943, p. 2.

26. Ibid., July 31, 1943, p. 10.

27. Ibid., July 10, 1943, p. 4.

28. *Age,* July 10, 1943, p. 1; *Daily Worker,* July 29, 1943, "Scrap Book," 249:107, FHLP.

29. La Guardia to Thomas E. Dewey, July 28, 1943, Box 2565, FHLP.

30. Helaine M. Cohen to La Guardia, July 1, 1943, Box 810, FHLP, and similar requests in this box.

31. A. Addessi postcard to La Guardia, July 15, 1943, and identically worded postcards, Box 810, FHLP.

32. White to La Guardia, July 17, 1943, Box 2574, FHLP. Why Powell was recommended as an alternate rather than a regular member of the proposed committee is unclear. Those submitting the recommendations were associated with La Guardia, thereby aware of Powell's challenge to their leadership and, more importantly, his rift with the mayor. In addition, his personality may have been considered too aggressive and opportunistic for a com-

mittee on race relations. Battle and Johnson were unable to participate in the decisions concerning regular and alternate committee members.

33. Channing H. Tobias telegram to Walter White, August 3, 1943, Box 2550, FHLP, for the implication that Tobias, White, et al. had requested the committee.

34. White to La Guardia, July 17, 1943, Box 2574, FHLP.

35. *Amsterdam News*, July 10, 1943, p. 1.

36. White to La Guardia, July 17, 1943, Box 2574, FHLP.

37. La Guardia to Roosevelt, June 27, 1943, OF 93-C, FDRP.

38. La Guardia to White, July 16, 1943, Box 2574, FHLP.

39. La Guardia to Roosevelt, June 27, 1943, OF 93-C, FDRP.

40. Joe Liring [?] to Roosevelt, July 2, 1943, OF 93-C, FDRP.

41. *Amsterdam News*, July 3, 1943, p. 10.

42. Ibid., July 17, 1943, p. 10.

43. Bass to J. Edgar Hoover, July 28, 1943, OF 93-C, FDRP. A copy was sent to FDR.

44. Memorandum to Miss [?] Thompson (from CAH), June 22, 1943, PPF 1820, FDRP.

45. Memorandum for the President (from Jonathan Daniels), June 22, 1943, PPF 1820, FDRP.

46. Bethune telegram to Roosevelt, June 22, 1943, PPF 1820, FDRP.

47. Memorandum to S. T. E. (from FDR), June 23, 1943, PPF 1820, FDRP.

48. Daniels to Granger, June 24, 1943, OF 4245-G, FDRP; Stokes to Roosevelt, June 26, 1943, Marcantonio to Roosevelt, June 16, 1943, and Murray to Roosevelt, June 18, 1943, OF 93-C, FDRP.

49. Roosevelt to Marcantonio, July 14, 1943, OF 93-C, FDRP, which was prepared by Secretary of Labor Frances Perkins and briefly reported in the *New York Times*, July 21, 1943, p. 1, probably at the Congressman's request.

50. Memorandum for the President (from G. G. T. [Grace G. Tully]), July 7, 1943, PPF 1820, FDRP.

51. Alfred McClung Lee and Norman Daymond Humphrey, *Race Riot* (New York, 1967), p. 62.

52. White telegram to Roosevelt, July 21, 1943, OF 4245-G, FDRP.

53. White to Daniels, July 22, 1943, OF 4245-G, FDRP.

54. *Age*, July 31, 1943, p. 1.

55. Biddle to Roosevelt, July 15, 1943, Box 213, HIP, which is based on extensive reports from C. E. Rhetts of the Attorney General's Office and J. Edgar Hoover, Director of the Federal Bureau of Investigation.

56. Biddle to Harold L. Ickes, July 22, 1943, Box 213, HIP.

57. Memorandum for the President (from Daniels), July 23, 1943, OF 4245-G, FDRP, for this and the following quotations.

58. Daniels to White, July 26, 1943, OF 4245-G, FDRP.

59. *Amsterdam News*, July 24, 1943, p. 1.

60. Biddle to Daniels, July 27, 1943, OF 4245-G, FDRP. The black candidates were Truman Gibson, Jr., Frank Horne, Robert Weaver, Leo Roston, Ted Poston, and William E. Clark; the white prospects included Robert A. Lovett, Adlai Stephenson [sic], Leon Keyserling, and Lawrence Appley.

61. Daniels to Monsignor Francis J. Haas, July 28, 1943, OF 4245-G, FDRP, for the form letter; "List of Persons Receiving Letters Concerning Minority Cooperation," OF 4245-G, FDRP.

62. For a comprehensive interpretation, see Harvard Sitkoff, "Racial Militancy and Interracial Violence in the Second World War," *Journal of American History*, 58 (Dec. 1971), 675–678.

63. Thomas Sancton, "Go North, Black Man!" *Negro Digest*, Aug. 1943, pp. 37–39.

64. Odum to Jonathan Daniels, Aug. 11, 1943, OF 4245-G, FDRP.

65. Frank Freidel, *FDR and the South* (Baton Rouge, 1965), pp. 72–73.

66. Louis Ruchames, *Race, Jobs and Politics* (New York, 1953), pp. 15, 71, 143, 163.

67. Quoted in Joseph P. Lash, *Eleanor and Franklin: The Story of Their Relationship, Based on Eleanor Roosevelt's Private Papers* (New York, 1971), p. 675.

68. *Pittsburgh Courier*, July 10, 1943, p. 5.

69. Quoted in Robert Shogan and Tom Craig, *The Detroit Race Riot: A Study in Violence* (New York, 1964), p. 31.

70. Memo for Mac [Marvin H. McIntyre] (from FDR), June 7, 1941, OF 93, FDRP.

71. Memorandum for the President (from McIntyre), Dec. 11, 1942, OF 93, FDRP.

72. Roosevelt to Embree, March 16, 1942, OF 93, FDRP.

73. James MacGregor Burns, *Roosevelt: The Soldier of Freedom* (New York, 1970), pp. 448–450 and 562.

74. White to Roosevelt, June 20, 1941, OF 2538, FDRP.

75. MacLean to Marvin H. McIntyre, Feb. 24, 1941, OF 93, FDRP.

76. A. Philip Randolph to Roosevelt, May 29, 1941, OF 93, FDRP, for an example.

77. Lash, *Eleanor and Franklin*, pp. 667–675; Edwin R. Embree to Marvin H. McIntyre, Feb. 3, 1942, OF 93, FDRP, and the numerous other letters in this file.

78. Shogan and Craig, *The Detroit Race Riot*, p. 13.

79. Ickes to Roosevelt, July 26, 1943, Box 213, HIP.

80. Lee and Humphrey, *Race Riot*, p. 76; Shogan and Craig, *The Detroit Race Riot*, pp. 8 and 115–118, for this interpretation of Jeffries.

Chapter 6. Harlem Boils Over

1. *PM*, August 3, 1943, p. 5, for the information in this paragraph.

2. Walter White, *A Man Called White* (New York, 1945), p. 223.

3. Walter C. Harding (Commanding Officer, 28th Precinct) to the Police Commissioner, Memorandum: Harlem Disturbance, Aug. 16, 1943, p. 2, Box 2550, FHLP (hereafter cited as Harding to Police Commissioner), for the information in this paragraph.

4. Ibid.

5. Jessie P. Guzman, *Negro Year Book, 1941–1946* (Atlanta, 1947), pp. 242–243.

6. *PM*, Aug. 3, 1943, p. 6.

7. Harding to Police Commissioner, p. 4; William Pickens, "A Useless and Excuseless Riot," c. Aug. 3, 1943, Box 752, FHLP, for reference to Bandy protecting his mother.

8. Walter White, "Behind the Harlem Riot," *The New Republic*, Aug. 16, 1943, p. 222, for the quote; Harding to Police Commissioner, p. 4.

9. *Amsterdam News*, Aug. 7, 1943, p. 4.

10. *PM*, Aug. 3, 1943, p. 6.

11. Claude Brown, *Manchild in the Promised Land* (New York, 1965), p. 13.

12. *Amsterdam News*, Aug. 7, 1943, p. 13.

13. *PM*, Aug. 3, 1943, p. 6.

14. Ralph Ellison, *Invisible Man* (New York, 1952), p. 406.

15. Pickens, "A Useless and Excuseless Riot," p. 1.

16. Harold Orlansky, *The Harlem Riot; A Study in Mass Frustration* (New York, 1943), p. 6.

17. Ellison, *Invisible Man*, p. 411.

18. *New York Times*, Aug. 2, 1943, p. 16.

19. Ibid., Aug. 3, 1943, p. 10; "Harlem's Wild Rampage," *Life*, Aug. 16, 1943, pp. 32–33, for photographs.

20. George Mulholland [?] (Commanding Officer, 6th Division) to the Police Commissioner, Memorandum: Report on Cause, Location, Crimes, Injuries, Police Details, Etc. in Connection with the Harlem Disturbance, Aug. 21, 1943 (refers to the 25th, 28th, and 32nd Precincts), pp. 2–4, Box 2550, FHLP (hereafter cited as Mulholland to Police Commissioner), for statistics in this paragraph not otherwise identified.

21. *New York Times*, Aug. 3, 1943, p. 1; William Carl Headrick, "Race Riots—Segregated Slums," *Current History*, 5 (Sept. 1943), 30.

22. *New York Times*, Aug. 3, 1943, p. 10, and Sept. 1, 1943, p. 22.

23. Harding to Police Commissioner, p. 14; for a record of the 28th Police Precinct's activities, the most accurate indication of the riot's pattern, see its radio messages, pp. 14–18.

24. William C. Beneke (Commanding Officer, 32nd Precinct) to the Police Commissioner, Memorandum: Harlem Disturbances, Aug. 16, 1943, p. 5, Box 2550, FHLP (hereafter cited as Beneke to Police Commissioner); for a record of the 32nd Precinct's activities, see its radio messages.

25. *New York Times*, Aug. 2, 1943, p. 16.

26. Harding to Police Commissioner, p. 15.

27. *New York Times*, Aug. 2, 1943, p. 16.

28. Joseph L. Reit (Commanding Officer, 23rd Precinct) to the Police Commissioner, Memorandum: Harlem Disturbance, Aug. 13, 1943, pp. 1–2, Box 2550, FHLP (hereafter cited as Reit to Police Commissioner); Christian L. Jommer [?] (Commanding Officer, 25th Precinct) to the Police Commissioner, Memorandum: Harlem Disturbance, Aug. 14, 1943, p. 2, Box 2550, FHLP (hereafter cited as Jommer to Police Commissioner).

29. *New York Times*, Aug. 2, 1943, p. 16.

30. *Amsterdam News*, Aug. 7, 1943, p. 4.

31. Reit to Police Commissioner, p. 2.

32. Complete text of La Guardia's first broadcast is in *New*

York Times, Aug. 2, 1943, p. 16; John K. Hutchens, "Couple of Matters," *New York Times,* Aug. 8, 1943, 2:7, for schedules of mayoral broadcasts of August 2.

33. White, *A Man Called White,* p. 237; *Amsterdam News,* Aug. 7, 1943, p. 4, for Yergan.

34. Press Release: Transcript of La Guardia's Broadcast from City Hall, Aug. 2, 1943, pp. 1–2, Box 2550, FHLP.

35. *New York Times,* Aug. 3, 1943, pp. 1, 10, for information in this paragraph.

36. *New York Times,* Aug. 3, 1943, p. 1.

37. Ibid., Aug. 4, 1943, p. 8, Aug. 5, 1943, p. 17, and Aug. 13, 1943, p. 11.

38. Edward M. Bernecker to Dr. George Baehr, "Report of Emergency Medical Service of New York City during Harlem Disturbance," Aug. 5, 1943, pp. 1 for the quotation, 2–3, OF 4245-G, FDRP (hereafter cited as Bernecker to Baehr), for information in this paragraph.

39. Harding to Police Commissioner, p. 16.

40. Bernecker to Baehr, p. 3, for information in this paragraph.

41. Press Release: Transcript of La Guardia's Broadcast from City Hall, Aug. 2, 1943, p. 2.

42. Daniel P. Woolley to La Guardia, Aug. 3, 1943, Box 2550, FHLP, for these statistics and the following quotations.

43. Memo: Phone from Commissioner Woolley to La Guardia, Aug. 3, 1943, Box 2550, FHLP.

44. Daniel P. Woolley, "Report on Food Conditions in Harlem," Aug. 6, 1943, Box 2550, FHLP.

45. Harding to Police Commissioner, pp. 15–18, 41–45, for information in this paragraph.

46. Harding to Police Commissioner, p. 45.

47. *People's Voice,* Aug. 7, 1943, p. 2, and *New York Times,* Aug. 3, 1943, p. 1, for agreement on this statistic.

48. Beneke to Police Commissioner, pp. 22–26.

49. William R. Bayes to La Guardia, Aug. 4, 1943, Box 752, FHLP; *New York Times,* Aug. 5, 1943, p. 17.

Chapter 7. Police, Hoodlums, Race, and Riot

1. "Babes in Harlem," *PM,* Aug. 2, 1943, p. 11.

2. Dyett to La Guardia, Aug. 5, 1943, Box 2550, FHLP.

3. Powell telegram to La Guardia, Aug. 2, 1943, Box 752, FHLP.

4. Eugene Faulkner to La Guardia, Aug. 30, 1943, Box 2550, FHLP.

5. Yergan to La Guardia, Aug. 5, 1943, Box 752, FHLP.

6. Walter C. Harding (Commanding Officer, 28th Precinct) to the Police Commissioner, Memorandum: Harlem Disturbance, Aug. 16, 1943, pp. 37–40, Box 2550, FHLP (hereafter cited as Harding to Police Commissioner); William C. Beneke (Commanding Officer, 32nd Precinct) to the Police Commissioner, Memorandum: Harlem Disturbances, Aug. 16, 1943, p. 21, Box 2550, FHLP (hereafter cited as Beneke to Police Commissioner).

7. Wilkins telegram to La Guardia, June 23, 1943, Box 2574, FHLP.

8. White to La Guardia, July 13, 1943, Box 2574, FHLP.

9. Walter White, "What Caused the Detroit Riots?" pp. 14, for this quotation, 13 and 16 for the following quotations, Box 2574, FHLP.

10. Phone Conversation between John O'Connell and Edward M. Butler, June 23, 1943, Box 2574, FHLP.

11. Memorandum: Information Received Regarding Racial Trouble in Detroit to the Police Commissioner (from Edward M. Butler and Emanuel Kline), June 28, 1943, p. 5, Box 2574, FHLP (hereafter cited as Butler and Kline, "Racial Trouble in Detroit").

12. Walter White, *A Man Called White* (New York, 1945), p. 230.

13. "Methods Used in Handling Disorder amongst Colored and Whites in the City of Detroit," n.d., Box 2574, FHLP, designated "Mayor" or "Police" to each suggestion, indicating responsibility for its implementation, and includes plans not associated with the police directly: quelling rumors, arraigning prisoners, and providing food in the riot area.

14. Elijah Crump to La Guardia, Aug. 2, 1943, Box 2550, FHLP.

15. Leonard Johnson to La Guardia, Aug. 10, 1943, Box 2550, FHLP.

16. *People's Voice*, Aug. 7, 1943, p. 3.

17. La Guardia to Dewey, Aug. 2, 1943, Box 2550, FHLP. By having the Guard on ready reserve, the four to six hours needed for mobilization would have been taken already.

18. Transcript of La Guardia's Broadcast, Aug. 2, 1943, Box 2550, FHLP, for this and the final quotation in this paragraph.

19. *People's Voice*, Aug. 14, 1943, p. 5.

20. La Guardia telegram to John T. McManus, Aug. 2, 1943, Box 2550, FHLP.

21. *Amsterdam News,* Aug. 7, 1943, p. 3.

22. Sylvia Breitberg to La Guardia, Aug. 4, 1943, Box 2550, FHLP.

23. Warren Brown, "Report on Harlem," Aug. 2, 1943, Box 2550, FHLP; La Guardia to Ernest Angell, Aug. 4, 1943, Box 2550, FHLP.

24. *PM,* Aug. 3, 1943, p. 6.

25. *Amsterdam News,* Aug. 21, 1943, p. 11.

26. *PM,* Aug. 3, 1943, p. 6.

27. *Amsterdam News,* Aug. 14, 1943, p. 11.

28. Shatsky to La Guardia, Aug. 5, 1943, Box 2550, FHLP.

29. "Review of the Month," *Monthly Summary of Events and Trends in Race Relations,* 1 (Aug. 1943), 2.

30. *Amsterdam News,* Aug. 21, 1943, p. 10.

31. Cleveland G. Allen to La Guardia, Aug. 3, 1943, and Elmer, Cora, and Lora Cummings to La Guardia, Aug. 3, 1943, Box 752, FHLP.

32. Harold Orlansky, *The Harlem Riot* (New York, 1943), p. 3.

33. "A Law-Abiding Citizen" to La Guardia, Aug. 8, 1943, Box 752, FHLP.

34. Bellena E. Davis to La Guardia, Aug. 7, 1943 (rec'd), Box 2550, FHLP.

35. Bishop J. Pierce Shields (pastor of Zion Gospel Church in Jamaica) to La Guardia, Aug. 14, 1943 (rec'd), Box 752, FHLP.

36. Quoted in *Amsterdam News,* Aug. 21, 1943, p. 10.

37. Brown, "Report on Harlem."

38. Simons to La Guardia, n.d., Box 752, FHLP.

39. Vivian C. Mason et al. to La Guardia, Aug. 6, 1943, Box 752, FHLP.

40. White to Harlem and Brooklyn Ministers, Club Presidents and Labor Organizations, June 28, 1943, "New York Situation: Correspondence" folder, NAACP.

41. Hall to La Guardia, Nov. 10, 1941 (rec'd), Box 752, FHLP.

42. "A Negro Resident of Harlem" to La Guardia, Oct. 4, 1941, and Ashley L. Totten to La Guardia, Dec. 1, 1941, Box 752, FHLP.

43. F. Jacobs to La Guardia, Nov. 6, 1941, Box 752, FHLP.

44. James H. Hubert to La Guardia, Nov. 7, 1941, Box 752, FHLP; *Amsterdam News,* Nov. 29, 1941, p. 8, for the quotation.

45. "A True Black American" to La Guardia, Aug. 3, 1943, Box 752, FHLP.

46. Orlansky, *The Harlem Riot*, pp. 10 and 22.

47. John J. O'Connell to the Police Commissioner, Memorandum: Ages of Persons Arrested during the Harlem Disturbances, Aug. 4, 1943, Box 2550, FHLP: of 88 women arrested, 63 were adult.

48. John T. Baissici [?] (Commanding Officer, 5th Division) to the Police Commissioner, Memorandum: Harlem Disturbances, Aug. 25, 1943, p. 1, Box 2550, FHLP (hereafter cited as Baissici to Police Commissioner).

49. "Press Statement by Walter White," Aug. 2, 1943, "New York Situation: Correspondence" folder, NAACP.

50. John J. Ryan (Assistant Chief Inspector, 18th Division) to the Police Commissioner, Memorandum: Harlem Disturbance, Aug. 14, 1943, pp. 1 and 2, Box 2550, FHLP.

51. Alex Haley and Malcolm X, *The Autobiography of Malcolm X* (New York, 1964), p. 102.

52. Neil J. Smelser, *Theory of Collective Behavior* (New York, 1962), p. 259.

53. Orlansky, *The Harlem Riot*, p. 10.

54. Baissici to Police Commissioner, p. 4, Harding to Police Commissioner, p. 35, Beneke to Police Commissioner, pp. 18, 19, Box 2550, FHLP.

55. Beneke to Police Commissioner, p. 24, for the statistic.

56. *People's Voice*, Aug. 28, 1943, p. 5.

57. Joseph Burns to La Guardia, Aug. 3, 1943, Box 752, FHLP.

58. Baissici to Police Commissioner, p. 2.

59. *Amsterdam News*, Aug. 14, 1943, p. 10.

60. Harding to Police Commissioner, p. 4.

61. Baissici to Police Commissioner, p. 1.

62. Orlansky, *The Harlem Riot*, p. 5.

63. Claude Brown, *Manchild in the Promised Land* (New York, 1965), p. 14.

64. Brown, "Report on Harlem".

65. Kenneth B. Clark and James Barker, "The Zoot Effect in Personality: A Race Riot Participant," *Journal of Abnormal and Social Psychology*, 40 (1945), 143–148, passim.

66. Anonymous to La Guardia, August 9, 1943 (postmarked), Box 2550, FHLP.

67. Robert K. Merton, *Social Theory and Social Structure* (rev.; New York, 1957), pp. 131–160.

68. Orlansky, *The Harlem Riot*, p. 21.

69. Smelser, *Theory of Collective Behavior*, pp. 257–261.

70. Orlansky, *The Harlem Riot*, p. 7.

71. Baissici to Police Commissioner, p. 6.

72. Young Citizens' Committee of New York City on Race Relations, "Digest: Racial Gang Warfare" (typewritten copy, 1943), p. 3, Box 2574, FHLP.

73. Allen D. Grimshaw, "Changing Patterns of Racial Violence in the United States" in his *Racial Violence in the United States* (Chicago, 1969), p. 493.

74. Russell Dynes and E. L. Quarantelli, "What Looting in Civil Disturbances Really Means," *Trans-action*, 5 (May, 1968), 13.

75. Harry Shatsky to La Guardia, Aug. 5, 1943, Box 2550, FHLP.

76. Clark to La Guardia, Aug. 2, 1943, Box 752, FHLP; letters of Mrs. Villaflar, Clarel A. Spearing, Walter R. Thomas and Elmer, Cora and Lora Cummings in Box 752, FHLP.

77. O. S. Ceola and B. Lee to La Guardia, Aug. 1, 1943, Box 2550, FHLP, and Minnie P. Littlejohn to La Guardia, Aug. 4, 1943, Box 752, FHLP.

78. Littlejohn to La Guardia, Aug. 4, 1943, Box 752, FHLP.

79. Joseph Pelot to La Guardia, Aug. 3, 1943, Box 752, FHLP.

80. *Amsterdam News*, Aug. 14, 1943, p. 11.

81. Kenneth B. Clark, "Group Violence," *Journal of Social Psychology*, 19 (May 1944), p. 321, indicates that forty blacks (comprising 60 percent of those interviewed) rejected the riot, feeling personal guilt and shame for its occurrence.

82. Mason to Roosevelt, Dec. 22, 1943, OF 93, FDRP.

83. Memo to the Mayor (from Lester B. Stone), Aug. 2, 1943, Box 2550, FHLP.

84. Michael J. Quill and Douglass L. MacMahon to La Guardia, Aug. 3, 1943, Box 752, FHLP, and similar telegrams and letters in this box.

85. *People's Voice*, Aug. 14, 1943, p. 5.

86. R. J. Campbell telegram to La Guardia, Aug. 2, 1943, Box 2550, FHLP; Joseph J. Yedowitz to La Guardia, Aug. 2, 1943, Box 752, FHLP; James H. Sheldon telegram to La Guardia, Aug. 2, 1943, Box 2550, FHLP.

87. Charles Garland telegram to La Guardia, Aug. 2, 1943, Box 2550, FHLP.

88. Thomas Myers to La Guardia, Aug. 9, 1943 (rec'd), Box 752, FHLP; Reverend A. L. Hughes to La Guardia, Aug. 3, 1943, Box 752, FHLP.

89. Percy Marks to La Guardia, Aug. 6, 1943, Box 2550, FHLP.

90. Henricks telegram to La Guardia, Aug. 2, 1943, Box 2550, FHLP.

91. Beulah Bell-Morris to La Guardia, Aug. 2, 1943, Box 752, FHLP.

92. Shapiro to La Guardia, Aug. 6, 1943, Box 752, FHLP.

93. Sam Diamond telegram to La Guardia, Aug. 2, 1943, and Melvina Scranton Eberle telegram to La Guardia, Aug. 2, 1943, Box 2550, FHLP.

94. One Hundred Negro and White New Yorkers, Wholesale and Warehouse Workers Union (Local 65) telegram to La Guardia, Aug. 2, 1943, Box 2550, FHLP.

95. Mary L. Fairley to La Guardia, Aug. 3, 1943, Box 2550, FHLP.

96. Anthony DiShapio to La Guardia, n.d., Box 2550, FHLP; "A Group of White People" to La Guardia, Aug. 3, 1943, and "Brooklyn" to La Guardia, Aug. 3, 1943 (rec'd), Box 752, FHLP.

97. Anonymous to La Guardia, Sept. 30, 1943, Box 752, FHLP.

98. "A Reader" to Editor, *New York Times*, Aug. 18, 1943, Box 2550, FHLP.

99. Walter White, "Behind the Harlem Riot," *New Republic*, Aug. 16, 1943, p. 222. During the riot, La Guardia had investigated a false rumor that whites were gathering near New York Central's 125th Street station.

Chapter 8. Conditions for Riot

1. James P. Comer, "The Dynamics of Black and White Violence" in *Violence in America: Historical and Comparative Perspectives*, ed. Hugh D. Graham and Ted R. Gurr (Washington, D.C., 1969), 2:349.

2. H. Otto Dahlke, "Race and Minority Riots—A Study in the Typology of Violence," *Social Forces*, 30 (May 1952), 419–425.

3. *PM*, Aug. 3, 1943, p. 8.

4. Vasquez to La Guardia, Aug. 10, 1943 (rec'd), Box 752, FHLP.

5. Harry Hartman to La Guardia, Aug. 3, 1943, Box 752, FHLP.

6. "The Reminiscences of Lester B. Granger" (COHC), 2:183.

7. *Amsterdam News,* Aug. 7, 1943, p. 13.

8. Allan to La Guardia, Aug. 4, 1943, Box 2550, FHLP.

9. *Amsterdam News,* April 17, 1943, p. 11; "This Is Our Common Destiny: Negro, Jew United thru History by Persecution," *People's Voice,* July 24, 1943, p. 6.

10. William Pickens, "A Useless and Excuseless Riot," c. Aug. 3, 1943, p. 2, Box 752, FHLP.

11. Jane Benedict to La Guardia, Aug. 3, 1943, Box 752, FHLP.

12. Margolis to La Guardia, Aug. 4, 1943, Box 2550, FHLP.

13. "A Group of White People" to La Guardia, Aug. 3, 1943, Box 752, FHLP.

14. Mrs. E. Brown to La Guardia, March 17, 1943, Box 752, FHLP.

15. Pauline Helfrich to La Guardia, April 20, 1943, Box 752, FHLP.

16. "A Citizen" to La Guardia, June 29, 1943, Box 810, FHLP.

17. La Guardia to Rear Admiral E. J. Marquart, Dec. 26, 1942, Box 2564, FHLP.

18. Forrestal to La Guardia, Jan. 11, 1943, Box 2564, FHLP.

19. Lawrence Ervin to La Guardia, Jan. 19, 1943, Box 2546, FHLP.

20. *New York Times,* Feb. 3, 1943, "Scrap Book," 235:19, FHLP.

21. La Guardia to William Wilson, Jan. 6, 1943, Box 2564, FHLP.

22. La Guardia to Leathe Hemachandra, Jan. 26, 1943, Box 2546, FHLP.

23. *Amsterdam News,* May 1, 1943, p. 1.

24. Ibid., May 8, 1943, p. 7.

25. Andy Razaf, " 'Guilty' Savoy," *People's Voice,* May 22, 1943, p. 26.

26. *Amsterdam News,* May 1, 1943, p. 1.

27. Joe Bostic, "What's Behind Savoy Closing?" *People's Voice,* May 1, 1943, p. 3.

28. *Amsterdam News,* May 8, 1943, p. 7.

29. Ibid., May 15, 1943, p. 1.

30. *People's Voice,* May 8, 1943, pp. 1, 3.

31. Quoted in *Amsterdam News*, May 1, 1943, p. 1.

32. *Amsterdam News*, May 8, 1943, p. 7.

33. *People's Voice*, May 1, 1943, p. 3.

34. John Anderson to La Guardia, June 2, 1943, Box 762, FHLP.

35. M. Harris to La Guardia, June 2, 1943, Box 762, FHLP.

36. Joseph Kertz to La Guardia, June 16, 1943, Box 762, FHLP.

37. Leonard E. Golditch to La Guardia, July 24, 1943, Box 762, FHLP.

38. Algernon Black, A. Clayton Powell, Sr., and Charles A. Collier, Jr., to La Guardia, Aug. 3, 1943, Box 752, FHLP.

39. David Levidow to La Guardia, Sept. 7, 1943 (postmark), Box 752, FHLP.

40. Memo Concerning Stuyvesant Town, Inc., Aug. 9, 1943, Box 2554, FHLP.

41. Memorandum for the Attorney General (from C. E. Rhetts), July 12, 1943, p. 8, Box 213, HIP.

42. Quoted in Fern M. Eckman, *The Furious Passage of James Baldwin* (New York, 1966), p. 93.

43. Kenneth B. Clark, "Group Violence," *Journal of Social Psychology*, 19 (May 1944), 329.

44. Walter C. Harding to the Police Commissioner (Commanding Officer, 28th Precinct), Memorandum: Harlem Disturbance, Aug. 16, 1943, p. 2, Box 2550, FHLP.

45. Victor H. Bernstein, "Opinion," *PM*, Aug. 3, 1943, p. 2.

46. Mrs. [?] Williams to La Guardia, Aug. 3, 1943, Box 2550, FHLP.

47. Eleanor Roosevelt to La Guardia, Aug. 4, 1943, Box 2572, FHLP.

48. Walter White, *A Man Called White* (New York, 1945), p. 234.

49. Warren Brown, "Report on Harlem Riot," Aug. 2, 1943, Box 2550, FHLP.

50. Leonard Johnson to La Guardia, Aug. 10, 1943, Box 2550, FHLP.

51. *Amsterdam News*, Aug. 28, 1943, p. 10.

52. Totten to La Guardia, Aug. 3, 1943, Box 752, FHLP.

53. Walton Frederick to La Guardia, Aug. 5, 1943, Box 2550, FHLP.

54. *Age*, Aug. 14, 1943, pp. 1 and 5.

55. Sidney J. Ungar to La Guardia, Aug. 3, 1943, Box 2550, FHLP.

56. Louis E. Milarto to La Guardia, Aug. 4, 1943, Box 2550, FHLP, for Pegler's column of August 4, which appeared in the *World Telegram*.

57. Eleanor Roosevelt to La Guardia, Aug. 4, 1943, Box 2572, FHLP.

58. La Guardia to Mrs. Franklin D. Roosevelt, Aug. 6, 1943, Box 2572, FHLP.

59. Ibid.; Gilbert J. Rhodes to La Guardia, Aug. 3, 1943, "New York Situation" folder, NAACP, for the estimate that according to population percentages black policemen should have numbered 3,000.

60. La Guardia to Mrs. Franklin D. Roosevelt, Aug. 7, 1943, Box 2572, FHLP.

61. La Guardia to Mrs. Franklin D. Roosevelt, Aug. 6 and Aug. 7, 1943, Box 2572, FHLP.

62. *Amsterdam News*, Aug. 14, 1943, p. 11.

63. Ibid., Jan. 17, 1942, pp. 1 and 25.

64. *People's Voice*, April 18, 1942, p. 21.

65. *Amsterdam News*, May 9, 1942, p. 1.

66. WMCA Radio Broadcast, "The Negro and the War," March 12, 1944 (mimeo. copy), p. 4, Series 1, Box 169, NULP.

67. *New York Post*, Aug. 3, 1943, p. 41.

68. *Amsterdam News*, June 19, 1943, p. 1.

69. *New York Post*, Aug. 3, 1941, p. 41.

70. White to Stimson, Aug. 6, 1943, "New York Situation—Correspondence" folder, NAACP.

71. Coleman to La Guardia, Aug. 20, 1943, Box 752, FHLP.

72. Quoted in *People's Voice*, Aug. 28, 1943, p. 5.

73. *Daily Worker*, Aug. 8, 1943, "Scrap Book," 250:63, FHLP.

Chapter 9. Aftermath: Official Response and Local Programs

1. John J. Harkins to Roosevelt, Aug. 2, 1943, OF 4061, FDRP; a letter from the National Federation for Constitutional Liberties, quoted in *Amsterdam News*, Aug. 7, 1943, p. 11.

2. M. Moran Weston in *Amsterdam News*, Aug. 14, 1943, p. 11.

3. Joe Casper Holland to La Guardia, Aug. 3, 1943, Box 2550, FHLP.

4. Memorandum for the President (from Jonathan Daniels), Aug. 2, 1943, JDP.

5. Daniels to John J. Harkins, Aug. 9, 1943, OF 4061, FDRP.

6. Memorandum for the President (from Jonathan Daniels), Aug. 10, 1943, JDP.

7. Memorandum for the President (from Jonathan Daniels), Aug. 2, 1943, JDP.

8. Biddle to Roosevelt, July 15, 1943, Box 213, HIP.

9. Ickes to Roosevelt, July 16, 1943, Box 213, HIP, for an example.

10. Memorandum: The Minority Situation Today, a Suggested Program to Daniels (from David K. Niles [?]), Aug. 1943, and Newman Jeffrey, "An OCD [Office of Civilian Defense] Plan to Alleviate Racial Tension," Aug. 5, 1943, OF 4245-G, FDRP.

11. "Findings of the Continuous Committees of the Durham and Atlanta Conferences," n.d., OF 4245-G, FDRP.

12. Odum to Daniels, Aug. 11, 1943, OF 4245-G, FDRP. The original idea for such a committee may have come from Edwin R. Embree of the Julius Rosenwald Fund, who proposed a presidential commission on race relations early in 1942. Richard M. Dalfiume suggests that Embree "probably passed along his idea to Odum." Dalfiume, "The 'Forgotten Years' of the Negro Revolution," *Journal of American History*, 55 (June 1968), 105, n. 71.

13. Odum to Daniels, Aug. 23, 1943, OF 4245-G, FDRP, for this and the following quotations.

14. Odum to Daniels, Aug. 23, 1943, and attached memorandum, OF 4245-G, FDRP. The list includes Will Alexander, Hugo Black, James B. Conant, Frank Graham, Charles Johnson, Howard W. Odum, Homer Rainey, Robert Sproul, and Donald Young. Daniels added Edwin Embree and Mordecai Johnson, and crossed out Lewis Mumford, Beardsley Ruml and R. R. Wright, although it is not clear why. Some of Daniels' notations are: "No Jew"; "bring in Spanish Americans"; "Labor?"

15. Daniels to Odum, Sept. 1, 1943, OF 4245-G, FDRP.

16. Odum to Daniels, Sept. 6, 1943, OF 4245-G, FDRP.

17. Daniels to Odum, Sept. 10, 1943, OF 4245-G, FDRP.

18. Ickes to Oscar L. Chapman, Aug. 11, 1943, Box 213, HIP, referring to F.D.R.'s disinterest in the racial crisis.

19. Memorandum for Daniels (from FDR), Aug. 16, 1943, and Aug. 17, 1943, OF 93-C, FDRP.

20. Memorandum for Daniels, Aug. 16, 1943, OF 93-C, FDRP.

I could find no record of Biddle's reaction to Daniels' memorandum; however, from the beginning Biddle influenced presidential decisions on the racial crisis and consistently advised against Roosevelt taking any vigorous public action.

21. Granger to Biddle, Aug. 19, 1943, OF 4245-G, FDRP.

22. Roosevelt, for example, had canceled the FEPC's southwest hearings on discrimination against Mexicans and Mexican Americans because the State Department contended they would hinder relations with Mexico: Sumner Welles to Roosevelt, June 20, 1942, OF 4245-G, FDRP.

23. Odum to Daniels, Aug. 11, 1943 and attached memorandum, n.d., OF 4245-G, FDRP.

24. Ickes to Roosevelt, July 26, 1943, Box 213, HIP. Ickes' long membership in the NAACP probably disqualified him, in Roosevelt's mind, as an adviser on the racial crisis.

25. Ickes to Roosevelt, Sept. 23, 1943, OF 93, FDRP.

26. Ickes to Roosevelt, Aug. 11, 1943, OF 88, FDRP.

27. Roosevelt to Granger, Sept. 7, 1943, PPF 902, FDRP; Memorandum to William D. Hassett (from Elmer Davis), Sept. 6, 1943, PPF 902, FDRP.

28. Compare Roosevelt's revised draft with Davis' original one, ibid.

29. *Amsterdam News*, Oct. 9, 1943, p. 10-A.

30. Memorandum (from A. M. B. [?]), Dec. 8, 1943, OF 4245-G, FDRP.

31. Memorandum: Sunday Broadcast, Unity (from Lester B. Stone), Aug. 7, 1943, Box 2636, FHLP. The series had been planned before the riot.

32. La Guardia to Colman, Sept. 20, 1943, Box 2691, FHLP.

33. La Guardia, Radio Address: Unity At Home—Victory Abroad, Sept. 9, 1943, Box 2586, FHLP.

34. La Guardia to Morris Kritzman, Oct. 22, 1943, Box 2574, FHLP, for information in this paragraph.

35. Quoted in *PM*, Oct. 19, 1943, "Scrap Book," 255:139, FHLP.

36. Robert Moses to La Guardia, Sept. 23, 1943, Box 2534, FHLP.

37. Text of Mayor F. H. La Guardia's Sunday Broadcast, Nov. 21, 1943, Box 2533, FHLP.

38. *Opportunity*, Oct. 1943, p. 177. On Aug. 11, an office was opened in Harlem at West 136 Street.

39. Memorandum: Sunday Broadcast (from Lester B. Stone), Aug. 15, 1943, Box 2636, FHLP.

40. *People's Voice*, Aug. 28, 1943, pp. 3 and 5.

41. *New York Times*, Sept. 14, 1943, "Scrap Book," 252:140, FHLP.

42. Memorandum: Sunday Broadcast (from Lester B. Stone), Aug. 15, 1943, Box 2636, FHLP, for these statistics and the following quotation.

43. *Amsterdam News*, Aug. 21, 1943, p. 1.

44. *New York Times*, Sept. 12, 1943, "Scrap Book," 252:122, FHLP.

45. *People's Voice*, Nov. 6, 1943, p. 4.

46. *PM*, Oct. 13, 1943, "Scrap Book," 255:65, FHLP, for this and the following information.

47. *Daily Worker*, Oct. 23 and Oct. 24, 1943, "Scrap Book," 256:39 and 51, FHLP.

48. Ibid., Oct. 23, 1943, "Scrap Book," 256:39, FHLP.

49. Muir to La Guardia, Sept. 21, 1943, Box 809, FHLP.

50. "Report of the Citizens Emergency Conference for Interracial Unity" (mimeo. copy, 1943), p. 6, for the statistics and "Call to Citizens Emergency Conference for Interracial Unity," n.d., p. 1, for the quotation, "Citizens Emergency Conference for Interracial Unity" folder, NAACP.

51. "Report of the Citizens Emergency Conference for Interracial Unity," p. 11, for this quotation, 11–15 for the following information.

52. "Pledge of Unity" Scroll, Aug. 29, 1943, Box 2574, FHLP.

53. Dr. Adele Sincular and Stella Holt to La Guardia, Dec. 7, 1943, Box 2574, FHLP.

54. Jeanette Katz to La Guardia, Sept. 27, 1943, Box 752, FHLP.

55. Michelesen to Roosevelt, Dec. 18, 1943, OF 93, FDRP. Roosevelt's heavy work load would not permit him to comply with her request.

56. *Amsterdam News*, Nov. 20, 1943, p. 12-A.

57. Stella Holt to Newbold Morris, Oct. 4, 1943, Box 2574, FHLP.

58. *Amsterdam News*, Nov. 13, 1943, p. 1-A; *Monthly Summary of Events and Trends in Race Relations*, 3 (Nov. 1943), 6.

59. Daniel P. Woolley, "Report on Food Conditions in Harlem," Aug. 6, 1943, Box 2550, FHLP.

60. Philipp to La Guardia, Aug. 9, 1943, Box 2550, FHLP; the emphasis is Philipp's.

61. Memorandum: Colonel Leopold Philipp for James Harten (from the Department of Investigation[?]), Aug. 23, 1943, Box 2550, FHLP; Philipp to Lehman, Nov. 22, 1941, reel 42, Governorship Papers, HHLP, for Philipp's genuine concern for Harlem residents.

62. Quoted in Louis H. Robinson to Harold C. Ostertag, Nov. 2, 1943, Box 2550, FHLP.

63. Memorandum: Uptown Chamber of Commerce Meeting to Assistant Chief Inspector (from George Mulholland), Sept. 1, 1943, pp. 1–3, Box 2550, FHLP.

64. *Uptown New York*, Aug./Sept. 1943, p. 4.

65. Ibid., p. 3.

66. Lazarus to Harold C. Ostertag, Nov. 10, 1943, Box 2550, FHLP.

67. Lazarus to Wilkinson, Nov. 12, 1943, Box 2550, FHLP.

68. Danahy to La Guardia, Nov. 8, 1943, Box 2550, FHLP.

69. "Petition: Fiorello H. La Guardia's Application for an Order Expurging from the Records of the County Court of Kings County a Certain 'Presentment' made by the Aug. 1943 Grand Jury of Kings County," Nov. 23, 1943, Box 2534, FHLP.

70. White to Nathan R. Sobel, Dec. 3, 1943, Box 2534, FHLP, for an example.

71. White to La Guardia, Nov. 30, 1943, Box 2574, FHLP.

72. Betty Cohen to Black and Cohen to Tobias, Dec. 3, 1943, Box 2574, FHLP.

73. Morris H. Horowitz to La Guardia, Dec. 1, 1943, Box 752, FHLP.

74. Arthur Goddard to La Guardia, Aug. 19, 1943, Box 752, FHLP, for an example.

75. La Guardia to White, Aug. 6, 1943, Box 2550, FHLP.

76. Algernon Black, Adam Clayton Powell, Sr., and Charles A. Collier, Jr., to La Guardia, Aug. 3, 1943, Box 752, FHLP.

77. La Guardia to Randolph, Aug. 6, 1943, Box 2574, FHLP.

78. Randolph and Mabel K. Staupers to La Guardia, Sept. 13, 1943, Box 2574, FHLP; Citizens' Committee on Better Race Relations, "Recommendations for Action," 1943 (printed program), n.p., "New York Situation" folder, NAACP.

79. La Guardia to Rockefeller, Dec. 27, 1943, Box 2549, FHLP.

80. Beardsley Ruml to La Guardia, Dec. 8, 1943, Box 2549, FHLP. Ruml was asked on December 6 to chair the Mayor's Committee on Unity.

81. White to La Guardia, Dec. 13, 1943, Box 2546, FHLP.

82. La Guardia to White, Dec. 15, 1943, Box 2546, FHLP.

83. La Guardia to Rockefeller, Dec. 27, 1943, Box 2549, FHLP.

84. Gunnar Myrdal et al., *An American Dilemma: The Negro Problem and Modern Democracy* (2 vols.; New York, 1944), had been in progress since 1938. Nor was evidence found of La Guardia having been influenced by the earlier ideas of Edwin R. Embree or Howard W. Odum.

85. Ruml to La Guardia, Dec. 8, 1943, Box 2549, FHLP.

86. Rockefeller to La Guardia, Dec. 30, 1943, Box 2549, FHLP.

87. La Guardia to Lehman, Feb. 5, 1944, Box 2549, FHLP.

88. *New York Times,* Feb. 28, 1944, p. 19; Dan W. Dodson to La Guardia, Sept. 14, 1943, Box 864, FHLP. Committee members included Edmond B. Butler, former NYC Housing Commissioner; Dr. Henry Sloane Coffin, president, Union Theological Seminary; Morris Hadley, president, NYPL; Fannie Hurst, author; Reverend John H. Johnson, St. Martin's Episcopal Church; Alfred McClosker, president, Mutual Broadcasting System; Nathan D. Perlman, Justice, Special Sessions Court; Allan M. Pope, Welfare Council; Channing Tobias. Dan W. Dodson was appointed executive director of research.

89. Memorandum to Roy Wilkins et al., May 1, 1944, "Racial Tension—Harlem" folder, and Minutes of Confidential Meeting with Mayor La Guardia, June 30, 1944, "Racial Situation—Harlem" folder, NAACP.

90. *New York Times,* Dec. 11, 1945, p. 17, and Dec. 8, 1948, p. 40.

Chapter 10. The Riot in Historical Perspective

1. For information in this and the next two paragraphs, see: Richard Maxwell Brown, *Strain of Violence: Historical Studies of American Violence and Vigilantism* (New York, 1975), pp. 205–235; August Meier and Elliot Rudwick, "Black Violence in the 20th Century," 2:307–316, and Morris Janowitz, "Patterns of Collective Racial Violence," 2:317–339, both in *Violence in America: Historical and Comparative Perspectives,* ed. Hugh D.

Graham and Ted Gurr (Washington, D.C., 1969); Allen D. Grimshaw, "Changing Patterns of Racial Violence in the United States" in his *Racial Violence in the United States* (Chicago, 1969), pp. 488–501; Louis H. Masotti et al., *A Time to Burn? An Evaluation of the Present Crisis in Race Relations* (Chicago, 1969), pp. 93–134.

2. Meier and Rudwick, "Black Violence in the 20th Century," p. 311.

3. For information in this paragraph, see Elliot M. Rudwick, *Race Riot at East St. Louis, July 2, 1917* (Carbondale, Ill., 1964), pp. 217–233; William M. Tuttle, Jr., *Race Riot: Chicago in the Red Summer of 1919* (New York, 1970), p. 261, for the quote below.

4. For comparisons of the Harlem riots of 1935 and 1943, from which I have drawn for this and the following paragraph, see: Allen D. Grimshaw, "A Study in Social Violence: Urban Race Riots in the United States" (Ph.D. diss., University of Pennsylvania, 1959), pp. 374–377; Robert M. Fogelson, *Violence as Protest: A Study of Riots and Ghettos* (Garden City, N.Y., 1971), pp. 17–22.

5. Adam Clayton Powell, Jr., *Marching Blacks* (New York, 1967), p. 72.

6. Hamilton Basso, "The Riot in Harlem," *New Republic,* April 3, 1935, pp. 209–210.

7. Roi Ottley and Willaim J. Weatherby, eds., *The Negro in New York: An Informal Social History* (New York, 1967), p. 276; Fogelson, *Violence as Protest,* p. 19, cites one dead and more than 100 injured.

8. Quoted in *People's Voice,* Aug. 14, 1943, p. 5.

9. Walter White, "What Caused the Detroit Riots?" p. 2, Box 2574, FHLP.

10. WMCA Radio Broadcast, "Democracy and Race Justice," May 24, 1943 (mimeo. copy), p. 3, Series 1, Box 169, NULP.

11. *Amsterdam News,* Aug. 14, 1943, pp. 1 and 10.

12. Memorandum for the Attorney General (from John Edgar Hoover), July 8, 1943, Box 213, HIP.

13. Memorandum for the Attorney General (from C. E. Rhetts), July 12, 1943, p. 7, Box 213, HIP.

14. La Guardia to Thomas E. Dewey, Feb. 27, 1943, Box 2565, FHLP, for 662 NYPD vacancies five months before riot; Memorandum for the Police Commissioner (from George Crumby [?]),

Dec. 7, 1943, Box 2533, FHLP, for 1455 NYPD vacancies four months after riot.

15. Rudwick, *Race Riot at East St. Louis*, p. 228.

16. Alfred McClung Lee and Norman Daymond Humphrey, *Race Riot* (New York, 1967), pp. 98–99.

17. Allen D. Grimshaw, "Actions of Police and the Military in American Race Riots" in his *Racial Violence in the United States*, p. 286.

18. Julius A. Thomas, "Race Conflict and Social Action," *Opportunity*, Oct. 1943, p. 166.

19. John S. Adams, "The Geography of Riots and Civil Disorders in the 1960's," *Economic Geography*, 48 (Jan. 1972), 33–38.

20. Janowitz, "Patterns of Collective Racial Violence," p. 337.

21. Stanley Lieberson and Arnold A. Silverman, "The Precipitants and Underlying Conditions of Race Riots," *American Sociological Review*, 30 (Dec. 1965), 888.

22. Neil J. Smelser, *The Theory of Collective Behavior* (New York, 1962), p. 249; Lee and Humphrey, *Race Riot*, p. xix.

23. Terry A. Knopf, *Rumors, Race and Riot* (New Brunswick, N.J., 1975), pp. 70–106.

24. Quoted in Orlansky, *The Harlem Riot*, p. 23.

25. Allen D. Grimshaw, "Urban Racial Violence in the United States: Changing Ecological Considerations" in his *Racial Violence in the United States*, p. 291.

26. Jules J. Wanderer, "1967 Riots: A Test of the Congruity of Events," *Social Problems*, 16 (Fall 1968), 193–198.

27. Russell Dynes and E. L. Quarantelli, "Looting in Civil Disorders: An Index of Social Change," *American Behavioral Scientist*, 11 (March-April 1968), 8–9.

28. Walter White to Henry L. Stimson, Aug. 6, 1943, "New York Situation—Correspondence" folder, NAACP.

29. Walter C. Harding (Commanding Officer, 28th Precinct) to the Police Commissioner, Memorandum: Harlem Disturbance, Aug. 16, 1943, p. 34, Box 2550, FHLP (hereafter cited as Harding to Police Commissioner); Christian L. Jommer [?] (Commanding Officer, 25th Precinct) to the Police Commissioner, Memorandum: Harlem Disturbance, Aug. 14, 1943, p. 3, Box 2550, FHLP; William C. Beneke (Commanding Officer, 32nd Precinct) to the Police Commissioner, Memorandum: Harlem Disturbance, Aug. 16, 1943, p. 18, Box 2550, FHLP.

30. Janowitz, "Patterns of Collective Racial Violence," p. 323.

31. Meier and Rudwick, "Black Violence in the 20th Century," p. 314.

32. Joseph Boskin, "Violence in the Ghettos," *New Mexico Quarterly*, 27 (Winter 1968), 331.

33. Russell Dynes and E. L. Quarantelli, "What Looting in Civil Disturbances Really Means," *Trans-action*, 5 (May 1968), 13.

34. John P. Spiegel, "Hostility, Aggression and Violence" in *Racial Violence in the United States*, ed. Grimshaw, p. 337.

35. John T. Baissici [?] (Commanding Officer, 5th Division) to the Police Commissioner, Memorandum: Harlem Disturbances, Aug. 25, 1943, p. 2, Box 2550, FHLP.

36. Joseph Boskin, "Aftermath of an Urban Revolt: The View from Watts, 1965–71" in his *Urban Racial Violence in the Twentieth Century* (2nd ed.; Beverly Hills, Calif., 1976), p. 175.

37. Joe R. Feagin and Harlan Hahn, *Ghetto Revolts: The Politics of Violence in American Cities* (New York, 1973), pp. 49 and 53.

38. Don R. Bowen and Louis H. Masotti, "Civil Violence: A Theoretical Over View" in their *Riots and Rebellion: Civil Violence in the Urban Community* (Beverly Hills, Calif., 1968), pp. 11–29.

39. Harold Orlansky, *The Harlem Riot* (New York, 1943), p. 29.

40. William Ryan, *Blaming the Victim* (New York, 1971), p. 228.

41. Joseph Boskin, "The Revolt of the Urban Ghettos, 1964–70," in his *Urban Racial Violence in the Twentieth Century*, p. 159.

42. Bryan T. Downes, "The Social Characteristics of Riot Cities: A Comparative Study," *Social Science Quarterly*, 49 (Dec. 1968), 507, for the above figure of 15%; the approximation of 24,000 persons for Harlem is derived by taking 15% of the riot zone's population for 1940.

43. National Advisory Commission on Civil Disorders, *Report of the National Advisory Commission on Civil Disorders* (New York, 1968), pp. 128–129.

44. Anthony Oberschall, "The Los Angeles Riot of August, 1965," *Social Problems*, 15 (Winter 1968), 329, for the example of Watts.

45. H. Edward Ransford, "Isolation, Powerlessness and Vio-

lence: A Study of Attitudes and Participation in the Watts Riot," *American Journal of Sociology*, 73 (March 1968), pp. 581–591.

46. Benjamin Muse, *The American Negro Revolution: From Nonviolence to Black Power, 1963–1967* (Bloomington, 1968), pp. 212, 296–298.

47. National Advisory Commission on Civil Disorders, *Report*, pp. 111–112.

48. Walter White, *A Man Called White* (New York, 1945), pp. 237–238; *New York Post*, Aug. 3, 1943, p. 41.

49. "Press Statement by Walter White," Aug. 2, 1943, "New York Situation" folder, NAACP.

50. "Report of the Citizens' Emergency Conference for Interracial Unity," 1943, p. 9, "Citizens' Emergency Conference for Interracial Unity" folder, NAACP.

51. Granger telegram to *Philadelphia Tribune*, Aug. 3, 1943, Series 1, Box 22, NULP; Griggs to La Guardia, Aug. 2, 1943, Box 752, FHLP.

52. James A. Geschwender, "Civil Rights Protest and Riots: A Disappearing Distinction," *Social Science Quarterly*, 49 (Dec. 1968), 484.

53. Rudwick, *Race Riot at East St. Louis*, p. 67; Lee and Humphrey, *Race Riot*, p. xxiii.

54. David O. Sears and T. M. Tomlinson, "Riot Ideology in Los Angeles: A Study of Negro Attitudes," *Social Science Quarterly*, 49 (Dec. 1968), 489, table 2, for the example of Watts.

55. Kenneth B. Clark, "Group Violence," *Journal of Social Psychology*, 19 (May 1944), 337.

56. Grimshaw, "Actions of Police and the Military in American Race Riots," p. 276.

57. Lee and Humphrey, *Race Riot*, p. xxii.

58. Clark, "Group Violence," pp. 330 and 333.

59. "Welfare Council Forum," March 12, 1944, p. 6, Series 1, Box 169, NULP.

60. Memorandum to Roy Wilkins et al., May 1, 1944, p. 2, "Racial Tension Harlem" folder, NAACP.

61. Gary Marx, *Protest and Prejudice: A Study of Belief in the Black Community* (New York, 1969), p. 115, table 70, for attitudes in 1964; Boskin, "Aftermath of an Urban Revolt," pp. 177–178, for the example of Watts.

62. National Advisory Commission on Civil Disorders, *Report*, p. 112.

63. Meier and Rudwick, "Black Violence in the 20th Century," pp. 311–312.

64. Janowitz, "Patterns of Collective Racial Violence," p. 335.

65. *New York Times,* Nov. 17, 1967, p. 1.

66. Milton Bloombaum, "The Conditions Underlying Race Riots as Portrayed by Multidimensional Scalogram Analysis: A Reanalysis of the Lieberson and Silverman Data," *American Sociological Review,* 33 (Feb. 1968), 90–91.

67. Philipp to Lehman, Nov. 22, 1941, reel 42, Governorship Papers, HHLP.

Selected Bibliography

The impact of World War II on black Americans and race relations is summarized in Richard Polenberg, *War and Society: The United States, 1941–1945*, pp. 99–130, and John Morton Blum, *V Was for Victory: Politics and American Culture during World War II*, pp. 182–220.* Three articles in *The Journal of American History* focus more directly on black protest during the war years: Richard M. Dalfiume, "The 'Forgotten Years' of the Negro Revolution," and Harvard Sitkoff, "Racial Militancy and Interracial Violence in the Second War," document the emergence of black militancy, while Lee Finkle, "The Conservative Aims of Militant Rhetoric: Black Protest during World War II," contends that the black press and leaders were more conservative than the black masses, whose militancy they sought to restrain. Finkle, *Forum for Protest: The Black Press during World War II*, elaborates his thesis. *The Afro-American and the Second World War* by Neil A. Wynn is a much needed synthesis of that topic.

A handful of studies provide a background for understanding the black community, particularly that of Harlem, during World War II. James Weldon Johnson, *Black Manhattan*, Claude McKay, *Harlem: Negro Metropolis*, and Roi Ottley, *"New World A-Coming": Inside Black America*, are standard. More recent and analytical are Gilbert Osofsky's *Harlem: The Making of a*

*Bibliographical data for titles discussed in the essay are given in the lists that follow.

Ghetto and Seth M. Scheiner's *Negro Mecca: A History of the Negro in New York City, 1865–1920.*

Government and private records present a relatively complete picture of the living conditions of black New Yorkers and the discrimination they confronted. The Schomburg Collection of Negro Literature and History in New York City is the most important depository of this material. It houses the research papers of the Federal Writers' Program that were collected for a history of blacks in New York City. Some of these papers make up Roi Ottley and William J. Weatherby, eds., *The Negro in New York: An Informal History.* More precise data are in "The Negro in Harlem: A Report on Social and Economic Conditions Responsible for the Outbreak of March 19, 1935," available as the Mayor's Commission on Conditions in Harlem, *The Complete Report of Mayor La Guardia's Commission on the Harlem Riot of March 19, 1935.* Copies of the original report and related data are in the La Guardia Papers. Reports on education, recreation, employment, health, and housing by the City-Wide Citizens' Committee on Harlem concentrate on the early war years. The public hearings and reports of the New York State Temporary Commission on the Condition of the Urban Colored Population document conditions in black communities throughout the state, offering a wider perspective in which to consider Harlem. Since most blacks lived in New York City, much of the material focuses directly on Harlem. For a comparison with the national situation in which black Americans found themselves, the annual reports of the National Association for the Advancement of Colored People and the National Urban League are useful. Their respective official publications, *Crisis* and *Opportunity,* are also of value.

The Fair Employment Practices Committee Papers are necessary to any study of black employment during the war and provide an insight into wartime morale. Numerous magazines, both popular and scholarly, also deal with black morale and the role of blacks in the war effort. The more important of these include Earl Brown, "American Negroes and the War," and Brown and George R. Leighton, *The Negro and the War.* See also the entire issue of the *The Annals* (Sept. 1942), *Survey Graphic* (Nov. 1942), *The Journal of Negro Education* (Summer 1943), and *The Journal of Educational Sociology* (Jan. 1944).

The Fiorello H. La Guardia Papers are the single most important source for any study of New York City during the war years.

They contain very detailed correspondence, reports, newspaper clippings, and miscellany. Especially important are the confidential letters and reports of administrative officials on issues like Stuyvesant Town or riot preparation that reflect La Guardia's close ties with black leaders such as Walter White. La Guardia himself corresponded with many residents of both races, and these letters provide information on middle- and lower-class attitudes. Because La Guardia's papers reflect the views of so many people—ranging in stature from President Roosevelt to an anonymous welfare recipient—they place race relations in a large context and amid other pressing problems. These materials, plus the penciled notes in their margins, sometimes in La Guardia's own hand, often reveal immediate, frank feelings on very controversial matters.

Other collections are invaluable for understanding race relations at state and national levels during World War II. Although Herbert H. Lehman left office in 1942, his papers, particularly those of the Governor's Commission on Discrimination in Employment, provide vital background information for the Depression and early war years. Franklin D. Roosevelt's papers are essential for understanding his view of the war effort and his response to the racial crises of 1943, which were intertwined. The papers of Harold L. Ickes reveal the kind of pressure put on Roosevelt by some administrative members who called for assertive presidential action in race relations. The papers of Jonathan W. Daniels record his efforts as race relations adviser to evaluate the crises and recommend programs for presidential consideration. Together, these papers identify Roosevelt's priorities, as well as the inner workings and decision-making process of his administration.

The black perspective is reconstructed from several sources, in addition to correspondence found in the collections described above. Papers of the National Association for the Advancement of Colored People and the National Urban League index the major events in race relations, though the former contains the more useful material for a study of the riots. These collections represent both the efforts of the oldest civil rights organizations and the concerns of their leaders, Walter White and Lester B. Granger. More local documentation is found in New York City's black newspapers. The *Age* (1940–1943) provides the most conservative view and the least amount of coverage, whereas the *Amsterdam News* (1940–1943) is much more vocal and gives the fullest coverage.

Adam Clayton Powell, Jr.'s the *People's Voice* (1942–1943) is more protest-oriented and at times serves his political needs. All of these newspapers employed perceptive columnists, such as Ludlow Warner, Roy Wilkins, W. E. B. DuBois, and A. M. Wendell Malliet, who present a cross section of opinion. Since almost none of the white-owned newspapers adequately covered events that affected black residents, the black press is absolutely essential for establishing chronology, as well as indicating the black community's concerns. *PM* (1943), a liberal weekly, was the only newspaper directed towards whites to give consistent objective and adequate coverage of black New Yorkers.

Information gleaned from autobiographies and reminiscences fills out the AfroAmerican perspective. Walter White, *A Man Called White* (New York, 1945), and an interview with Roy Wilkins (New York City, January 29, 1968) contain their personal feelings and the official position of the National Association for the Advancement of Colored People. Lester B. Granger's reminiscences (COHC) do much the same for him and the National Urban League, while those of Benjamin McLaurin pertain to the Brotherhood of Sleeping Car Porters (COHC). The recollections of George S. Schuyler (COHC) are wider in scope, perhaps reflecting his concerns as a journalist. Those of Samuel J. Battle (COHC) are briefer and less critical, although they focus in part on the police department and municipal government. Fuller, more informative accounts, which are essential for an understanding of black politics and protest in New York City, are Adam Clayton Powell, Jr., *Marching Blacks: An Interpretive History of the Rise of the Common Black Man*, and the early chapters of his more self-serving *Adam by Adam: The Autobiography of Adam Clayton Powell, Jr.* Similar in tone, but more ideologically oriented is Benjamin J. Davis, Jr., *Communist Councilman From Harlem: Autobiographical Notes Written in a Federal Penitentiary.* To understand the feelings of the mass of black citizens, Claude Brown, *Manchild in the Promised Land,* Malcolm X and Alex Haley, *The Autobiography of Malcolm X,* and Ralph Ellison, *Invisible Man,* are indispensable. These are supplemented by letters from black correspondents in the La Guardia Papers and studies of black public opinion, such as the Office of Facts and Figures, "The Negro Looks at the War: Attitudes of New York Negroes Towards Discrimination Against Negroes and a Comparison of Negro and Poor White Attitudes Toward War-Related Issues."

Only a handful of studies focus directly on the Harlem riot of 1943. Harold Orlansky, *The Harlem Riot: A Study in Mass Frustration,* is the most comprehensive and perceptive. It is nicely supplemented by Kenneth B. Clark, "Group Violence: A Preliminary Study of the Attitudinal Pattern of Its Acceptance and Rejection: A Study of the 1943 Harlem Riot," which provides a very limited measurement of black opinion on the disorder. Clark and James Barker, "The Zoot Effect in Personality: A Race Riot Participant," gives the profile of one person involved in the upheaval, while the aims and objectives of other participants can be found among the sources cited above. Coverage by the black press and *PM* and, especially, the police reports in the La Guardia Papers are the best materials for piecing together the riot's chronology and events.

For an overview of the various forms of racial violence and their historical periods, see Richard Maxwell Brown, *Strain of Violence: Historical Studies of American Violence and Vigilantism.* Several studies are of special value in understanding race riots. The best historical models are Elliot M. Rudwick, *Race Riot at East St. Louis, July 2, 1917,* and William M. Tuttle, Jr., *Race Riot: Chicago in the Red Summer of 1919.* "Black Violence in the 20th Century: A Study in Rhetoric and Retaliation" by August Meier and Elliot M. Rudwick is important for identifying trends and placing race riots in historical perspective, while "Patterns of Collective Racial Violence" by Morris Janowitz is the best single comprehensive treatment of that subject; both articles are part of the report, compiled by Hugh Davis Graham and Ted Robert Gurr for the National Commission on the Causes and Prevention of Violence, *Violence in America: Historical and Comparative Perspectives.* For the sociological and psychological meaning of race riots, the work of Allen D. Grimshaw is indispensable. His "A Study in Social Violence: Urban Race Riots in the United States" (Ph.D. dissertation, University of Pennsylvania, 1959) is the place to begin. It is nicely supplemented by the articles and bibliography in Grimshaw's edited volume on *Racial Violence in the United States.* See Robert M. Fogelson, *Violence as Protest: A Study of Riots and Ghettos,* for the contemporary riots. As for so many other aspects of AfroAmerican history, the most useful guide to the enormous literature on the race riots of the 1960s is James M. McPherson et al., eds., *Blacks in America: Bibliographic Essays,* pp. 389–396.

Manuscripts, Collections, and Interviews

Jonathan W. Daniels Papers. Southern Collection. University of North Carolina Library. Chapel Hill, North Carolina.

Fair Employment Practices Committee Papers. Record Group 228. National Archives. Washington, D.C.

Harold L. Ickes Papers. Manuscript Division. Library of Congress. Washington, D.C.

Fiorello H. La Guardia Papers. Municipal Archives and Records Center. New York, New York.

Herbert H. Lehman Papers. Columbia University. New York, New York.

National Association for the Advancement of Colored People Papers. 1940–1955 (General Office). Manuscript Division. Library of Congress. Washington, D.C.

National Urban League Papers. Manuscript Division. Library of Congress. Washington, D.C.

Franklin D. Roosevelt Papers. Roosevelt Library. Hyde Park. New York.

Columbia Oral History Collection. Columbia University. New York, New York.

Schomburg Collection of Negro Literature and History. New York, New York.

Interview with Charles Poletti. New York City. March 8, 1968.

Interview with Roy Wilkins. New York City. January 29, 1968.

Municipal and State Records

"Local Laws of New York City, 1942–1943." Unpublished compilation. c. 1944. Municipal Reference Library.

"Local Laws of New York City, 1944–1945." Unpublished compilation. c. 1946. Municipal Reference Library.

Mayor's Commission on Conditions in Harlem. "The Negro in Harlem: A Report on Social and Economic Conditions Responsible for the Outbreak of March 19, 1935." FHLP, 1936. This report has been published recently as Mayor's Commission on Conditions in Harlem, *The Complete Report of Mayor La Guardia's Commission on the Harlem Riot of March 19, 1935.* In Mass Violence in America Series, Robert M. Fogelson and Richard E. Rubenstein, eds. New York: Arno Press and The New York Times, 1969.

Proceedings of the City Council of New York. 1940–1944. 2 vols each. Municipal Reference Library.

The City Record: Official Canvass of the Votes Cast in the Counties of New York, Bronx, Kings, Queens, and Richmond at the General Election Held November 5, 1940. Municipal Reference Library.

The City Record: Official Canvass of the Votes Cast in the Counties of New York, Bronx, Kings, Queens and Richmond at the General Election Held November 4, 1941. Municipal Reference Library.

New York City Housing Authority. *Tenth Annual Report: 1944.* New York: NYCHA, 1945.

New York State Temporary Commission Against Discrimination. *Report of the New York State Temporary Commission Against Discrimination.* Albany, New York: Williams Press, 1945.

New York State Temporary Commission on the Condition of the Urban Colored Population. "Public Hearings." 9 vols. SCNLH.

——. *Report of the New York State Temporary Commission on the Condition of the Urban Colored Population to the Legislature of the State of New York.* Albany, New York: J. B. Lyon Company, 1938.

——. *Second Report of the New York State Temporary Commission on the Condition of the Urban Colored Population to the Legislature.* Albany, New York: J. B. Lyon Company, 1939.

Other Reports and Documents

City-Wide Citizens' Committee on Harlem. "Preliminary Report of the Sub-Committee on Education and Recreation." Unpublished report, SCNLH, 1942.

——. "Preliminary Report of the Sub-Committee on Employment." Unpublished report, SCNLH, 1942.

——. "Preliminary Report of the Sub-Committee on Health and Hospitals." Unpublished report, SCNLH, 1945.

——. "Preliminary Report of the Sub-Committee on Housing." Unpublished report, SCNLH, 1942.

——. "The Story of the City-Wide Citizens' Committee on Harlem." Unpublished report, 1943, Series 1, Box 38, NULP.

Eastern Seaboard Conference on the Problems of the War and the Negro People. "Program." Mimeographed copy, FHLP, 1942.

Frost, Olivia P. *An Analysis of the Characteristics of the Popula-*

tion in Central Harlem. New York: Urban League of Greater New York, 1946.

Hampton Institute Conference on the Participation of the Negro in National Defense. "Findings and Principal Addresses." Mimeographed copy, FHLP, 1941.

National Association for the Advancement of Colored People. *Annual Report. 1940, 1943, 1948, 1949, 1950*. New York: NAACP, 1941, 1944, 1949, 1950, 1951.

National Urban League. *Annual Report of the National Urban League for 1942: Interracial Cooperation in Action*. New York: National Urban League, 1943.

———. *Freedom's Seed: Annual Report of the National Urban League for 1943*. New York: National Urban League, 1944.

———. *Racial Aspects of Reconversion: A Memorandum Prepared for the President of the United States*. New York: National Urban League, 1945.

———. (Lorenzo F. Davis, Jr.). "Semi-Annual Report: Negro War Worker—Asset or Liability?" Mimeographed copy, FDRP, 1943.

Negro Press Conference. "A Digest of Proceedings: The Negro Press Conference, May 7–8, 1943." Mimeographed copy, FDRP, 1943.

New York Urban League. *Annual Report for 1940*. New York: Urban League, 1941.

Nichols, Franklin O. *Harlem Housing*. New York: Citizens' Housing Council of New York, Inc., 1939.

Office of Facts and Figures. "The Negro Looks at the War: Attitudes of New York Negroes Towards Discrimination Against Negroes and A Comparison of Negro and Poor White Attitudes Toward War-Related Issues." Mimeographed copy, SCNLH, 1942.

Ottee, Joanne. *Food Costs More in Harlem*. New York: NAACP, 1943.

United States Senate Subcommittee of the Committee on Education and Labor. *Wartime Health and Education*. Washington, D.C.: Government Printing Press, 1944.

Welfare Council of New York City. *Census Tract Data on Population and Housing, New York City: 1940*. New York: Welfare Council, 1941.

White, Walter, and Marshall, Thurgood. *What Caused the Detroit Race Riot?* New York: NAACP, 1943.

Magazines, Newspapers, and Newspaper Clippings

Age (New York). 1940–1943.
Amsterdam News (New York). 1940–1943.
Crisis. 1940–1943.
A Monthly Summary of Events and Trends in Race Relations. 1943–1948.
New York Times. 1940–1943.
Opportunity. 1940–1943.
People's Voice (New York). 1942–1943.
Phylon. 1940–1943.
Pittsburgh Courier. 1940–1943.
PM. (New York). 1943.
"Scrap Books." FHLP. 1940–1943.
"Clippings." HHLP. 1940–1942.

Books and Pamphlets

American Management Association. *The Negro Worker: An Analysis of Management Experience and Opinion on the Employment and Integration of the Negro in Industry.* New York: American Management Association, 1942.
Anderson, Jervis. *A. Philip Randolph: A Biographical Portrait.* New York: Harcourt, Brace and Jovanovich, 1973.
Barbeau, Arthur E., and Henri, Florette. *The Unknown Soldiers: Black American Troops in World War I.* Philadelphia: Temple University Press, 1974.
Bernstein, Barton J., ed. *Towards a New Past: Dissenting Essays in American History.* New York: Pantheon Books, 1968.
Blum, John Morton. *V Was for Victory: Politics and American Culture during World War II.* New York: Harcourt, Brace and Jovanovich, 1976.
Boskin, Joseph, ed. *Urban Racial Violence in the Twentieth Century.* 2d ed. Beverly Hills, Calif.: Glencoe Press, 1976.
Bowen, Don R., and Masotti, Louis H., *Riots and Rebellion: Civil Violence in the Urban Community.* Beverly Hills, Calif.: Sage Publications, 1968.
Bradley, Phillips, et al. *Fair Employment Legislation in New York State, Its History Development and Suggested Use Elsewhere.* New York: Associated Press, 1946.
Bronz, Stephen H. *Roots of Negro Racial Consciousness, The 1920's: Three Harlem Renaissance Authors.* New York: Libra Publishers, Inc., 1964.

Brown, Claude. *Manchild in the Promised Land.* New York: The Macmillan Co., 1965.

Brown, Earl, and Leighton, George R. *The Negro and the War.* New York: Public Affairs Pamphlet, 1942.

Brown, Richard Maxwell. *Strain of Violence: Historical Studies of American Violence and Vigilantism.* New York: Oxford University Press, 1975.

Burns, James McGregor. *Roosevelt: The Lion and the Fox.* New York: Harcourt, Brace and World, Inc., 1956.

——. *Roosevelt: The Soldier of Freedom.* New York: Harcourt, Brace and Jovanovich, Inc., 1970.

Clark, Kenneth B. *Dark Ghetto: Dilemmas of Social Power.* New York: Harper and Row, 1965.

Clarke, John Henrik, ed. *Harlem: A Community in Transition.* New York: The Citadel Press, 1964.

Cronon, E. David. *Black Moses: The Story of Marcus Garvey and the Universal Negro Improvement Association.* Madison: University of Wisconsin Press, 1955.

Dalfiume, Richard M. *Desegregation and the U.S. Armed Forces: Fighting on Two Fronts, 1939–1953.* Columbia: University of Missouri Press, 1969.

Daniels, Jonathan. *Frontier on the Potomac.* New York: Macmillan Co., 1946.

Davis, Benjamin J., Jr. *Communist Councilman From Harlem: Autobiographical Notes Written in a Federal Penitentiary.* New York: International Publishers, 1969.

Davis, James A. *How Management Can Integrate Negroes in War Industries.* New York: New York War Council, 1942.

Eckman, Fern Marja. *The Furious Passage of James Baldwin.* New York: M. Evans, 1966.

Edwin, Ed, and Hickey, Neal. *Adam Clayton Powell and the Politics of Race.* New York: Fleet Publishing Corp., 1965.

Ellison, Ralph. *Invisible Man.* New York: Random House, Inc., 1952.

Essien-Udom, E. U. *Black Nationalism: A Search for an Identity in America.* Chicago: University of Chicago Press, 1962.

Feagin, Joe R., and Hahn, Harlan. *Ghetto Revolts: The Politics of Violence in American Cities.* New York: Macmillan Co., 1973.

Finkle, Lee. *Forum for Protest: The Black Press during World War II.* Rutherford, N.J.: Fairleigh Dickinson University Press, 1975.

Fogelson, Robert M. *Violence as Protest: A Study of Riots and Ghettos.* Garden City, N.Y.: Doubleday and Co., Inc., 1971.

Franklin, John Hope. *From Slavery to Freedom: A History of Negro Americans.* 3d ed. revised. New York: Alfred A. Knopf, 1967.

Frazier, E. Franklin. *The Negro in the United States.* 2d ed. revised. New York: Macmillan Co., 1957.

Freidel, Frank. *FDR and the South.* Baton Rouge: Louisiana State University Press, 1965.

——. *Franklin D. Roosevelt: The Triumph.* Boston: Little, Brown, and Co., 1956.

Garfinkle, Herbert. *When Negroes March: The March on Washington Movement in the Organizational Politics of FEPC.* Glencoe, Ill.: The Free Press, 1959.

Garrett, Charles. *The La Guardia Years, Machine and Reform Politics in New York City.* New Brunswick, N.J.: Rutgers University Press, 1961.

Graham, Hugh Davis, and Gurr, Ted Robert, eds. *Violence in America: Historical and Comparative Perspectives.* 2 vols. Washington, D.C.: U.S. Government Printing Office, 1969.

Grimshaw, Allan D., ed. *Racial Violence in the United States.* Chicago: Aldine Publishing Co., 1969.

Guzman, Jessie P., ed. *Negro Year Book: A Review of Events Affecting Negro Life, 1941–1946.* Atlanta, Ga.: Foote and Davies, Inc., 1947.

Hair, William Ivy. *Carnival of Fury: Robert Charles and the New Orleans Race Riot of 1900.* Baton Rouge: Louisiana State University Press, 1976.

Haley, Alex, and Malcolm X. *The Autobiography of Malcolm X.* New York: Grove Press, Inc., 1964.

Haynes, Robert V. *A Night of Violence: The Houston Riot of 1917.* Baton Rouge: Louisiana State University Press, 1976.

Higbee, Jay Anders. *Development and Administration of the New York State Law Against Discrimination.* University, Alabama: University of Alabama Press, 1966.

Isaacs, Harold R. *The New World of Negro Americans.* London: Phoenix House, 1963.

James, G. G. M. *The Fate of Black People Under Germany.* New York: G. G. M. James, 1941.

Johnson, James Weldon. *Black Manhattan.* New York: Alfred A. Knopf, 1930.

Johnson, John H. *Harlem, the War and Other Addresses.* New York: Wendell Malliet and Co., 1942.

Knopf, Terry Ann. *Rumors, Race and Riot.* New Brunswick, N.J.: Transaction Books, 1975.

La Guardia, Fiorello H. *The Making of an Insurgent: An Autobiography.* Reprint. New York: Capricorn Books, 1961.

Lane, Ann J. *The Brownsville Affair: National Crisis and Black Reaction.* Port Washington, N.Y.: Kennikat, 1971.

Lash, Joseph P. *Eleanor and Franklin: The Story of Their Relationship, Based on Eleanor Roosevelt's Private Papers.* New York: W. W. Norton and Co., Inc., 1971.

Lee, Alfred McClung, and Humphrey, Norman Daymond. *Race Riot (1943).* Revised edition. New York: Octagon Books, 1967.

Lee, Ulysses. *The Employment of Negro Troops.* Washington, D.C.: Government Printing Office, 1966.

Lehman, Herbert H. *Public Papers of Herbert H. Lehman, 1940.* New York: Publishers Printing Company, 1945 [?].

——. *Public Papers of Herbert H. Lehman, 1941.* Albany, N.Y.: Williams Press, 1946.

——. *Public Papers of Herbert H. Lehman, 1942.* Albany, N.Y.: Williams Press, 1947.

Lewinson, Edwin R. *Black Politics in New York City.* New York: Twayne Publishers, Inc., 1974.

Lewis, Claude. *Adam Clayton Powell.* New York: Gold Medal Books, 1963.

Locke, Alain, ed. *The New Negro: An Interpretation.* New York: Johnson Reprint Corp., 1968.

Logan, Rayford, *What the Negro Wants.* Chapel Hill: University of North Carolina Press, 1944.

McKay, Claude. *Harlem: Negro Metropolis.* New York: E. P. Dutton and Co., 1940.

McWilliams, Carey. *Brothers Under the Skin.* Boston: Little, Brown and Co., 1943.

Mann, Arthur. *La Guardia: A Fighter Against His Times, 1882–1933.* New York: J. B. Lippincott, 1959.

——. *La Guardia Comes to Power: 1933.* New York: J. B. Lippincott, 1965.

Marx, Gary T. *Protest and Prejudice: A Study of Belief in the Black Community.* New York: Harper Torchback, 1969.

Masotti, Louis H.; Hadden, Jeffrey K.; Seminatore, Kenneth F.; and Corsi, Jerome R. *A Time to Burn?: An Evaluation of the*

Present Crisis in Race Relations. Chicago: Rand McNally and Co., 1969.

Melby, Ernest O., ed. *Mobilizing Educational Resources for Winning the War and the Peace.* New York: Harper and Brothers, 1943.

Merton, Robert K. *Social Theory and Social Structure.* New York: Free Press, 1949; revised, 1967.

Milbank Memorial Fund. *Postwar Problems of Migration.* New York: Milbank Memorial Fund, 1947.

Murray, Florence, ed. *The Negro Handbook.* New York: Wendell Malliet and Co., 1942.

Muse, Benjamin. *The American Negro Revolution: From Nonviolence to Black Power, 1963–1967.* Bloomington: Indiana University Press, 1968.

Myrdal, Gunnar, et al. *An American Dilemma: The Negro Problem and Modern Democracy.* 2 vols. New York: Harper and Brothers, 1944.

National Advisory Commission on Civil Disorders. *Report of the National Advisory Commission on Civil Disorders.* New York: E. P. Dutton and Co., 1968.

Nevins, Allan. *Herbert H. Lehman and His Era.* New York: Charles Scribner's Sons, 1963.

Orlansky (Orlans), Harold. *The Harlem Riot: A Study in Mass Frustration.* New York: Social Analysis Report No. 1, 1943.

Osofsky, Gilbert. *Harlem: The Making of a Ghetto.* New York: Harper and Row, 1966.

Ottley, Roi. *'New World A-Coming': Inside Black America.* New York: The World Publishing Co., 1943.

———, and Weatherby, William J., eds. *The Negro in New York: An Informal Social History.* Dobbs Ferry, N.Y.: Oceana Publications, Inc., 1967.

Parsons, Talcott, and Clark, Kenneth B., eds. *The Negro in America.* Boston: Houghton Mifflin, 1966.

Polenberg, Richard. *War and Society: The United States, 1941–1945.* New York: J. B. Lippincott Company, 1972.

Powell, Adam Clayton, Jr. *Adam by Adam: The Autobiography of Adam Clayton Powell, Jr.* New York: Dial Press, 1971.

———. *Marching Blacks: An Interpretive History of the Rise of the Common Black Man.* New York: Dial Press, 1945; revised, 1973.

Rainwater, Lee, and Yancey, William L., eds. *The Moynihan Report and the Politics of Controversy.* Cambridge, Mass.: The M.I.T. Press, 1967.

Record, Wilson. *The Negro and the Communist Party.* Chapel Hill: University of North Carolina Press, 1951.

Roosevelt, Elliot, ed. *F.D.R.: His Personal Letters, 1928–1945.* 4 vols. New York: Duell, Sloan and Pearce, 1950.

Ruchames, Louis. *Race, Jobs and Politics.* New York: Columbia University Press, 1953.

Rudwick, Elliot M. *Race Riot in East St. Louis, July 2, 1917.* Carbondale, Ill.: Southern Illinois University Press, 1964.

Ryan, William. *Blaming the Victim.* New York: Vintage Books, 1971.

Scheiner, Seth M. *Negro Mecca: A History of the Negro in New York City, 1865–1920.* New York: New York University Press, 1965.

Shogan, Robert, and Craig, Tom. *The Detroit Race Riot: A Study in Violence.* New York: Chilton Books, 1964.

Simon, Arthur. *Stuyvesant Town, U.S.A.: Pattern for Two Americas.* New York: New York University Press, 1970.

Smelser, Neil J. *Theory of Collective Behavior.* New York: Free Press, 1962.

Sternsher, Bernard, ed. *The Negro in Depression and War: Prelude to Revolution.* Chicago: Quadrangle Books, 1969.

Tuttle, William M., Jr. *Race Riot: Chicago in the Red Summer of 1919.* New York: Atheneum, 1970.

Waskow, Arthur I. *From Race Riot to Sit-In, 1919 and the 1960's: A Study in the Connections Between Conflict and Violence.* Garden City, N.Y.: Doubleday and Co., Inc., 1966.

Weaver, John D. *The Brownsville Raid.* New York: W. W. Norton and Co., Inc., 1970.

White, Walter. *A Man Called White.* New York: Viking Press, 1945.

Wilson, James Q. *Negro Politics: The Search for Leadership.* New York: The Free Press, 1960.

Wolters, Raymond. *Negroes and the Great Depression: The Problem of Economic Recovery.* Westport, Conn.: Greenwood Publishing Corp., 1970.

Work, Monroe N., ed. *Negro Yearbook, 1937–1938: An Annual Encyclopedia of the Negro.* Tuskegee, Alabama: Negro Yearbook Publishing Co., 1939.

Wynn, Neil A. *The Afro-American and the Second World War.* New York: Holmes and Meier Publishers, 1976.

Zinn, Howard. *La Guardia in Congress.* Ithaca, N.Y.: Cornell University Press, 1958.

Articles

Adams, John S. "The Geography of Riots and Civil Disorders in the 1960's." *Economic Geography* 48 (Jan. 1972): 24–42.

"The American Negro." *The Annals* (of the Academy of Political and Social Science) 140 (Nov. 1928).

"The American Negro in World War I and World War II." *The Journal of Negro Education* 12 (Summer 1943).

Banner, Warren M. "Profiles: New York." *The Journal of Educational Sociology* 17 (Jan. 1944): 272–279.

Basso, Hamilton. "The Riot in Harlem." *The New Republic* 82 (Apr. 3, 1935): 209–210.

Bellush, Jewel. "Roosevelt's Good Right Arm: Lieutenant Governor Herbert H. Lehman." *New York History* 41 (Oct. 1960): 423–443.

Bennett, Lerone, Jr. "Adam Clayton Powell: Congressman Is an Enigma on Capitol Hill." *Ebony* 18 (June 1963): 25–28.

Bloombaum, Milton. "The Conditions Underlying Race Riots as Portrayed by Multidimensional Scalogram Analysis: A Reanalysis of the Lieberson and Silverman Data." *American Sociological Review* 33 (Feb. 1968): 76–91.

Boskin, Joseph. "Violence in the Ghettos." *New Mexico Quarterly* 37 (Winter, 1968): 317–334.

Brown, Earl. "American Negroes and the War." *Harper's Magazine* 184 (April 1942): 545–552.

Cayton, Horace R. "Negro Morale." *Opportunity* 19 (Dec. 1941): 371–375.

——. "What Strategy for Negroes: Patience or Pressure?" *Negro Digest* 1 (Aug. 1943): 49–52.

Clark, Kenneth B. "Group Violence: A Preliminary Study of the Attitudinal Pattern of Its Acceptance and Rejection: A Study of the 1943 Harlem Riot." *The Journal of Social Psychology* 19 (May 1944): 319–337.

——, and Barker, James. "The Zoot Effect in Personality: A Race Riot Participant." *The Journal of Abnormal and Social Psychology* 40 (1945): 143–148.

"Color: Unfinished Business of Democracy." *Survey Graphic* 31 (Nov. 1942).

Dalfiume, Richard M. "The 'Forgotten Years' of the Negro Revolution." *The Journal of American History* 55 (June 1968): 90–106.

Dahlke, H. Otto. "Race and Minority Riots—A Study in the Typology of Violence." *Social Forces* 30 (May 1952): 419–425.

Daniels, Lee A. "The Political Career of Adam Clayton Powell: Paradigm and Paradox." *Journal of Black Studies* 4 (Dec. 1973): 115–138.

Davenport, Walter. "Harlem: Dense and Dangerous." *Collier's* 114 (Sept. 23, 1944): 11–13+.

Downes, Bryan T. "The Social Characteristics of Riot Cities: A Comparative Study." *Social Science Quarterly* 49 (Dec. 1968): 504–520.

Dunbar, Ernest. "The Audacious World of Adam Powell." *Look* 27 (May 7, 1963): 30–34.

Dynes, Russell, and Quarantelli, E. L. "Looting in Civil Disorders: An Index of Social Change." *American Behavioral Scientist* 11 (March–April 1968): 7–10.

———. "What Looting in Civil Disturbances Really Means." *Transaction* 5 (May 1968): 9–14.

"Employment Conditions, January–March, 1943." *The Employment Review* 5 (April 1943): 84–90.

Finkle, Lee. "The Conservative Aims of Militant Rhetoric: Black Protest During World War II." *The Journal of American History* 60 (Dec. 1973): 692–713.

Fishel, Leslie H., Jr. "The Negro in the New Deal Era." *The Wisconsin Magazine of History* 48 (Winter 1964–65): 111–126.

Frazier, E. Franklin. "Negro Harlem: An Ecological Study." *The American Journal of Sociology* 43 (July 1937): 72–88.

Geschwender, James A. "Civil Rights Protest and Riots: A Disappearing Distinction." *Social Science Quarterly* 49 (Dec. 1968): 474–484.

Habe, Hans. "The Nazi Plans for Negroes." *Nation* 152 (March 1941): 232–235.

Hamilton, Charles V. "Riots, Revolts and Relevant Response," in William M. Chace and Peter Collier, eds. *Justice Denied: The Black Man in White America.* New York: Harcourt, Brace and World, Inc., 1970. 511–518.

Headrick, William Carl. "Race Riots—Segregated Slums." *Current History* 5 (Sept. 1943): 30–34.

High, Stanley. "Black Omens." *The Saturday Evening Post* 210 (May 21, 1938): 5–7+.

Jones, Lester M. "The Editorial Policy of Negro Newspapers of 1917–18 as Compared With That of 1941–42." *The Journal of Negro History* 29 (Jan. 1944): 24–31.

Kesselman, Louis C. "The Fair Employment Practice Movement in Perspective." *The Journal of Negro History* 31 (Jan. 1946): 30–46.

Lieberson, Stanley, and Silverman, Arnold H. "The Precipitants and Underlying Conditions of Race Riots." *American Sociological Review* 30 (Dec. 1965): 887–898.

Locke, Alain. "Harlem: Dark Weather-Vane." *Survey Graphic* 25 (Aug. 1936): 457–462+.

McKay, Claude. "Harlem Runs Wild." *The Nation* 140 (April 3, 1935): 382–383.

"Minority Peoples in a Nation at War." *The Annals* (of the Academy of Political and Social Science) 223 (Sept. 1942).

Muraskin, William. "The Harlem Boycott of 1934: Black Nationalism and the Rise of Labor-Union Consciousness." *Labor History* 13 (Summer 1972): 361–373.

"Negro Internal Migration, 1940–1943." *Monthly Summary of the Events and Trends of Race Relations* 1 (Sept. 1943): 10–12.

"The Negro in the North During Wartime." *The Journal of Educational Sociology* 17 (Jan. 1944).

Oberschall, Anthony. "The Los Angeles Riot of August, 1965." *Social Problems* 15 (Winter 1968): 322–341.

Osofsky, Gilbert. "The Enduring Ghetto." *The Journal of American History* 55 (Sept. 1968): 243–255.

"Placement of Negroes in the State." *The Employment Review* 5 (May 1943): 235–239.

"The Position of the Negro in the American Social Order," "Yearbook edition." *The Journal of Negro Education* 8 (July 1939).

Ransford, H. Edward. "Isolation, Powerlessness and Violence: A Study of Attitudes and Participation in the Watts Riot." *American Journal of Sociology* 73 (March 1968): 581–591.

Reddick, L. D. "What the Northern Negro Thinks About Democracy." *The Journal of Educational Sociology* 17 (Jan. 1944): 296–306.

Salmond, John A. "The Civilian Conservation Corps and the Negro." *The Journal of American History* 52 (June 1965): 75–88.

Sears, David O., and Tomlinson, T. M. "Riot Ideology in Los

Angeles: A Study of Negro Attitudes." *Social Science Quarterly* 49 (Dec. 1968): 485–503.

Sitkoff, Harvard. "The Detroit Race Riot of 1943." *Michigan History* 53 (Fall 1969): 183–206.

———. "Racial Militancy and Interracial Violence in the Second World War." *The Journal of American History* 58 (Dec. 1971): 661–681.

Swan, L. Alex. "The Harlem and Detroit Riots of 1943: A Comparative Analysis." *Berkeley Journal of Sociology* 16 (1971–1972): 75–93.

Wakefield, Dan. "Adam Clayton Powell, Jr.: The Angry Voice of Harlem." *Esquire* 70 (Nov. 1959): 119–123.

Wanderer, Jules J. "1967 Riots: A Test of the Congruity of Events." *Social Problems* 16 (Fall 1968): 191–198.

Weaver, Robert C. "Negro Labor Since 1919." *The Journal of Negro History* 35 (Jan. 1950): 20–38.

White, Walter. "Behind the Harlem Riot." *The New Republic* 109 (Aug. 16, 1943): 221–222.

———. "What the Negro Thinks of the Army." *The Annals* (of the Academy of Political and Social Science) 223 (Sept. 1942): 67–71.

Williams, Charles. "Harlem at War." *Nation* 156 (Jan. 16, 1943): 86–88.

Wilson, James Q. "The Flamboyant Mr. Powell." *Commentary* 41 (Jan. 1966): 31–35.

———. "Two Negro Politicians: An Interpretation." *Midwest Journal of Political Science* 4 (Nov. 1960): 346–369.

Wynn, Neil A. "The Impact of the Second World War on the American Negro." *The Journal of Contemporary History* 6 (1971): 42–53.

Zangrando, Robert L. "The NAACP and a Federal Antilynching Bill, 1934–1940." *The Journal of Negro History* 50 (April 1965): 106–117.

Dissertations and Unpublished Manuscripts

Grimshaw, Allen D. "A Study in Social Violence: Urban Race Riots in the United States." Unpublished Ph.D. dissertation, University of Pennsylvania, 1959.

Kifer, Allen F. "The Negro Under the New Deal, 1933–1941." Unpublished Ph.D. dissertation, University of Wisconsin, 1961.

Pollard, Myrtle Evangeline. "Harlem As Is." I: "Sociological Notes on Harlem Social Life." Unpublished Baccalaureate thesis, City College of New York, 1936. II: "The Negro Business and Economic Community." Unpublished M.B.A. thesis, City College of New York, 1937.

Shannon, William V. "Projected Biography of Herbert H. Lehman." Unpublished ms, HHLP, n.d.

Index

Please remember that this is a library book,
and that it belongs only temporarily to each
person who uses it. Be considerate. Do
not write in this, or any, library book.